IN THE WILDS
OF WESTERN CANADA

Tyrone
Danlock

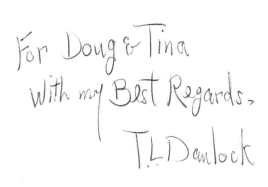

For Doug & Tina
With my Best Regards,
T.L Danlock   September 5th, 2005.

Printed in Victoria, British Columbia, Canada.

First copyrighted on May 1, 2002. Registration #1002034

A cataloguing record for this book that includes the U.S. Library of Congress Classification number, the
Library of Congress Call number and the Dewey Decimal cataloguing code is available from the National
Library of Canada. The complete cataloguing record can be obtained from the National Library's online
database at: www.nlc-bnc.ca/amicus/index-e.html
ISBN 1-4120-3447-7

TRAFFORD

This book was published *on-demand* in cooperation with Trafford Publishing.
On-demand publishing is a unique process and service of making a book available for retail sale to the public
taking advantage of on-demand manufacturing and Internet marketing.
On-demand publishing includes promotions, retail sales, manufacturing, order fulfilment,
accounting and collecting royalties on behalf of the author.

Suite 6E, 2333 Government St., Victoria, B.C. V8T 4P4, CANADA
Phone 250-383-6864 • Toll-free 1-888-232-4444 (Canada & US) • Fax 250-383-6804 • E-mail sales@trafford.com • Web site www.trafford.com

Trafford Catalogue #04-1275 • www.trafford.com/robots/04-1275.html

TRAFFORD PUBLISHING IS A DIVISION OF TRAFFORD HOLDINGS LTD.

10 9 8 7

Author's
Edition

CONTENTS

"Nature gives to every time and season
Some beauties of its own."
Charles Dickens

DEDICATION

This book is dedicated to whomever appreciates
The positiveness that Nature expresses and gives to us all;
It is also no less dedicated to our wildlife
Which like children, need our caring.

Acknowledgments

During this book's five years of writing several people have been most helpful.

My much appreciation and thanks to:

Mike J. Benz and Chrissy Benz of Coldstream Creek and Vernon, B.C., for your generous hospitality and computerizing of the book's first manuscript, running paper printouts and transferring onto CDs;

Patricia Butler of Slocan Lake, West Kootenay, B.C., for your computerizing of improvements to the book's main text;

Beth Young of Port Alice and Comox Valley, B.C., for your computer work on the book;

Shelley Glaus of Courtenay, B.C., for your computerizing of the book's final draft, running paper printouts for proofreading and transferring the completed book onto CDs.

INTRODUCTION

The events described in this book occurred at various places in Western Canada over a thirty-one year span from 1969 until 1999…while I was at work, prospecting or just out enjoying Nature. During those years much of my time passed alone in the woods, meadows and on mountain slopes. Out there, wild inhabitants would often meet, entertain and teach me about their wild ways and the ways of Nature.

As the years passed, I noticed how little time the greater majority of people had to be out directly experiencing our natural realm. But since I was fortunate to have more time than most in our wild western Canadian regions…thought it would be worthwhile sharing some of these uncommon and rare experiences. More than anything else, these short descriptions are an effort to express both the reality of and my great appreciation for the multifarious life that we call Nature.

Much separated in time and place, these real life short-stories are therefore not presented as a continuum, so can be read in any order. Also, I have been intentionally vague about most locations for several reasons but primarily to protect the wildlife that lives there.

Nature and wildlife give far more to humanity than is generally realized…the main reason for Planet Earth's deteriorating condition today. I apologize to no one for liking wild animals just as they are — alive— and for wanting Nature's ecosystems to remain intact and alive. But since interpretations vary regarding the meaning of Nature, wildlife and humanity's role in it all…I expect these writings to be much enjoyed and appreciated by some readers but not so by others.

Southern British Columbia

A Deep Rumbling

It was a dark June night in 1969. Powerful engines, three units of the 5,000 series rumbled along with an incredibly deep, solid vibration of nine thousand horsepower generated by the V-16 units. One's whole body, heart included, shook in unison…giving three trainmen a sense of being all-powerful, as if we were an intimate part of these huge diesel engines!

The engineman sat alone on the right side, with the controls. I sat on the left front seat, the brakeman's spot, in front of the fireman, watching for signals ahead…each time calling out the signal's meaning, which too, the fireman and engineman did in turn. We were taking a train of empty coalcars to North Bend, slowly winding our way alongside the Fraser River upstream from Yale. The triple-engine roared steadily as forty-eight huge pistons plunged up and down, pulling the long heavy train through solid-rock tunnels near Hell's Gate…their deep throbbing sound echoing up and down the river's nearly perpendicular canyon.

I had to keep alert and awake, fighting against this continuous, monotonous drumming that could easily lull one into sleep. Through the dark gorge…slowly, slowly the train meandered. Now about two o'clock in the morning, mottled black cliffs and flat black fir trees outlined the bottom edge of a silent star-filled sky, lit with twinkling countless billions above.

Below too, the river was black and grey with faint hints of motion in everchanging patterns. Now a few miles downstream from North Bend, creeping upslope at about ten miles per hour, we entered the first of two adjacent tunnels that were cut through the vertical granite cliff. In bright headlights, steel rails glowed silvery. Black shadows formed sharp triangular abstract patterns that rapidly changed, appeared and disappeared on the tunnel walls and ceiling. Leaving this tunnel, a tumbling white waterfall glowed momentarily on our left as we entered the second tunnel.

Passing through…another magical dance of light, shadow and night played before our eyes in the jagged, dynamite-sculpted tunnel. As we emerged from the north end, a long wooden trestle stretched in a slight curve high above a rocky whitewater creek, to a third tunnel cut into another perpendicular rock cliff barely visible in the dark distance.

Far out on the trestle, there appeared a faint motion within the blackness. Something indistinct seemed to be there, moving. It stopped. Was this optical illusion from tired eyes? As we approached, a pale object quickly began to take vague shape, emerging from the black space of night. Then a tan-coloured animate form appeared, standing motionless…with glowing emerald-green eyes…staring at our brilliant headlights. Now recognizable was the distinct shape of a large cat!

The big cougar crouched down flat on its belly between rails in centre of the trestle…just staring towards us! Then its ears flattened back. It began to snarl. Immediately standing, I stepped to the front door. The engineman began blowing the whistle in sharp, short bursts!

But the cougar was frozen into a crouch with claws out, cheeks curled and wrinkled, steadily snarling! Its long pointed, creamy yellow teeth and pink curled tongue glistened as it growled inaudibly from within the locomotive's deep rumbling roar! Closer, closer we crept towards this unfortunate animal. At such short distance, even at slow speed the train was impossible to stop. The big cat's emerald-green eyes were no doubt blinded by the train's bright white headlights. Its flattened ears heard naught but a deep, loud rumble. Light and sound had the cougar trapped!

I yelled to the engineman: "Turn out the lights! Turn out the lights!…It can't see!" He instantly switched off the headlights while keeping on with quick short whistles. Now the big cat was barely visible from the engine's small white running-lights. Our huge orange engine rolled slowly along…relentlessly shortening space between the hapless cat and big iron cowcatcher blade. As I watched helplessly, an emotion of desperation shot through my body and mind. Sorrow soon followed. It seemed the inevitable end of a cougar's life were a few moments away!

Quickly opening the front door, I stepped out and ahead. Standing at the engine's front rail, I thought hard to the cougar: "Move off to the side! It's a wooden trestle!"

The creek was a hundred feet below — too high to jump safely. With headlights off…in a few seconds the cougar's eyes adjusted enough to see what was approaching inexorably closer and closer. But in the dim light I could see it still crouched flat…looking at me and snarling aggressively! Yet simultaneously the cat's aggressive self-defense was no doubt tinged with fear.

Now we were just five yards away…I thought this beautiful wild animal would certainly die! But then, in an instant the big cougar jumped sideways into absolute darkness! A split-second later, we rolled over the cat's crouching-spot.

As the cougar lunged in midair into blackness and out of visibility, it appeared to have left the trestle! I consoled myself with the thought that fortunately, a small wooden ramp and water barrel were jutting out of the trestle's west side where the cougar had leapt! Maybe it was safely there with claws dug into wood, crouching in the darkness. I hoped; I wished.

Or did it jump to its death a hundred feet below? To me, that possibility seemed less probable since the trestle was wooden and this was a cat. But we could not know the answer until next day when we would be taking a southbound train during daylight over the trestle. I wanted to think that this big beautiful cat did reach safety by the water barrel and had sense enough not to panic while eighty-plus coalcars rolled by, just one yard away! After all, with long sharp claws, the cougar could have easily climbed down and under the trestle to safety.

Next day, on a warm blue-skied afternoon we took our train slowly southward, leaving North Bend. Only about fifteen minutes passed until we were through the northernmost tunnel and rumbling out onto the long curving trestle. As we crossed this high trestle slower than usual… we looked hard at the rocky creekbed below! All three of us were much eased that no sign of a dead cougar was to be seen! It had indeed survived! Now, to me the night before seemed almost a dream…as if it never really happened!

Tension and fearful expectation had suddenly vanished and a calm relaxed energy surrounded us. Suddenly, I felt especially happy about this unusual event! Cougars were and are to me an important part of my identity as a Western Canadian. They are wild expressions of qualities that we should develop at least to some degree within ourselves. This cougar certainly was self-controlled, independent, courageous in face of the unknown and had a particular strength of both mind and body…all very real. Although its role in Nature is to kill for food, we human beings do not need to necessarily but can develop those other qualities, since we are superior… supposedly.

Swishing and Snapping

Puffy white and grey clouds were drifting across a deep blue September sky. Below them, pale grey and rust-coloured tetrahedral rocky peaks jutted up all around the broad valley…their upper scree fans dotted with pale orange and ruby red, while heavily treed lower slopes were patched in bright yellow and dark green. Filtering down from the clouds were faint sounds of sandhill cranes, croaking and squawking their familiar sour-notes to each other.

Looking up, I could barely discern them winging from the northwest very high up in long, angled single-file lines, vees and double-yoos. I stood watching…listening and counting them as they approached, passed over, then continued away into the distant southeast horizon. There were about one hundred seventy-five birds in this flight! Enroute from their Arctic summer residence, they sounded excited and happy! Their social chitchat dissolved away my aloneness and I felt cheered, too.

As their sounds faded, the rustling of pale green, yellow and golden aspen leaves mingled with distant echoing far below from a whitewater creek…as if vying with the silence of still, erect lodgepine trees that I was passing under. I was walking along a partly grown-in logging road, looking at rocks in the semi-open area of an old clearcut where kinnikinick and tiny dwarf huckleberry bush grew profusely. The ground seemed to dance with wee coloured spots of shiny green, yellow, pink and maroon oval leaves. Among these, low to the ground in the millions were bright orange-red and black shiny berries. This was perfect habitat for mice, voles and grouse!

Peacefully, silently for some unknown minutes I proceeded along this large flat glacial bench…until sudden swishing bushes and snapping twigs brought me to alert! These sounds were on my right just thirty yards away! Glancing over, I glimpsed a large fuzzy blond animal dashing through the bush, paralleling the old road. Its long shoulder-and-neck hair stood almost vertically, tips curving back over in the selfmade wind as it ran. Aspen saplings, willow brush and orange-fruited wildrose bushes shook, bent and crackled as the bear rushed through and by them!

I slowed my pace but kept walking…thinking that since the bear was afraid and on the run, the best strategy would be to exert my apparent dominance by not stopping. The big bruin glanced back a few times as it hastened to gain distance! A conspicuous shoulder hump, thick neck ruff and wide flat face were the marks of grizzly, the most feared animal in Western Canada!

Adrenalin ran through my arteries. But for the moment I was less afraid than this most impressive grizzly was! When it had gained another thirty yards of space, it curved over to the old road, slowed…then stopped right on the road! There, now about forty yards distant and standing broadside…the bear turned its large wide head to have a good look at me. What a beautiful bear! Almost fully-grown, still young and in the prime of its life, it looked almost five feet tall at the shoulder!

I kept moving towards it, stepping slowly with one hand on a pepperspray holster. It stood staring for maybe five seconds…then bound off through tall willow clumps towards the creek bank dropoff, disappearing from sight down the steep gravelly slope. I thought this bear must have recently come here from the remote mountain area to the south, thus unfamiliar with human beings: the reason it had spooked so easily. But again, it could have had some experience with hunters, another reason for fear.

The speed that the big grizzly had vacated told me it would be running probably a long way to the creek, which was fifty yards or more down. Now I had to decide whether to keep with my planned route or change strategy. I kept with it, gambling on the probability that was in my favour. Even so, as my footsteps intersected with the bear's crossover point, I held the pepper spraygun in hand just in case my assessment was wrong.

Long tense moments enveloped my walk for about one hundred yards until I veered onto another trail, moving away from the creek and the big-clawed beauty. Pacing quickly to increase distance between us, I wandered through the poplar and evergreen woods minding my business and hoping the bear would be minding its own. For over three hours I explored the undulating ridges looking for ore-bearing rock. During that time, I met two ruffed grouse and discovered a beaver pond backed up by a series of four well-constructed mud-and-stick dams.

A dozen large poplar trees had been recently felled by these living representatives of our much-maligned Canadian symbol. Now lying in the woods and across the pond…bark, branches and fresh yellowgreen leaves were a ready food supply. The beavers used one of these trees for dam material, having pushed mud and sticks directly under it for a dam, which became a convenient bridge to me. Straight shafts of bright sunlight penetrated this shady poplar grove, reflecting off the mirror-surface in brilliant sparkles while simultaneously, in places shallowly penetrating the cloudy brown water. All was calm and quiet in the pond, as the locals were now resting safely for the day in their cool dark lodge somewhere nearby.

The only other social company I had in this peaceful forest were squirrels. They chattered, squealed and scurried after each other over the mossy green ground, up and down lodgepine and hemlock trees. Busily snipping off evergreen cones and branch-tips high in the trees or with tails held high and curling, playfully bouncing over the moss and logs…they stashed their winter's food cache into little mossy holes, under rotten old logs or at the base of trees. A real pleasure these squirrels were! Some caches were many years old: heaps of greybrown bracts ten feet wide and two feet high, still in use with fresh green cones added to them. These energetic little animals cheered me up…as they carried fir cones clenched between front teeth in a manner looking like a big cigar protruding from their mouths, or with hemlock branch-tips loaded with little cones stuffed into mouths, their cheek pouches bulging! Squirrels almost always look happy, even when they are being serious defending territory and food supply.

Now on the way back out, while walking through one wildrose patch I picked two pockets full of ripe, orange-red rosehips, conscious not to take much since these too, are important food for rodents, birds and sometimes even bears. Returning via the same route that I had come, all the while nibbling on the soft tasty outer pulp, I slowed my pace when nearing the creekbank. Again holding pepperspray in hand, I cautiously passed the grizzly's feeding area…in case it had returned! Luckily, it had not.

I walked quickly for some distance then at the orange and black spotted flat, knelt down taking a few minutes to savour the berries of ground-level kinnikinick and low-growing dwarf huckleberry, which the big blond bear had no doubt been eating. Kinninick berries were dry, sugary and mild tasting. But the black dwarf huckleberries were juicy and had the most exquisite taste, as if not of this earthly realm! I found the best way to eat them was one handful at a time…mmmm…deeelicious!

Although these berries were such a treat, I was careful to take very few, knowing how crucial they are for wildlife as food source, directly or indirectly. From wee to very large, a variety of beings eat them: ants, various other insects, mice, voles, Canadian jays, grouse and the huge grizzly that I had good fortune to see here. And indirectly dependent are the carnivores that feed on sooner or later, those berry-and-seed-eaters, such as: weasels, marten, fox, coyotes, owls and hawks. So…with them in mind, I left this secret place…with happy thoughts and lively memories, even though the rocks around gave me no excitement!

WILD NEIGHBOURS: SILENT AND VOCIFEROUS

One cool, sunny autumn day everything was right for a walk in the woods. Thinking that wild mushrooms may now be growing I decided to explore a little nearby hill treed with arbutus and second-growth fir. Pushing through thick young alder lower down, I slowly zigzagged up the open slope among red-maroon mahonia and shining green shalal bushes. Below to my left, a crystal-clear creek flowed in everchanging curves and curls over rounded grey, brown and green mottled rocks. The larger stones forced air and water together into whitewater bubbles and shishing, gurgling sounds. Here, in the distant past salmon and steelhead would spawn...but not anymore.

Up on top, the hill levelled into a flattish gently sloping bench. I had chanterelle and pine mushrooms in mind but so far, saw none. Only a few unknown species were up, which were worthy of just a glance...being probably inedible and possibly poisonous. Following a faint deer trail through shalal and huckleberry brush, I paced along under beautiful old arbutus trees. Stopping for a short rest beside one arbutus, I ran my hands over the smooth rusty-coloured bark. It felt more like soft skin than tree bark, giving a most pleasant tactile sensation!

Wrapping my arms around the trunk, I leaned a cheek against it and gazed upward. The leaf-pattern arched over as ten thousand or so, green ovals and curves...some shining, some translucent, others dark and opaque; among them were clusters of bright orange-red, round berries hanging like grapes. Here and there among the leaves, little gaps opened to the zenith of deep blue sky...where sunshine entered, penetrated and reflected its starlike brilliance. Although silent and still, this all seemed so much alive!

After enjoying this peacefulness awhile, my mind returned back to the ground. Letting go of the tree, I continued farther along the deer trail paralleling the creek but far above near its vertical solid rock canyon walls. Now its flow and tumble echoed loudly through the deep rockcut. I walked up and up for some long distance...seeing no mushrooms of the kind I wanted. Then finally I took the hint, turned around and headed back along this same path!

Passing by my hugging tree, I did not then realize that a few years later someone in the wood products industry and their media cohorts would dream up "tree hugger" as a derogatory term for concerned people: citizens who could — clearly or not — see the negative effects of fifty-plus years of excessive corporate-style clearcuts. But the shining orange-red berry clusters demanded to be looked at, hanging among oval leaves as if offerings to Steller bluejays, bandtailed pigeons and grouse. But our only wild native pigeon, the beautiful bandtailed...which I had often seen as a boy...was now extremely rare, probably due to its long migrations through overpopulated countries to the south where it usually winters.

Continuing my way down, within ten minutes I was back at the truck. Starting up, I slowly drove the bumpy gravel road until at an open flat, a glimpse of something moving caught the corner of my eye. Instinctively, instantly my head turned towards it. What a pleasantly exciting surprise! A tall lanky wolf had just emerged from thick alder saplings and was beginning to cross the gravel flat, moving in the same direction as me!

Loping a short way, it stopped...standing broadside. Excited and energized, I stepped on the brake and turned off the motor. It just stood in the open...staring back! Big-pawed, long legged and skinny, it looked half-starved. Even so, this wolf's long-stranded, unkempt fur coat was beautiful in a rare multicolour of grey, white, black, rusty brown and cream!

I grabbed my twenty-power spotting scope off the seat, leaning it against the window. Although the wolf was about thirty yards away the scope pulled it in so close that its sparkling, pale copper-coloured eyes were clearly visible! Through motionless steady eyes, this intelligent being fearlessly, intently looked back at me...unaware of how close I was to it through the special eye of optical science. Through its black pupils I could see the living intelligence of a conscious being — watching, observing me as much as I did it! It standing and I sitting motionless...for more than a minute, this beautiful wolf allowed me to observe, enjoy and immensely appreciate its presence.

A most pleasing meeting this was because I had not seen a wolf in the wild since summer of 1955 near Sproat Lake. Then I was a boy of ten years, with a group of six other boys hitchhiking home after a day of swimming. Two adult timber wolves, one black and one white, walked out of the fir and wild cherry forest to stand momentarily in the roadside clearing, just twenty yards directly across from us...before loping away to the east about thirty yards then crossing the gravel road onto our side and disappearing forever...into the fir and dogwood forest below. Now this lone wolf, seeing my lack of ill-will, just casually jogged away into the standing timber and out of sight under fir, maple, dogwood and shalal...but this time, not forever.

The next spring I was fortunate enough to see this same wolf a second time, recognizable by its unique colouration and slim body. Again while out for a walk in the woods...the shaggy-maned beauty was also out trotting along the railway tracks on conspicuously large paws, loping long legs, with shoulder blades pumping up and down! The typical wolf-style bouncing trot was fascinating! It stopped to look back for a half-minute, then loped away with steady purpose another hundred yards before turning down into maple and spruce woods. Now I knew that this animal was local and thought it probably subsisted on deer and grouse.

A month later as I walked along the creekside looking into crystal-clear water for signs of wild fish — especially steelhead — at one point, bright red spatterings on the gravelbar caught my attention. Here was a blood trail...and a very fresh one! The blood was still wet! Following the ruby red spatters downstream, I noticed a little white feather, then another. Since a nearby farm had domestic geese, ducks and chickens that were often not penned in, I suspected one of them had been taken either by my wolf or some other animal, maybe a mink, marten or cougar. These blood spatters pointed in the farm's direction...very suspicious.

Continuing to follow the spotted trail, it led onto a large half-rotten log that crossed over the creek. Walking over this log, I could see red spots dotted along sandy loam alongside the creek, now leading upstream...then onto a small mossy green log, over a thick moss patch and into a muddy dip among tall pink-flowered salmonberry bushes. Here was my answer! Impressed into the mud were the large pawprints of a wolf. The tracks and blood trail were just too recent. It was certainly not far away!

Needless to say, I did not venture any farther...with visibility being so restricted by salmonberry bushes and also not wanting to disturb or chase it out from a safe hiding place. This lean wolf needed that farm bird more than the overly-fat man who farmed merely for enjoyment, since he was actually a businessman by trade. I told no one about this wolf for fear that someone would shoot it.

Two pair of large birds nested each year in this beautifully forested wild neighbourhood. These eagles and ravens were always a pleasure to see and hear. The big birds often perched in large sea-level grand fir and Douglas fir trees. For years the two purple-black ravens were a constant in the local environment, livening it with deep croaks, raspy screams and twenty-plus other uniquely raven sounds! The eagles too, expressed their lively presence with high-pitched calls almost daily...although they were more visible than audible, often perching on favourite treetop branches in early morning and at sunset.

The quasi-farmer had mentioned to neighbours that he lost a goose and a couple of ducks. He did not know who or what took them. Then one day a neighbour found half of a large white eggshell near the quasi-farm's gateway. He showed it to me, not sure what kind and I suggested it be an eagle's eggshell. But even so, he assumed it to be a stolen goose egg, telling the fat-man that he thought ravens were taking eggs and had maybe killed the goose and ducks, too. So...the inevitable conclusion resulting from that misinformation: the hobby farmer shot two innocent ravens!

They had missed the fact that a raven is not capable of killing and carrying away a large farm goose or even farm ducks, and that the eggshell was too large for a goose egg. The eggshell was actually from the eagles' nest where two chicks had just hatched; one eagle parent had carried that piece of shell away from the nest, dropping it by chance at the gate. Since then...raven calls have seldom been heard and no new nesting pair has moved in. But I maintained silence about the wolf...knowing its fate would be the same if the locals knew.

Four seasons passed and the following summer I was again out for a morning walk, carrying my camera and hoping to see an elk. A small herd of Vancouver Island elk had been moved to this area in an effort to increase their numbers, so there was a good chance of meeting them. Walking along an old seldom-used sideroad, I came to white and greybrown feathers and fluff dispersed on the ground in ones, twos and little clumps, strung out in a line for at least one hundred yards along the road. This time, they were grouse feathers.

Although the road was hardpacked rust-coloured gravel and dirt, here and there were faint scrapes and scratches on the ground alongside the feathers. At least two animals had jogged along this morning, no more than a few hours ago while eating-on-the-move, apparently. Crouching down, I looked closely. These were definitely wolf tracks. And my wolf was not alone this time: one track was that of a juvenile pup! Upon seeing this...a happy energy began flowing through my mind and body.

"These wolves are definitely survivors," I thought, "able to find food and a place to hide even when strong efforts from humen are aimed at decimating them! The Provincial government's wolf-kill action on northern Vancouver Island has not got them all. A small pack has moved into this rural area and made the powerline clearing a part of its hunting territory. I wonder how successful the little elk-transplant will be, since it seems the wolves have arrived simultaneously with the elk. These wolves are here not merely by coincidence." I hoped both elk and wolves would thrive but knew the chance was slim...having seen too many years of government mismanagement working hand-in-hand with excessive, predatorial commercialism: our wild carnivores were invariably the dead scapegoats!

After a few minutes of such thought my mind came back to earth, to these scuff-marks in the rusty dirt. Then I walked towards a semi-open forest of small second-growth fir and dogwood. Following old partly grown-in logging roads, I kept as quiet as possible. Between fir and amabilis trees were patches of shalal and huckleberry, both with green and half-ripe berries. A little flock of chirping, peeping kinglets were feeding in these low bushes and trees. A few squirrels were also about, chattering and squealing in the near and far distance. But during two hours of walking, seeing old elk droppings and tracks at times — no elk presented themselves. So, I finally gave up on the elk. Since wolves had passed by this morning, they were probably a long distance away.

Three months later, early one frosty morning I took my camera into these same woods, yet had no expectation of seeing anything in particular. Walking along another old unused logging road...gravel crunched underfoot as the inch-high frost crystals broke, making my approach not-so-stealthy. So I moved off the road, stepping onto frozen moss which was relatively quiet. In no hurry, I stopped now and then to pick a handful or two of frozen blue-black or orange-pink berries, observing them for worms before putting them all at once into my mouth. But these were much less tasty than earlier in the season!

With each breath, little clouds of minute white crystals hovered in front of my face a moment, then trailed behind. The ice-cold air was most refreshing and invigorating. Frosty brush and trees were beautiful pastel greens, browns and yellows, all covered with long blades of hoarfrost: a silent, frozen little bit of paradise!

When maybe a hundred yards into the forest, distant sounds of splashing water began filtering through the trees. I stopped, listened...somewhat puzzled, not expecting water anywhere nearby. Could it be a pond with ducks or trumpeter swans splashing? Wetting my right index finger in my mouth, I held it to the air, checking wind direction. A cool sensation indicated a breeze coming from the same direction as the sounds...I was in luck, downwind from the animate unknowns.

Slowly...slowly, I moved towards the splashes under cover of small fir trees, shalal and tall huckleberry bushes. Persistent loud multiple, simultaneous splashes indicated several large animals. What these animals were I could not tell. Now I thought they could be either deer, wolves or elk!

Excited and with high hopes, I crept closer, setting the camera for the dim early light. Soon one small opening through fir trees allowed a clear view. And there, fifteen yards away stood a big bull elk! He and the others were yet unaware of my presence. I stood still...watching. This bull, three younger bulls, six cows and one yearling were peacefully loitering about in the shallow water. But there were no newborns of this year; I wondered if the local wolves were a factor.

The elk were down in a shallow old bulldozer-cut gravel pit that had partly filled into a large foot-deep puddle of clean water. At their ankles thin ice and broken wedges bobbed about, sparkling in the golden shafts of early morning sunlight filtering low through distant alder, pine and dogwood trees. White mist drifted slowly from their nostrils, curled and billowed about. A real pleasure to see at such close range, they were...with big eyes sparkling, black noses wet and shining! Their coats were dark brown and the two larger bulls had antlers of a scraggly look, bent at odd angles. These rare and beautiful moments completely absorbed my awareness for several minutes as the elk quietly, peacefully lounged about. They seemed to be quite enjoying the sunrise, too.

It was a setting perfect for photography. But to get a good photo I would have to show myself since brush and treeboughs were so thick. Stepping into the open, I focussed my three hundred mm telephoto and clicked-away as much film as possible! Seeing me now and hearing the camera, the elk were surprisingly in no panic but on alert. Curious though, they looked back a short while...then trotted away westward into the pine and fir forest almost in single-file. Left behind by their breath, little transparent sparkly white ice-crystal clouds curled and trailed into the woods behind them. At a mere twenty yards in, now mostly hidden by shalal and huckleberry brush, the elk stopped momentarily then just casually walked away. They certainly had no fear of me!

In the big solitary puddle, sparkling ripples and tiny wavelets peaked, swirled and bounced... gradually slowing to a halt among faint squeaks of bobbing broken ice. Brush rustled now and then in the near distance as the elk made their casual escape towards several very large ancient Douglas fir trees. I stood in the cold silence, listening and mentally thanking the elk for being here...for bringing me a few minutes of their presence and a happiness that would definitely last much longer.

And what happened to my multicoloured wolf? A couple of years later, one day I was in a Courtenay cafe having coffee and socially chitchatting with a few familiars. We were talking about wildlife. Perchance, a young lady in the group mentioned that a man she knew in Cumberland had shot a wolf that was frequenting the powerline and that she had seen its pelt.

Questioning her about the wolf...she described its motley fur. Her comment brought a sudden jolt of pain, of sadness to my body and mind: her description sounded just too much like my wolf! I told her that it was probably the same one I had enjoyed so much seeing two years previously and...it was most likely shot illegally! But I knew if I called the local conservation officer, nothing would be done about it...the "C" in "C.O." being a misnomer in the extreme.

Someplace Remote

The month was October and wild mushrooms of all sorts were coming up in good numbers. Told by a mushroom company's owner that I could make a good income picking pine mushrooms in an area where they were now growing well, it seemed worth trying. I drove hundreds of miles at my own expense to this well-known area where various companies' field-buyers were set up. I worked hard and persisted for three days, but finding few mushrooms. Other pickers were not doing well either…even the more experienced ones. After these few days of wandering in the woods for almost nothing, I decided to go for a seven hundred mile drive to another place that purportedly had a good crop coming. There too, everything was new to me so on the first day had to scout a lot, again making little money for my efforts.

On the second day under warm sunshine and a wide blue sky, I found a gently sloping conifer and aspen forest that showed several small patches of creamy white buttons. This area seemed to have good potential, with extensive forest continuing on and on in all directions! Now my hopes were up a wee bit. Many species of mushroom were scattered in large numbers throughout these pinewoods…some that I recognized, others not. It was all quite beautiful! The ground everywhere was a cacophony of colour from literally thousands of mushrooms in red, orange, yellow, cream, white, brown, rust, purple and even blue! Coloured patterns dotted the ground in little clusters, singles, curves and sometimes fairyrings in circles or ovals…some contrasting with patches of green moss and whitish reindeer lichen, yet others blending in nearly invisible as if trying to hide.

For some unknown time I wandered through this natural paradise, albeit not randomly, focussed mainly on the pine mushroom…while also enjoying the beauty of these other, non-dollar mushrooms, stopping at times to observe them closer. At one point I stood looking out across the wide silent valley at white, grey and deep blue rhomboidal mountain peaks that jutted up many miles away. And I was beginning to feel good since I had stumbled onto several pine mushroom spots that were in multiples, not merely singles. Now standing under one large lodgepine tree, thinking to check downslope from it…the peace and quiet ended abruptly. Just below, maybe a hundred yards down, a loud deep throaty howl exploded from the forest!

This was the unmistakable sound of a lone wolf! Although the first time hearing a wolf, I instantly recognized its unique sound. It let out four very deep-voiced, short howls that would be heard for a mile or so! This adult wolf was too close for comfort, so I decided to immediately leave! Having little previous direct experience with wolves I was uncertain about its present purpose and thought there were probably more wolves nearby. By now late afternoon, time enough remained in the day to scout elsewhere so I drove about five miles to a flat pine-treed bench for another scout.

Lucky again, enough buttons were showing to finish the day there. Back at the buyers' camp in early evening I was rewarded with a hundred fifty dollars for my day's pick. But the local fellow in line just in front of me was paid a thousand dollars for his pick!

Returning next day to a half-mile from where the wolf howled, I worked a slope that had some nice solid buttons coming, along with mushrooms at various stages all the way to large old open flags. This day was another pleasantly warm sunny one after a beautiful starry, almost freezing night. The wolf's presence lingered in my mind…and I now had a wish that this wolf would let me see it! Slowly, I zigzagged uphill…loading my green nylon backpack with buttons and two plastic grocery bags with open lower grades. Working up a sweat, the sunshine was no longer pleasant, but hot! Soon though, I entered a thick subalpine fir clump on a small flat higher up, where the shade was refreshingly cool!

Besides the most welcome shade, under these trees was a pleasant surprise: an animal trail passed through, about two feet wide and three inches deep, tampled into the evergreen needle bed…and very recently used. It was a wolf trail! Kneeling down, I looked closely at the churned-up needles. Though indistinct, a variety of paw sizes were discernible: I was definitely in the home territory of a wolf pack!

Unstrapping the heavy full backpack, I placed it against one treetrunk then sat down in the soft needles beside the trail for a much-needed cooldown and rest, leaning my back against another small balsam trunk. Gazing at their pathway, I wondered where the wolves were…how close I was. Within a few minutes though, I was recharged and ready for another walk. Taking off my blue canvas western jacket, I draped it over the backpack then paced westward along this wolf trail under the balsam trees until an expanse of open huckleberry and rhododendron bushes. This brushy area had little chance of mushroom growth, so I turned back, retracing my steps along the wolf trail. Upon returning to the backpack I was feeling badly that biological force of having to urinate. I did so at the trailside…not giving any thought about how wolves mark boundaries and leave messages.

Then walking along the trail eastward, I stopped where it dropped down steeply beside a large rounded granite boulder. The much-used pathway wound around below it, then down into a narrow pine-treed gully and out of sight. Here again, in the dirt I could see both large adult tracks and small distinct pup tracks. I thought, "A den must be not far away!" Now, I thought it would be prudent to avoid going down into this deep shady gully!

So instead, I pushed uphill through thick clumps of copperbush towards a stand of conifer and poplar trees. Sunshine, fresh leafy smells and the soothing, relaxing silence dominated my senses as I wended upward through this jungle of tough buckbrush. Two minutes later I was under an old lodgepine tree about thirty yards above my backpack and jacket. I stood there debating about how much farther up to go, while gazing at the lovely snow-capped bluegrey mountains far away to the south.

Then the peaceful silence ended. A loud high-pitched yipping burst from the trees below! Four or five wolf pups yipped-and-yapped in wild, youthful excitement right by my backpack and jacket! I stood still, also intensely excited in my own way, enjoying it all for about ten short seconds…until joining in from the same spot: one loud deep-voiced, long howl that abruptly stopped! Silence suddenly regained its gentle dominance of the mountainside.

I stood under this ancient pine tree listening for sound and watching for any movement of the brush below. The pepperspray, I took from its holster and held it — ready. Listening and waiting for about five minutes, the only sounds around were intermittent soft rustlings of trembling aspen leaves. And silence prevailed. Realizing that I had upset this wolf family by the presence of human objects and the smell of strange urine by their trail, I thought it best to leave the area now...so they could continue their normal routine. Thinking it should now be safe, I returned slowly, cautiously, through copperbush and huckleberry buckbrush that allowed almost no visibility.

Back down on the trail, I could see that freshly disturbed duff and needles had stopped just a few feet from my backpack! The wolf pups had come up from the gully, past the boulder, up to the little shady flat under subalpine fir trees...where they were stopped by a sight and smell of something unknown. Almost immediately they vented their surprise in the high-pitched youthful chorus that had some minutes ago also surprised, but immensely entertained me! The one adult must have been a short way behind them. It soon caught up and put them in order with its deep-voiced statement! Then the wolves retreated back down into the gully.

Now I stood at the big rounded boulder. Leaning my left hand against it...I took one last look down their trail. Feeling most happy about this rare experience in life, I vowed to never tell anyone where this wolf family lived. Then stepping over to my jacket and backpack, I strapped on the heavy load — about twenty pounds of buttons — then began a slow, careful descent down the steep slope. Since the sunshine was so hot my jacket was strung through the backpack's straps, dangling behind, which also freed one more hand for grasping brush or branches...a necessity on such steep terrain. And the pepperspray was back into its holster...my wolf neighbours obviously having no ill-will towards me! Since their home range was so rugged, thankfully, there would be little chance anyone else would discover this inconspicuous wolves' denning area.

Present and Past

In the mid 1970s I worked for British Columbia's largest wood products company out of Franklin River Camp. One weekend, leaving early Saturday afternoon I went for a drive along the gravel logging roads. Such was my usual entertainment: exploring new places, watching wildlife and looking at rocks. Taking the mainline towards old Sarita River logdump site, in no hurry I stopped by the river to enjoy the antics of two little whitewater birds. Water ouzels were busily chasing each other and chatting in their unique raspy piping-sound!

Perfectly designed for swimming underwater in rapids, they were picking insect larvae from the bottom among boulders. When the birds resurfaced, rounded transparent water droplets quickly rolled off greyish-blue feathers. Their feathers looked dry and smooth, more like soft velvet, being so fine and tightly together. Now standing on a small mottled grey boulder, bobbing up and down with their backwards knees constantly bending in little pushups, the ouzels looked so energetic and full of enjoyment! Smiling…I too, felt pleasure and energized by their unique expressions and exuberance for life!

After watching this little natural drama, I continued along the winding road until an odd-looking cliffside hole caught my attention. It had been dug long ago a short way into solid brownish rock and was much overgrown with green lichen and moss. Just inside, I could see traces of turquoise-coloured copper bloom here and there on the cave walls. This tunnel had been a shortlived mining attempt, by appearance maybe one hundred years ago. Outside, I picked up a little rusty rock mottled with bluegreen carbonate…a nice keepsake. Two larger rocks I broke open with a small sledgehammer, exposing silvery white iron ore and specks of golden yellow copper ore.

After this interesting discovery, driving onward I kept a keen eye on the mossy rockbluffs along the way. By the time I arrived at the old logdump and Alberni Inlet near where it meets Barkley Sound, the Sun was setting…so thought it a good place to stay the night. Next morning, the light and heat of sunshine awoke me early. The tide was out and air fresh with smells of the living saltwater seashore! After wolfing down some cold breakfast, I slipped on high rubber boots then walked westward along the beach. Loose gravel crunched underfoot. Clams and crabs were making their wee, lowtide clicking sounds. Crows cawed and picked among the rocks and the high-pitched call of an eagle drifted on a cool breeze from across the inlet. In the far-off distance a speck of unusually bright colour momentarily appeared, then vanished.

Something reddish-pink was moving near waterline. What it was, I could not tell. I had my twenty-power spotting scope in hand and looking through it…could see a dark animal coming my way purposely stepping from rock to rock at a stop-and-go pace. As it approached closer, its identity became apparent as a blackish-brown mink carrying in its mouth a squid that was about half the size of itself! As the mink wended over and around boulders, the squid's limber tentacles were bouncing and bending like soft rubber over the cream-coloured barnacles and yellow-ochre rockweed. It kept coming my way, yet unaware of me.

Thinking to give it some space I walked back to the car. There I waited cheerfully, watching through the scope. Its bouncy gait, body movement and head position gave the mink a happy look. Closer and closer it came, then disappeared awhile until reappearing about fifteen yards away as it ran up onto the old logdump pier. Its long brown-black body and tail curved gracefully in a smooth undulating motion. Stopping momentarily to look at me through shining small eyes…it then bound across the gravel road and up into bushy green woods, out of sight under shalal and huckleberry. No doubt, there was a nest of baby mink nearby! Thinking about how this mink could catch a squid…apparently the only way would be if the squid were trapped in a tidal pool, since mink can easily swim short distances underwater.

Again walking back to waterline of the little bay, I turned westward. Here in shallow water lay a brownish, circular metal object coated with turquoise spots of copper carbonate and little creamy-white barnacles. It was a large brass cogwheel — from what, I did not know. Made with mathematical precision, the curving cogs gave it a beauty that would probably have it acceptable as artistic sculpture! And a few yards away lying flat among the rocks was another circular brass object, also dashed with pale blue. Two nice keepsakes, these were little bits of tangible history from Sarita River's early logging days.

My next exploration focussed on a small tidal island to the northeast which was not an island at low tide, now separated only by a narrow muddy channel. I walked along the beach towards it. At one point along the bay a circular grey metallic object, maybe a foot in diameter, was barely visible above gravel and under about two feet of water. It looked like grey lead but had several rusty nuts in a circle. I puzzled over this for awhile and thought that it was probably a part of some old logging machinery; but a second thought came that it may be a beach mine from World War II. If so, was it still alive? I suddenly lost interest in wading out to it!

Now…I kept walking towards the little island! The air was so fresh with the ocean's lowtide smells! On the breeze came another high-pitched call of an eagle. The sound did not match the bird's size but seemed appropriate for its long-distance communications. Nearing the island's western end, instead of crossing the twenty-yard wide muddy channel, I climbed up through tall green and bluegreen grass above high-tide line to sit under a large old alder tree, leaning my back against it. The warm sunshine felt so good on my face and arms! I just sat fully enjoying the soothing natural peace that filled the space of this little natural paradise. Some pleasant time passed…as I slipped into a comforting semi-sleep.

But eventually as all things earthly or heavenly do, everpresent change arrived…this time brought by a fly that was buzzing nearby…bringing me quickly back to the waking state! Directly in front grew a large clump of tall thick bluegreen grass. As I looked through it towards an unlogged ancient fir forest across the inlet, a greyish object began bobbing up and down among rounded black and grey boulders on the island's northwest beach. Some smallish animal was coming towards me from the other side of the island, moving back and forth, stopping and starting among the large barnacle-mottled rocks. Finally its head raised up to sniff the air, with black shiny nose twitching from side to side. It was a young bandit with black eyemask, the raccoon's most unique feature!

It had not seen me as I sat still and low, peeking through tall grass. The raccoon was busily searching for small crabs, mud clams and such. A pleasure to watch, it was moving quietly, slowly closer until almost directly across the mud channel. Again it sniffed the air, head and nose held high…this time more persistently. Standing tall on its hind legs with front paws up then leaning onto a large brown boulder, the raccoon began staring to the northeast along the mud channel's island edge. Now with ears erect, it stared hard…while remaining motionless, suddenly frozen to the spot!

What caught its interest, I could not see at first. I carefully parted some more grass. There it was! A large sow blackbear calmly grazing in an open patch of thick green tidal grass…stood only twenty-five yards from where I sat! Beside her were two tiny cubs, looking soft and delicate in their fuzzy black fur! The raccoon did not look at them long. Ducking its head, it turned and tiptoed away in a hurry — back along the island's rocky beach, soon disappearing around the bend and boulders.

The cubs were very lively, chasing through tall grass as they played follow-the-leader up over rocks and onto dry grey logs. One cub climbed onto, then padded along a large branchy old treetop snag that lay on the ground. The snag's narrow pointed top angled upward off the ground to maybe six feet in the air. The other cub followed on its sibling's heels. Up they went…with uncertain steps all the way to the narrow, precarious top! That was a crowded little space with nowhere to go but straight down to the ground!

Now they were just twenty yards away, straight across the mud channel from me. Their hungry mother kept voraciously grazing…oblivious of my presence nearby. I suddenly realized that this was a potentially dangerous circumstance, if she decided to cross over from the island or became aware of where I was. We were too close for comfort! And my car was at least one hundred yards away. The big alder behind me could be climbed to doubtful safety: bears being strong, agile climbers.

The cubs continued their childlike enjoyment moving about among twisting grey branches, testing their dexterity while their little young minds learned about the natural realm…this all-new world where pleasure and pain were being discovered and lived! After inspecting the snagtop, somehow without falling off…they carefully padded back down in single-file, then jumped off over their heads into the tall grass. Although these little cubs did not know, their playful antics were also my pleasure!

Then the mother bear raised her head with nostrils held high, twitching side to side, up and down. Standing still, she persisted sniffing the breeze for a couple of minutes while slowly turning her head back and forth…ears perked and listening. It now became obvious to me that she had detected my scent but was not yet aware of my position. I kept motionless…watching through the tall thick grass. Now her demeanor became less relaxed and more serious.

The human smell was no doubt too strong, too close! Slowly, she turned towards the brush and trees. Padding into a little thicket of twinberry, hawthorn, spruce and fir…her two wee cubs tagging closely behind, one by one, they vanished into the brushy shadows. Their silent world of nonverbal gesture-communication was a real wonder! And this mother bear, I thought to be quite intelligent, having chosen the tidal island as safe haven for her cubs while simultaneously a ready food supply for herself.

With them out of sight, it was now my turn to move…stepping quietly away and smiling from a morning so full of uncommon experience, happiness seemed to envelop the whole environment inside and all around. For the moment…we were all safe and each enjoying our own little world. Back at the car, the mink reappeared by roadside, hesitated there…loped across then scooted in a hurry down to the beach again, moving with urgency as a parent naturally would! Saying a mental, "Goodbye and thankyou," to these exciting wild animals for just being here…I turned the key and drove towards a small oceanside village that was built half on floats and half on rock bluffs.

As I drove along dodging dry potholes now and then, thoughts came: of how alive this seaside forest is, with animals in greater variety and number than farther inland; of how important it is for wildlife to have some long stretches of saltwater beach that has gravel, sand, mud and tidal pools as component parts; of adjacent land that is forested, being necessary as living space, for a good distance inland; of the ocean as great provider of food necessary for so many species of land mammals and birds.

With such thoughts, time passed quickly and I soon arrived at the tiny seaside hamlet inhabited mostly by fishermen, called Bamfield. It was — I had been told — during the 1800s and early 1900s, a whale-killing station until too few whales were left. Now just above the floating buildings, I stood on a mossy rockbluff thinking about the immaturity of humanity: how sad that human beings have not learned to live in a balanced way.

But now, this was a lovely scenic little place still dominated by Nature's powerful natural forces. A delicious fresh saltwater smell mingled with aromatic fir tree pitch. I thought how fortunate I was to not be a bigcity denizen, whose experience is foreign to this! Random calls of seagulls, crows and eagles punctuated the silence…as did a rhythmic soft splashing of waves against vertical rock cliffs and wooden floats. A gentle tinkling of bells echoed up from the fishing boats below. Here, humanity and Nature met with not much disagreement. And here, Nature was allowing and giving to humanity in its silent, subtle ways…while yet maintaining its position of power.

After an hour of appreciating the life and beauty of Barkley Sound, the time came to venture inland on another pothole logging road. This road led through a small block of shady old forest of very big red cedar, western hemlock and balsam, then wound across a broad low area of little hills. These had been mostly clearcut in several stages over the years. The older clearcuts were much grown-in with berry bushes now in bloom: huckleberry dotted with tiny white and pale pink flowers and salmonberry with larger deep pink, star-like blossoms. Some huge flaring old, partly rotten stumps were beautifully decorated with these flowery bushes and pale green ferns, rooted into their tops and sides. Hummingbirds were busily buzzing and zipping around, licking up nectar and minute insects while their brilliant iridescent green, yellow, red and orange feathers flashed on-and-off among the bushes!

Rounding a tight curve, the road entered a broad long valley then ran straight for at least half-a-mile. In the far distance, barely visible on the road was a black dot. Mildly surprised, I thought it was probably a bear. Proceeding slowly closer and closer I kept my eyes on potholes and the motionless black dot. Soon recognizable, the form was sure enough of a blackbear causally standing broadside…looking back at the approaching car. Then it turned, walking away but remaining at the road's centre. I slowed down. The closer I got, I could see that it was in no hurry. At sixty yards away the bear's pigeon-toed walk became clearly discernible.

Now it stopped, turned around and stood facing me with ears perked straight up! Pushing the brake pedal hard, I stopped the car. This bear seemed determined to remain on the road! I was driving a vw Beetle, a small challenge to a self-confident bear. I watched and waited as it stared back. A skinny, long-legged animal with scruffy fur, maybe a hundred fifty pounds…it looked half-starved! I felt sorry for it. Shutting off the motor, I sat watching and waiting for the bear to make up its mind where to go next. But it stood firm…holding position!

After about two minutes I stepped out and stood by the car…keeping the door open. Just then the bear began to snarl, showing its creamy white teeth! Its ears moved back flat against its head. It growled a medium-high-toned: "R-r-r-r-r-r-r-r...r-r-r-r-r...r-r-r-r-r!" A long distance away, about fifty yards, I wondered why so angry. This bear was in a very bad mood...so had no fear of me and no intention to move off the road!

Then of all things, it began to bark — sounding just like a dog! Its bark was of a medium-high-pitch similar to a Collie's. This was a completely unexpected sound for a bear! I got back into the car, thinking to turn around and leave the bear alone. Obviously, I had crossed an invisible personal boundary and impinged upon its sense of safety: its comfort space. The bear continued to bark and snap its jaws with black lips tightly back and pointed ivory teeth flashing! And with stiffened front legs, it alternately stamped paws hard onto the gravel — warning me to keep back! It continued sending these signals for a minute or so as I sat still in the car observing and learning about blackbear behaviour...yet with hand on the ignition key ready to escape, if need be!

I could see that this poor animal had been having a rough time and was no doubt hungry. It may have had some bad memory of contact with people or maybe had tapeworms or some other health trouble. Possibly the previous summer was too dry, producing little food and the winter had been difficult for it. Now early spring, this very thin bear appeared to have not yet found enough grubs, ants and hornet larvae to regain normal metabolism and strength. The bear was considerably underweight and I really felt sorry for the poor grouchy animal: it seemed so alone and uncared about!

After a short while the bear began to relax slightly, quit stamping and snapping...seeing that I was no threat just sitting still and quiet in the car with motor off. Its ears perked back up. Then it turned around. Now walking away slowly but still in a tense manner the half-starved bear angled towards roadside northward where it stepped off and down, moving out of sight under the bright flowery brush. I waited a few minutes in case the hungry animal returned to the road...but it did not. So, firing up the motor I continued along my planned route, looking for the bear as I passed its point of departure. But it was hidden from view under the little brushy forest of huckleberry, shalal and tall salmonberry bushes.

Another tiny winged gem flashed across — bright emerald green and metallic yellow, bringing the thought of how beauty, pleasure and pain coincide in both animal and human environments. I hoped this unfortunate bear would soon find a good feeding area and so regain its health and balance. This road led towards Nitinat Lake which was next on my agenda. The drive would be long, with several potholed sideroads and views of vast clearcuts growing in with sapling evergreens and alder. At times it was difficult to ascertain which road was the mainline leading to the lake. Since no logging was on, there was no road maintenance and few signs were up. But eventually I found my way back to another familiar mainline that went to the lake's southeastern shore.

Finally arriving, I stopped for lunch at a stoney beach along this unique tidal lake. To the west and southwest beautiful forest of huge ancient conifers stood still and silent. Looking across to the northwest side, the view was an old clearcut as far as the eye could see along the lake's length...now a vast young forest of small fir, hemlock, cedar and alder...the tallest being about thirty feet high. And towering above just behind me were old-growth red cedar, balsam, western hemlock and fir...all wrapped with thick moss and long black or pale yellow beard-lichen.

Beneath and between them grew younger trees of various ages, sizes and species all the way down to wee one-inch seedlings sprouting atop rusty brown ancient logs. These seedlings were accompanied by four or five species of tiny lichen in colours of tan, black, white, pale green, yellow, orange and red; here was another realm of miniature curving geometric shapes, branching antlers, round or oval spheres topping thin vertical threads, or little shining cups. Here too were shalal, huckleberry and salmonberry growing sporadically and now offering a few blossoms to hummingbirds, butterflies, flies and wee wild black honeybees…then later in the year would provide berries for bluejays, Canadian jays, bears, insects, voles and mice.

Sitting on this warm rocky shore, I thought about and compared the open young forest I had seen an hour or so ago and the one across this lake, with the ancient forest just behind me — of huge old trees and much more shade. The life forces of Nature are omnipresent…with various species ready to grow or reproduce whenever an ecosystem alters, be it man-made or natural, slowly or suddenly…it is obvious that changes in sunlight will effect changes in plant, lichen and fungus species, some increasing, others decreasing, thus likewise with the local animal species. The clearcut is a sudden change bringing more sunshine to ground level, higher temperatures, quicker water evaporation and runoff…all dictating what plants, insects and animals will or will not be there.

This inner focus was then drawn back outward by four goldeneye ducks quietly paddling by, keenly observing me through bright yellow eyes! They looked cheerful and happy in a childlike way, inducing similar feelings in me. Slowly, they paddled away…out of sight behind overhanging shoreline willow and red osier brush. Shortly afterward as I finished lunch and returned to the car, a kingfisher flew by, rattling its loud coarse call along lakeshore. Firing up the car, I drove onward. Just then a Steller's bluejay glided past sapling cedar trees chattering its coarse call! These birds were a real pleasure to see and hear: alive and well in this yet fairly intact ecosystem.

My next destination was high up, along a new branch-road where I had been working two days before as a cat-swamper. The big orange-red D-12 Cat was ideal for cutting the road through soft sandstone and shale, moving quickly into the three hundred-plus year-old forest. One day as we were working at a hairpin curve I noticed above on a low greybrown rock cliffside, two most unusual objects. About ten feet up, they projected in relief from the smooth siltstone. Shockingly beautiful — they were the perfect forms of ancient seashells!

Side by side, they curved and rippled the rock with their flowing flared shapes. With bulged hinge-ends at the top, the shells curved outwards and down, ending with a wide wavey front edge. Probably top and bottom halves of the same seashell, they were the same size: about ten inches wide on front and thirteen inches long! These were truly ancient works of art, manifested by Nature's boundless forces of life and intelligence! I had never seen that particular fossil anywhere…not in museums, books or magazines. So, on this day I had my camera.

The higher I went, the slower…as the newly built road became quite rough with jagged broken pieces waiting to cut a tire. Driving over one part, I thought about the four large highgrade Douglas fir and some hemlock logs varying from two-and-a-half to four feet in diameter, that were underneath the road. Some high-quality wood from two hundred to three hundred year-old trees were gone to waste as roadfill. I knew they were there because I had watched in dismay as the bulldozer operator buried them! It was an unnecessary manoeuvre since the shale rockbank was soft enough for the D-12's huge blade to easily cut through for fill. I learned that this was common practice for sake of expediency in time; the company would lose a lot of money, probably not known by the highest echelons, in order to save a bit of money by shortening building time. And of course, the British Columbia government also lost money. But we did pull out several five and six-foot diameter fir logs from that small dip on the grade…before the D-12's big blade pushed tons of broken shale and siltstone over the others.

Continuing slowly up…winding around the southeast side of the slope, in the distance another large lake shining like a brilliant white diamond, came into view. Far below to the southwest and west, ancient forest stretched to the far distant, shining pale blue and white Pacific Ocean! That was the Carmanah forest where unknown to me, marbled murrelets were nesting. The grade straightened and steepened then at the top a hairpin curved to the left. But first, I stopped lower down to look for fossils in recently broken sandstone. Yes, this rock too, was loaded with pockmarks and variously-shaped holes, some with bits of white limestone mixed in…the remnant remains of sea creatures from an ancient time; how long ago, I did not know.

I checked a cracked rock outcropping along the road's lower side where open fissures varied from one inch to eight inches wide, most of which being natural openings, here long before the bulldozer had bladed it over. Leaning forward I noticed something glowing in the shade. Snow-white, it was a foot inside one of the cracks. Kneeling down to have a better look, what I saw was a complete surprise! Tiny crystals, clear and white, lay in a perfect spiral about one inch in diameter. Quartz-like crystals projected outward in all directions yet kept the definite spiralling shape of an ancient land-snail!

At that moment…not thinking to get the camera to photograph this little gem, I reached in with both hands. Carefully, I slid it with my left index finger into the palm of my right hand. In so-doing a few crystals broke off. Drawing my hand back, the curled form sparkled brilliantly in the sunshine! This snail's shell was composed completely of minute crystals in the hundreds! For a few moments, I admired the ancient beauty… then with thumb and forefinger tried picking it up. But it crumbled into a little white pile of sparkling powder! To my immense disappointment the beautiful crystal snail had disappeared! At this, the middle of my chest tightened; I shook my head at my stupidity. Heavy sadness overcame mind and body.

I belatedly realized that it was composed of fragile calcite crystals, not quartz! Nature had probably taken millions of years to form this little treasure and it had probably lain inside the rock cavity for more millions. But I the human, destroyed it in an instant with a finger-touch. How sad. And I thought no one would ever accept this incident as true if I told them of it: a snail made of calcite crystals?

After that short-lived positive-to-negative experience, I drove up to the hairpin curve. There, my mind and body were subjected to another big shock. The two large seashell fossils had also vanished! I could not believe my eyes! And the smooth-faced cliff had changed shape, not as steep or high. Getting out of the car, I walked to the spot where the big shells were two days before. Now I knew. Fresh bulldozer tracks marked the shattered ground. A big blade-edge had been ran along the soft siltstone cliff-face, tumbling those most impressive natural sculptures to the ground!

Now I was irate! Obviously the cat operator had worked overtime the day before, no doubt alone — just to erase this ancient fossil bed from obvious view! It was a depressing sight. I could see how far this company would go to prevent a few acres of Crown Land where grew a three hundred fifty year-old forest…from being designated for some other use; they had legal rights to the wood but nothing else. The hairpin curve was already plenty wide for loaded trucks so cutting out this cliff was not necessary.

Calming myself, I shrugged my shoulders and looked into the infinite blue sky above. Then looking at the rock rubble directly below the fossilized slope I picked up several broken pieces, some that fit together, slightly smaller seashells of the same type. Other rock pieces contained little cavities of ammonite forms varying in size from one to three inches in diameter. The rock was mostly a soft greybrown siltstone while some was fine sandstone; it had very little white seashell calcium, since that had dissolved out over many millenniums.

Another interesting natural phenomenon was in open-faced display just beyond where the D-12 was parked...and on a high vertical sandstone cliff, presently out of the bulldozer's reach. Perfectly spherical balls of various-sized sandstone rock, mostly cannonball sized, some smaller and one larger, projected randomly from the cliff-face. This was another most unusual formation! Naturally, I wondered how these had come to be but never found a possible answer until many years later after seeing similar round stones called concretions.

But now feeling somewhat down, taking a few photoes never entered my mind...so I ended up with none. Again looking awhile at the broken siltstone pieces scattered about, there were several seashell shapes either in relief or as little hollows. A few of these fossils I gathered up to take home. As I drove back down heading to camp, I wished I had kept my mouth shut that first day...about seeing the two giant seashell sculptures.

Maybe they would have been there a bit longer if I had not questioned the cat skinner: "Did you see those big fossils?"

"Fossils? What fossils...what are fossils?" he replied.

I thought..."How could he not see them? How could he not know a fossil?"

Then I replied, "Ancient seashell shapes in the rock."

"No...I never saw any. Where?" he replied.

"Just back there on the cliff-face...two beautiful big seashells," I said, while twisting sideways and raising my left arm pointing to them.

"I don't know what fossils are. I've never seen any," he said, playing dumb.

At first I was a bit puzzled that he had apparently not noticed them...so blatantly and perfectly projected they were out of the smooth rockface that he had cut the day previously! But now I knew the reason, so never mentioned this incident for fear of losing my job. And maybe not by coincidence — two days later I was transferred to a different job, so never again saw those fossil and cannonball cliffs.

Tap-Tap-Tap

High above, thin white clouds were drifting slowly across a deep blue sky. On this September morning the air was almost cold. With legs and knees straining, chest heaving out and in, out and in…I climbed gradually, zigzagging up the steep forest slope. My knees were beginning to burn at the joints. Even so, this hard work was made less difficult by the fresh clean forest smells: young saplings of pine, fir and hemlock trees were emitting from their green needle-boughs refreshing aromas that saturated the almost-still air. Among these, now and then came a little invisible olfactory cloud of another sort, strong and pleasant, generated by yellow pitch drips that oozed out of…and very slowly trickled down…the thick grooved bark of three hundred to five hundred year-old conifer trees that were towering above in all directions.

Stopping for a rest, I leaned against one four-foot diameter fir that was festooned with black and yellowgreen beard lichen on the trunk and limbs, right to its top. Sunlight shone through the bigtree canopy in bright narrow beams. Here was a special reality that few people ever experience! These were moments of peace, beauty and comfort unknown in the human realm. Now halfway up the mountain, looking through little openings between huge treetrunks I could see to the south one beautiful glacier-capped rocky peak…bright white with a touch of new snow.

A clump of hemlock saplings stood to my left and below, their flat needle-boughs dotted with tiny spherical dewdrops. Where the sunbeams shone onto them, minute brilliant stars were sending forth long thin rays outward in the purest clear prismatic colours one could possibly see: colourless white, deep blue, emerald green, ruby red and deep yellow! Blinking steadily on-off-on…they were as if wee lights emanating from an invisible realm of absolute purity! I had just entered a little paradise.

One sapling held a spider's web lined with dewdrops, also sparkling and shimmering colourless and silvery white with tiny stars flashing on and off…red, green or blue. From just beyond these small trees came the steady shishing of a little creek, its transparent clear water tumbling over large angular rocks as it flowed and swirled into white foam along the steep descent. Then not far above in the big trees there began multiple high-pitched chirping and peeping. I stood still, listening…but could not see the wee winged beings.

Their constant chatting, like sweet music to me became gradually louder as a flock of tiny birds flitted and hopped from branch to branch, lower and lower in their search of food. Soon they were visible among lower boughs: about ten pale yellowish-green kinglets, both male and female, the males having a bright yellow and red feathery crown. Three flew down into hemlock saplings right beside me busily inspecting branches and needles while seemingly oblivious of my presence. One male, constantly flitting wings and tail, came along an eye-level branch until two feet from my now-happy face...allowing a rare close-up view of our most tiny mountain bird!

It was near this spot several days before that I heard a blackbear whoofing at me from behind a thick treeclump only twenty yards upslope! Now I had to be cautious, knowing it could be still in the area. After my entertaining kinglets had flown away...doing their valuable but thankless job of keeping trees healthy, I moved higher upslope to a small pine mushroom patch. I picked several nice solid buttons, each time filling in the stemholes with dirt. A benign monetarily-oriented activity...this was my reason for being in this beautiful ancient mountainside forest.

Then I moved westward paralleling the slope, finding more mushrooms in little groups. But soon the stoney, moss and lichen covered ground became poor for about two hundred yards. Next I had to bull my way through a couple of thickly treed parts; such were times of no visibility but of some apprehension. At one point while crossing the top edge of a small grey rock-cliff...a feeling of being watched came upon me. Looking around...I saw nothing and heard nothing. But now I was more alert than usual! Just upslope there were more thick little evergreen trees and bushes growing in clusters. My apprehension increased with such restricted visibility!

Moving back under the pine forest where it was more open, I looked down from the cliff's edge. Barely visible in thick green moss below was a patch of mushrooms that glowed a dim white in the shade. Leaving my button backpack, I climbed down over mossy boulders to them. A few big open ones peeked out of the deep moss while others hid, unseen. Here, a couple of wormy flags had been picked and partly eaten. By what, I could not discern. Looking around... all that I saw were trees, large angular rocks and moss. I picked a plastic grocery bag half-full then climbed back up to the clifftop, all the while still feeling a bit apprehensive.

Following this cliffedge westward to its end, I entered an open space where one very large bump in the pale brown dirt brought a sudden jolt of excited energy...and an expectant smile! Down onto knees, with hands swishing off the dirt — I was pleased to see the bubblegum dome of one very large pine button! Plunging fingers to the stem's bottom, I pried it up and out. Squeezing the stem hard, it was solid: no maggots in this one! It looked and felt to weigh about one pound! After filling in the stemhole I checked somewhat farther westward, finding nothing, so returned to the area of big glowing flags that were just below the cliff. Again, that sense of danger entered my awareness but could see nothing. This was a feeling familiar to me, one that I had experienced several other times over the years...and it was usually accurate.

Now, since my button backpack was full I walked back westward to the more open shrubby forest, went downslope about fifty yards, then leaned it and two flagbags against a conspicuous lodgepine tree which was a good stashing spot. Holding my sixth-sense at arm's length, I angled back up and eastward to enter an area of rolling humps under small hemlock trees. Circling around the base of one hump, I moved slowly upward. At the top an image that always induces excitement and energy greeted me: a large fairy-ring of pine mushrooms! Still that sense of danger lingered. Yet again...I heard and saw nothing unusual.

At this time, pepperspray was not yet available so I was carrying my Canadian Centennial 30-30 rifle as self-defence. It was my equivalent of teeth-and-claws when out in cougar and bear country. Laying the rifle down, I pulled a plastic grocery bag from one boot, kneeled on hands and knees then began testing the mushrooms for worms. Almost all of them were wormy! Even so, I salvaged a few big solid flags out of thirty-five or so mushrooms. While I was so engrossed with this ring of fungus...the unseen watcher arrived...unknown to me.

From directly behind — a quick regular tap-tap-tap-tapping sound of wood on wood brought my back instantly upright! Turning my head immediately left, I saw the spike-top of a little dry lodgepine ground-snag bouncing up and down, striking another beneath it. That same moment I glimpsed a little black furry object disappearing at ground level behind the three-foot diameter treetrunk, just ten yards away! My first thought was of a pine marten...but it seemed too dark, too black. Waiting and watching for maybe thirty seconds for something to show...my curiosity grew as nothing appeared at the base or higher up along the deeply grooved reddish brown bark. Remaining on my knees, I waited...a bit puzzled.

Then at the big trunk's right edge about three feet up, the fuzzy black object reappeared oh-so-slowly from behind the tree, as if growing out of the thick ribbed bark. First a fuzzy ear, then a brown eye, then a shiny black nose appeared. Half of a bear's face now peeked shyly for a few moments. Then its whole head moved out, looking somewhat humorous with the rest of its body hidden! I could not help smiling.

Since this circumstance appeared nonthreatening, my spontaneous response was a softly spoken: "Oh! Hullo there!...You sure are pretty, aren't you!"

Of course, the bear's reply was nonverbal: just a steady stare of its sparkling brown eyes. After some moments thus, it gained courage and stepped out...standing boldly in full view. It stood facing directly at me with ears straight up, eyes firm and unblinking and with front paws towards me, albeit slightly pigeon-toed. It was a healthy-looking young blackbear, maybe three years old, weighing about two hundred pounds and with a beautiful shining thick coat of fur.

Now I waited and watched. The bear waited and watched. For quite some time...we silently stared at each other. After awhile though, I could see that this bear had no fear and no intention to move away! Its expressionless fuzzy face had an air of seriousness, even so. I pulled the rifle to my side and cocked it. Still crouched on knees, I kept barrel-tip pointed at the bear. It stood staring keenly, silently, at me. During all of this mutual observing, the bear's wide eyes never blinked once! Its front legs now looked solid and tense even through thick fur!

Finally...very slowly I stood up...watching for any change of expression or hint of motion while keeping the rifle pointed at it. Not wanting to shoot this bear, I silently hoped it would decide to leave. These were tense moments because I knew how lightning-fast a bear could move! At this close range it could be on me in one short second! Knowing this, I hoped it would not charge. The bear seemed to be waiting me out...I was not certain what to do.

A thought came of trying one step away from it to see what would result, if anything. I slowly stepped away sideways. The bear's nonvocal reply was one firm step towards me...while maintaining its steady unblinking stare! Now I knew this was a very serious predicament! Here, I understood why people had told me to never run from a bear! It was better to hold one's ground. So...I waited and waited...while the bear made no attempt to come closer, also holding its position.

Over these long three or four minutes of silence and stillness, the psychological atmosphere gradually changed. It understood that I was not inferior: since I held my position, I was not a safe chase. And it also realized that I was no danger to it, so need not fight in self-defence. The bear seemed to relax bit by bit and accept my presence, somewhat.

Finally...slowly turning to its right, the bear walked a few paces back to the bouncy lodgepine snag, turning its backend to me but with ears perked straight up as it went, listening intently for any movement of mine. Pawing softly and muzzling the ground, it began foraging for I-don't-know-what: either insects, roots or pine mushroom buttons. While it muzzled the ground I thought of trying again to increase the distance between us. As I began stepping back one side-step, raising my left leg, the bear's head instantly whipped around to the left, looking back at me while my leg was still in the air halfway through the step! Its hearing and awareness were so keen that it heard the faint sound of my bluejeans bending at twelve yards distant, responding instantly to it! And that sound was to me, inaudible!

This time the bear looked back just a short while but kept its butt my way. Again, I ceased movement for a minute while it continued snuffling its snout in the needles and dirt. Then it took a few casual steps away, seemingly more interested now in the tasty things than in me. Once more, I stepped sideways back one step. This time...the bear merely turned its ears slightly back while muzzling the ground. With that I began feeling less tense and more relaxed, knowing that I was accepted and no longer considered as a possible threat to it. The bear kept feeding as I continued stepping silently one step and stopping, one step and stopping, down and away.

At about twenty yards downslope from the bear I turned towards my stashed backpack, angling downward but again visible to the bear. Looking sideways down at me, it stood motionless with head still low to the ground. When I came to be directly below, the bear surprised me again by beginning to walk along the slope at the same pace and same direction, westward, while keeping directly above me! As I angled away and down gradually increasing distance between, the bear remained at one level but kept straight upslope! This continued for about forty yards of parallel distance. I found that response to be a fascinating aspect of bear behaviour. When the space between had stretched to about fifty yards and due to treetrunks and low brush we were losing constant sight of each other, the bear lost interest and turned uphill. I stood watching as it vanished behind huckleberry brush and vertical grey treetrunks.

I sent it a goodbye thought: "Thankyou for being so polite. It was a pleasure meeting you!"

Quickly I paced down to the backpack and bags. There, both eased and excited, I unloaded the rifle to empty the barrel then reloaded the magazine chamber. Slipping on the heavy full backpack and carrying rifle and bags, I headed downward in a not-too-direct line, still looking for pine flags. As I went, I pondered about the reason this bear had been so tense. Apparently I had wandered too closely into its feeding area, so in consequence it felt somewhat threatened; the way this wild black beauty responded seemed appropriate: since food is a matter of life-or-death to a bear.

Fortunate I was that it had been so accepting of my presence at such close proximity...yet while picking mushrooms that it may have wanted! This potentially dangerous mountainside event was a good education about how I should behave when meeting bears at close range. In most cases — if a bear is not blatantly charging — the best strategy would be to remain still and silent while holding my position, wait out the bear and let it decide what it wants to do. By my remaining fearless, neutral and nonaggressive, the bear will usually respond likewise. It will eventually just walk away. Then would be the time to also leave but in another direction...just in case the bear changes its mind!

A Snap and a Track

The morning drive along a remote winding mudpuddle logging road was long and slow. Passing several miles of old and recent clearcuts, these had naturally grown in thickly with various-sized young fir, pine, cedar, wild cherry and alder. Beneath and between them grew blackberries, blackcaps, thimbleberry, huckleberry, mahonia, elderberry and various wild herbs and grass. Now late August, fruit was visibly abundant on shrubs: some yet green, others showing shiny black, deep blue and orange-pink. Nature was doing very well here repopulating the clearcuts, providing food for a great variety of animal life from the very smallest insects to birds to herbivorous mammals.

Continuing slowly on upward, dodging potholes all the way...finally a large block of oldgrowth forest appeared, looking beautiful with lichen-draped snaggly tops touching a clear blue sky! The road passed though this forest of two to four-foot diameter mountain hemlock, amabilis and Douglas fir. Between these trees there appeared on my left a rivulet spraying white, tumbling past and below the steep grey and rust-stained rock bluffs, while on my right within the deep rocky gorge a little creek of pale green clear water swirled and tumbled, yet almost inaudibly.

Now late morning, thin mist and drifting fog...remnants from last night's rainfall...were being rapidly reabsorbed by the warming air currents. Sunshine had already cleared away much of the dew but here and there, ochre green moss and deep green tree boughs still sparkled with a myriad pure white lights reflecting from countless tiny water droplets. All around, the huge snaggly mountain hemlock and amabilis were just sparkling with these wee brilliant white stars blinking off and on...with the odd droplet momentarily, randomly shining pure green, blue, red or yellow. Here was an ancient forest of giant living Christmas trees! But this rare beauty would be as ephemeral as the quickly evaporating dewdrops, so to be enjoyed now!

The cliffside above looked to be potential ore-carrying rock, so I thought to check it out. Parking the truck at a wide spot, I took my small sledgehammer and followed the little spraying rivulet upward a short distance. Sure enough...one boulder was partly coloured with indistinct spots and streaks of turquoise blue! Seeing this brought instant energy and a more enlivened presence of mind! So I climbed higher...up over white and cream lichen-coated scree to the cliff's bottom edge, then followed it upward until more copper bloom showed on the cliff-face in thin vertical streaks and spots; this ore-showing was almost hidden by yellow and black lichen which too, appeared as vertical streaks and large irregular patches. Here was another example of how Nature disguises things! The vein ran downward at a sixty-degree angle and dipping to the west. But as usual...it was too small, being a maximum of only one foot thick.

Directly below this vein were several pieces of ore rock in the scree slope. Some chunks I sledgehammered into small pieces then eyed them through my twenty-power magnifier. It was beautiful-looking ore: shining bright silvery-grey among turquoise green and cobalt blue carbonate, mixed with a dark grey parent-rock. Tiny golden yellow specks of chalcopyrite added to this microscopic natural beauty. Quite excited at first, I thought it to be silver ore! But on closer examination it was primarily lowgrade grey copper ore, only about two percent maximum of copper.

Even so, for quite some time I scrambled farther up and over the upper rocky bluffs looking for something better. Nothing else appeared, though. So, on the way back down I took an armful of ore from the scree as a keepsake. This vein was not big enough for a lone prospector to bother staking. The area would need diamond drilling to prove what may be hidden deeper in.

Back at the truck I had a quick bite to eat, then with goldpanning tools in my backpack went down the steep slope below, dragging and sliding a large heavy hexagonal iron prybar. Reaching bottom where this same rivulet entered the pale green creek, I loaded the pan with gravel and panned it out. Well, well…one tiny golden colour shone brightly from among fine magnetite, reflecting sunshine like a wee curved yellow mirror! It was gold: not mica, not pyrite! Encouraged by this I waded across the creek where a gravel bar looked to have good potential. Rolling rocks around I moved gravel until as deep as I could get, then filled the pan. Taking my time panning, in about five minutes the pan was down to mostly magnetite, pyrite, a few pink garnets and some nice shiny yellow gold in little specks and a few thick flakes!

Now I understood from experience what gave our early gold miners so much energy and the seemingly-crazy courage to brave their way into the vast unknown of British Columbia's and Yukon's wild river valleys and huge rugged mountainsides. I transferred this few dollars worth of gold into a clear plastic thirty-five millimeter film container…then panned a few more shovels of gravel, saving the little gold pieces each time. This exercise was most enjoyable even though my lower back became sore from it! But not being my sole purpose on this day, after an hour of panning I returned up the very steep slope to the truck.

Firing up, I drove the logging road some distance higher then crossed the same creek. Coming to a low rock cut, I stopped to observe the rock-face. Here was another thin vein of something unusual. This time though, the substance was earthy but bright orange-red. "Must be cinnabar," I thought. I took a few pieces but never touched it with bare fingers in case it actually was mercury ore, using cotton gloves and rock pick. Once again I proceeded slowly along, mostly in first gear…now almost on top of the mountain ridge.

Nearing the road's end at subalpine elevation I turned left along a recently bulldozed branch into an extensive piece of unlogged ancient rainforest. Standing silent, still and beautiful were snag-topped, twist-limbed mountain hemlock, yellow cedar and fir…all time-shaped and draped with long pale yellowgreen and black beard lichen. These large mountaintop trees seemed to be growing up into — penetrating the deep blue sky! Here, I had just entered another little piece of our northern westcoast rainforest…expressing as a touch of visual paradise.

Finding a wide spot on the road, I parked the truck about one hundred yards before a switchback that led higher and back above. This forest was quite open, with good visibility. I had planned only a short walk to check for pine mushrooms so left my 30-30 rifle — which I sometimes carried merely as self-defence — in the truck. Putting on my little yellow nylon daypack I decided to go upward under these beautiful giant trees.

After about one minute of walking through huckleberry and copperbush…yes, a familiar creamy glow caught my eye. It was a good-sized pine mushroom button, hiding between the large exposed roots of a four-foot diameter mountain hemlock! Using a screwdriver, yet with some difficulty I pried it out from between two sturdy roots — without breaking it! Two more buttons appeared but barely visible between tough surface roots under this same tree. They too, were difficult to pick intact. But shortly, I had in my backpack three nice solid buttons weighing about one-quarter pound each.

Again proceeding slowly upward, most enjoyable was the high-pitched peeping conversation of chickadees among the big twisting branches above...as they flitted about eating insects, larvae and insect eggs. I thought of how valuable are these tiny predators, keeping insects from overpopulating thus benefitting these huge old trees and in general the whole forest. And of course it was mutual: with the forest returning the favour by providing for the wee birds food, shelter, protection, nesting material and nest space. The ecosystem here was beyond merely survival-of-the-fittest...but was more so, a system of beneficial exchange!

Continuing upward around huge trunks and past widely spaced copperbush, my initial excitement gradually abated as not another pine mushroom was to be seen. Even so, the shrubby moss-covered ground was coloured with many mushrooms, names unknown to me, of various shapes and sizes: some orange, brown, white or cream. One beautiful big fungus looking more like a strange flowery cluster glowing iridescent purple and blue, I recognized as the edible black clustered chanterelle. This one, I called the purple-blue chanterelle since that be its predominant colouring when it is young and good to eat; by the time it turns black, it is often too old to eat. Since this was the only one, I left it to grow and seed the wind with its microscopic spores.

Soon I was scrambling up onto the gravelly upper switchback. Here the road ended and broadened out into a small blast-rock landing site where a grapple yarder or Madill steel spar would eventually be located. Standing on the road, I could see just above an eight-foot high rockcut, a patch of tall tiny-leaved bushes loaded with pinkish-orange huckleberries glowing in the sunlight. Having worked up a sweat and a thirst, this sight enticed me into a short climb upward through thick white rhododendron brush. Pushing my way to the berries, I picked a handful then sat down on a little mossy log a few paces away. Throwing berries in threes and fours into my mouth, their tart thirst-quenching juice was very much enjoyed and appreciated!

Now I was at the ridge's highest point. Looking westward...very steep, heavily treed bluish slopes plunged down into the valley. Beyond them, grey and bluegrey rocky peaks jutted up and away to the west and north. This whole wild horizon from south to west to north was a vast geological beauty far beyond words!

"How fortunate," I thought, "to be able to experience and enjoy Nature's form, colour, silent peace and living presence." Here, far from human doings, happiness arose within. No stupidity here...no small-minded jealousy...no unnecessary criticism. Nature's delicious neutrality and endless beauty eased my inner pain, giving some positive meaning and inspiration to life.

This open huckleberry patch stopped about five yards from where I sat. At that point a thick clump of young fir and cypress from eight to twenty feet tall grew at the ridge's top edge, then the same young forest continued on steeply downward a long, long way. This western slope was the site of an old forest-fire burn that had started low in the valley and stopped here; it was now fairly grown in with sapling and slightly larger trees: a mix of Douglas fir, amabilis and yellow cedar species. And between them grew various open-ground, sunloving plants and bushes.

The sunshine felt pleasantly warm, as was a fresh gentle breeze that drifted by without a sound. I walked back to the huckleberry clump, picked another handful and returned to the mossy log. This time throwing in berries all at once, I quietly sat...feeling as if an integral part of the silent, powerful mountain calmness. I was drifting too...into a relaxed, dreamy state...

36

induced by the warm sunshine and the almost tangible silence.

This peacefulness was of short duration, though. From just within the thick evergreen sapling treeclump came a loud muffled snap! A small snag on the ground suddenly broke — I had company! And it was something big! Swivelling eyes to the right but keeping my head still, I looked hard…searching the green fir boughs and dim shadows. Nothing animate was visible. Deciding that instant, I slowly stood up then calmly but quickly longstepped directly back down towards the logging road, skirting past the eight-foot vertical rockcut to my left. As I stepped onto the sharp-edged gravel, glancing back…still nothing showed. I was in luck, so far!

Having no self-defence made me more apprehensive than otherwise. I knew immediately that such a loud muffled sound was probably made by a large leathery paw, not the open solid hoof of a deer or elk! A big furry paw would muffle the sound whereas an open hoof would usually not. Only bear or cougar could break a ground-snag that large…with such deep-toned snap that a three to five inch diameter breaking stem would make!

Moving quickly across the blast-rock road then down into the open timbered slope, stepping as quickly and quietly as possible, I distanced myself before the animal could decide whether or not I was a danger to it…or if I would be an easy prey item. The sooner I moved away, the better! Sidestepping behind the first large tree, I momentarily stopped and listened…then kept pacing downslope towards the truck which was still fifty yards away. I was certainly glad of the four-foot-plus diameter mountain hemlock and Douglas fir trunks that I could use as a blind! Stepping behind the next large tree to block off visibility from above, I hesitated, listening… then looked back up.

Just then, two gravelly crunches in quick succession came from the road above in direction of the eight-foot rockcut — proof that my wild company was interested in me! With that, I was certain this animal must be a cougar! It had leapt onto the road from the high rockcut, something a bear would not do…and was now only twenty yards away! I kept walking as quietly as possible, looking up frequently over my left shoulder and stepping sideways behind every tree that I passed. I had expected to see the animal looking down from the roadside, but it did not appear. My apprehension lessened somewhat.

Moving as I did — immediately — was the best thing that I could have done: getting out of the big cat's line of vision, not giving it enough time to assess my potential as either danger or prey. But it was being cautious not knowing what strength I may have, so stayed above near the landing…although I was sure it could hear me moving away below. Within a minute or so I was back at the truck and feeling much less tense! Waiting, I listened and watched for several minutes…seeing and hearing nothing other than a flock of crossbills chirping in the distance.

My chances of seeing this animal now seemed remote. I drove to the switchback, turned around and parked about one hundred yards from the landing where the cougar had hit the road with a crunch. But wanting more confirmation about its identity, I decided to look for tracks in the dirt and mud. Sure enough, the answer was right there…down in the ditch! Very fresh cat tracks with front paws about four inches in diameter were clearly formed in the damp rusty red earth. Paw size indicated that it was probably a juvenile cougar, maybe three years old.

At this point though, the lovely mossy green forest to the east looked just too enticing as potential habitat for pine mushrooms. So I went up an easy slope away from where the cougar was but this time carrying the rifle as protection! I thought the big cat had no interest in me now…so would stay away for the time-being, not knowing whether or not I was a danger to it.

Here this ancient forest was partly open and a mix of large hemlock, yellow cedar, balsam fir and Douglas fir. The ground under tighter-growing trees was carpeted with pale emerald and deep green moss, interspersed with little groups of tiny maroon-spotted, white orchids growing in the shade. Kneeling down, I had a good close look at them. Then onto fours with nose touching, I sniffed their faint out-of-this-world perfume and could see the deep yellow inside of their throats. This heavenly scent was, I thought, one more of Nature's hidden beauties that unfortunately few people ever experience! This particular orchid was quite rare and I had seen it only in shaded mossy evergreen forest.

Keeping mindful of my purpose I continued on…looking for mushrooms and enjoying this little paradise…with its orchid-flowered, sunshine-mottled mossy greens under the trees. In more open areas grew rhododendron and copperbush with little wintergreen and pipsissewa plants low to the ground, still showing some white and pink blossoms. Walking was unusually easy on this gentle slope and on the low rolling humps that were covered with soft thick moss. I thought it a wonder that this rare old tree-mix was not a Class A park! It was a perfect place to have a walking trail for the people of British Columbia and tourists to enjoy and experience. As I walked…more and more I could see this forest's unique aspects, being of such mixed vegetation. Never before had I seen a section of forest as varied as this one! Its value was certainly far greater than the wood-as-dollar worth which it had been designated for in a Victoria office long ago, sight unseen.

For some unknown time I wandered through this lovely, peaceful forest of mostly four hundred to six hundred year-old trees. Pine mushrooms and orange chanterelles grew in a few more spots but in general mushrooms were sparse. Heading back to the truck, I kept a pathway of good visibility…just in case the big cat's curiosity or hunger had overcome its initial fear of the human. But I was alone walking a flowery path between the huge silent trees.

Once safely back at the truck, many thoughts ran through my mind. This forest was on the corporate chopping-block: due to be logged off in the not-too-distant future. Emotions of disappointment, disgust and anger flowed through my body and mind. About ninety percent of this subalpine area was already logged off! Thoughts ran on about the foolish, ignorant, inconsiderate people who were in decision-making positions of government and business. I thought about corporate-style logging that started in the 1930s and 40s when a handful of companies were granted so-called timber rights on vast expanses of Crown Land.

My thoughts went much like this: "Unfortunately, since then no politician has had the courage nor intelligence to tell the companies that nothing else on Crown Land is theirs: not the land, not the water, not the wildlife, not the shrubs and wildflowers. Timber rights are neither land rights nor water rights. Nor do such legal contracts give the company a right to log the forest in whatever manner it wants, i.e. not the right to clearcut! Aren't politicians supposed to intelligently govern? Is not Crown Land in the ownership of British Columbia's citizens? Too bad that clearcuts effectively nullify most other land use! Likewise, how is it that those companies also had a legal right to sell 'timber rights' to foreign companies — thus giving foreigners control over our Crown Land? Seems like politically and socially suicidal policy, to me."

Like a bad habit — blind and unabated — clearcutting continued into the highest reaches of this forest. But after such thoughts, I soon overcame the emotional negativity and started back down the bumpy road. It was not long until some recently broken rock caught my interest. The bulldozer used for building the road had churned over some brown and grey sandstone that was speckled with variously-shaped white objects. Stopping, I got out and walked around for a closer look. Curving and rippling white forms of seashells filled the sandstone, remnants of a forty million-plus year-old seafloor: a reminder of how long life in many forms has been on our planet Earth, while how short the life of one individual is!

Among this rock rubble I found a piece of flat brown sandstone just small enough to carry and having a perfect cockleshell indentation…this was my final discovery on a most unusual day! As I drove down the mountain winding slowly along the rough road, thoughts and emotions came and went: pleasure from the beauties experienced and pain from knowing that the cougar's beautiful ancient forest would soon be no more.

Two Mistakes

After a steady night of rain this Thanksgiving Day morning was cool and damp. I was alone… thinking of the happy families who were together, hopefully enjoying a day of feasting…as I drove along the puddle-filled logging road. Some distance along I turned onto a side branch, heading uphill. After a mile and a few switchbacks the road forked two ways. Between these forks, from the distance I could see a yellow object perched on top of an old grey sawn stump. Coming closer, it became recognizable as a new-looking thermos. On a remote seldom-used road this seemed odd!

But as I rounded the curve left, the thermos' owner was standing there motionless, atop another old sawn stump…grasping his faintly steaming plastic coffee mug! I was mildly surprised but much more amused and my lips spontaneously formed a slight smirky smile. The fellow was dressed up clown-like in bright orange, red and yellow. His glaring eyes peered at me from a fat pink face. His oversized rifle with scope, the sure sign of a non-marksman, leaned against his stump-perch.

My rumbling truck had certainly disturbed the morning silence and his hunt; I was quietly pleased with that! He had the look of a bigcity boy…of the type brainwashed by hunting magazines, archaic tradition and social pressure. Out trying to be a man in accordance with the gun dealers' and outdoor suppliers' commercial definition — my unexpected appearance raised his ire! Even so, he managed a semblant smile for me. Smiling back I held up my right hand, fingers and thumb up as a greeting. Then after passing by, I chuckled with the thought that I may be saving a deer's life.

A short while later, after a slow bumpy drive trying to dodge impossible potholes for half-a-mile another hunter — the clown's partner — appeared…walking along the road in the same direction I was going. He showed no animosity though, smiling as I passed. Farther up, a partial road washout slowed me down. I got by it only to meet a quarter-mile later an unpassable huge granite boulder that had slid from the clay cutbank onto the road. Three years previously I had picked a good area of pine mushrooms a fair distance beyond the boulder…too far to walk now. So this abrupt halt made a change of plan necessary. Luckily though, a block of old conifer forest just below looked to have some potential.

Road barely wide enough, I manoeuvred the truck around to face back downhill. Meanwhile the hunter caught up, so we chatted a few words. He told me that he wanted a big buck. I told him that I was not hunting and was going to look for mushrooms below the road from my truck, so not to shoot into that bit of forest. He was pleased that I was not hunting and agreed to not shoot my way.

Then as he walked on I said: "I hope you don't get a deer!"

He laughed, saying: "Good luck with the mushrooms!" and continued on his way.

Pulling out the keys and stepping onto the road, I stuffed four plastic grocery bags into high rubber boots then slid two pepperspray holsters onto my brown solid-leather belt. Next, on went my raggedy old blue canvas jacket and yellow souwester rainhat. Grabbing the green backpack, I stood awhile observing a steep semi-open forest above…for mushroom potential and any presence of large animals. Then I visually scanned the large clearcut below and one small piece of distant evergreen forest, still watching for any movement or large animal. As it appeared, there was no nonhuman company nearby. Here the road showed no sign of a bear or cougar…only a few deer tracks.

Looking across the main valley…stretching in a curve for miles the lovely rocky snow-capped mountains expressed themselves in silence, stillness and power. Pale grey and tan clouds hovered in the deep blue infinite sky beyond, ever-so-slowly drifting into various rounded or curving shapes. Below those snowy peaks stretched a vast greygreen and bluegreen conifer forest…with long gentle curves of rolls and dips outlining the less rugged lower mountainsides.

After this brief enjoyment I stepped carefully but quickly down into the semi-open big-treed hemlock, fir and cedar forest, anxious to see if any pine mushrooms grew there. About forty yards down I stepped up to a most pleasing, exciting surprise: faint whitish lights were glowing from amid little bumps on the ground, which I instantly recognized! A sight like this always induces a smile, invigorating energy and a sense that…yes, sometimes I can be successful even if in a small way.

Kneeling beside one bump, I thought: "Thankyou mushrooms for being here. Thankyou forest and all beings that helped to produce these mushrooms." Always…I try to show some positive appreciation to Nature: to what Nature gives and does for me and all of humanity.

Carefully rolling back moss, twigs and needles…a tight cluster of rusty-topped creamy buttons appeared — as if bubblegum blowing upward from the ground! Looking up and around, now I could see more little mounds here and there over a fifteen yard radius! Pushing two forefingers of each hand alongside stems, feeling the bottom point then curling my fingers back up…the buttons were eased out. Cleaning each stemtip with a few finger twists above the hole then rolling back the surface and pushing it into its original place, I was careful to protect the mycelium.

I repeated this procedure at several bumps, piling the buttons and a few semi-open mushrooms at each spot. They were growing in clusters of three to ten buttons! Pulling a couple of bags from my rubber boots, buttons went into one while the semi-opens went into the other. This first patch gave me about fifty buttons and some fewer opens. It seemed that this might be a good payday if a few more like-patches were nearby!

Downward I went towards a small creek that rapidly descended in a series of little noisy waterfalls…while closely eyeing the ground for that creamy white glow and likewise the forest horizon for large carnivores. Now closer to the creek, I had to depend totally on my vision for safety…with the steady tumbling of water dominating the audible sense. Twenty yards down another subtle telltale appeared, inciting the same response as minutes before! Yes, here was another loaded spot! After this, three more such spots presented themselves and with the backpack full of buttons I started back up towards the truck.

Halfway up, there appeared another spot of mushrooms forming a large circle. Taking off the heavy backpack and leaning it against a large fir tree, I began working this fairyring which consisted of all five grades and several big, fully open, wormy mushrooms. Actually, the worms were not worms but maggots. Usually these larvae were of small flies but sometimes beetles which had lain eggs, mostly in the stem. Squeezing each stem, I assessed for the presence or absence of larvae.

When I had an obviously wormy mushroom I broke the top into pieces, throwing them some distance away so that spores were distributed somewhat. Most often on the ground at the base of these open mushrooms would be a pale whitish-grey powder: spores in the millions. If the ground were dry I would swish my hand back and forth…sending spores drifting on the wind. But if wet, I scooped up the surface material and saved it to be thrown around in another area of forest later. Sometimes I wiped spores onto my shirt, jacket or pantleg, knowing that my body motion would release them gradually to drift away on the wind. In this way I was promoting the continuation of pine mushrooms…having seen many times, billions of spores green with mould on the damp ground beneath old flags or hats, that is, older open-topped mushrooms.

After picking this fairyring I left the heavy backpack to scout nearby upslope. About twenty yards up was another small spot with flags and buttons. Now on my hands and knees as I worked it, a rustling sound coming from some distance above caught my attention! Standing up, in a crouch I ducked behind the nearest treetrunk. Hidden behind a three-foot diameter hemlock, I peeked with my right eye to see the dark form of a deer moving downslope straight towards me! It was a three-point blacktail buck!

Not noticing me, it continued directly towards my hiding place. White mist blew from its nostrils and trailed along behind in little thin clouds. And through the forest above this deer, billowing puffs of thin whitish fog were drifting in from the southwest. As the deer came closer I could see that its left rear leg was dragging behind…making that rustling sound as its hoof dragged along through twigs, moss and needles. The leg was completely nonfunctional.

The buck stopped just ten yards above at a little flat under a clump of sapling hemlock trees. Attempting to lay down…its broken leg gave some difficulty since the leg was straight out, not bending. As the deer tried to lay down, moving back and forth and sideways, I could see that the femur of its left leg was pushing up from under the skin but not through. The bone had snapped cleanly straight across, a few inches below the hip and had not broken through. No blood was visible.

Finally, the buck's movements worked the leg into position so it could lay down. Out of breath, it needed a rest and oxygen! Puffing and panting…steam rapidly exited from its flaring nostrils and mouth. The long pink tongue curled up, licking its shiny black nose then drooped down, hanging to the left side. The deer continued to pant hard and fast, yet held its head high and ears out and up, facing northward. Then with mouth open and tongue back in, a sudden spray of green liquid puke ejected straight out for about two feet! Its tongue again drooped out, hanging down to the side. Heavily panting nonstop, it threw-up three more times in short succession.

Seeing the type of break and having heard no gunshots, this deer must have either broken the leg in a battle with a larger buck or had been attacked by a bear or cougar. I thought the latter was more probable. And knowing that a large carnivore could be following the deer, I became quite apprehensive — being so close to its prey! This was a potentially dangerous circumstance!

I had to get this deer to move away as soon as possible! So I stood out from behind the big treetrunk. Now seeing me, the deer slowly struggled up onto its feet then hobbled away northward on its three good legs, with the fourth dragging behind. At twenty yards distant it turned straight down towards the little noisy whitewater creek, as fog continued drifting by in sporadic but thicker little clouds. Sadly…I watched this beautiful dying buck disappear behind tall huckleberry brush and into the dip below.

Here before me was the harsh aspect of Nature: the reality of life and death, of beauty, pain and viciousness. This buck was in its prime of life…looking so strong yet so fragile and impermanent: like a bubble in a rainpuddle. My eyes filled with hot tears. I just stood still for a few minutes, feeling very helpless. I could not help this beautiful deer. I was powerless. I consoled myself…eased my sorrow by thinking of the lifegiving sustenance its body would give to one or more carnivore. But now I had to quickly plan an escape route in case a large carnivore did appear! The deer had come down directly from my truck above so my best route out was towards the clearcut to my right, away from the buck's scent trail.

I walked quickly down to my backpack of mushrooms and brought it back up to the little patch where the deer and I had met. Keeping a watch upslope all the while, nothing unusual appeared near the deer's path nor anywhere else. All that I saw was the cold pale grey fog moving slowly, silently between big balsam, hemlock and fir trees. From below, sounds of tumbling water continued to dominate the forest…drowning out all other sound. Seeing no danger, I decided to quickly pick the last couple of open mushrooms. I knelt in the moss and looking downward, pulled out one flag then began swishing my right hand back and forth across the big creamy white top, cleaning off twigs and needles.

As I did this…barely audible within the shishing creek's noise, a different unrecognizable sound began: soft distant thumping. Almost instantly I mentally located the direction. It was coming at a slight angle from ahead and above me to the east. These thumps were in a steady beat that was quickly getting louder and louder! Now I knew they were the muffled steps of large soft-padded feet in a run — pounding on the spongy forest ground!

In a split-second of spontaneous motion, I looked upward to see a very large bear sliding directly towards me with its butt-end on the ground and two big front paws stretched forward on the ground — spraying two fans of dirt and needles towards me! Wide eyes staring straight at me and ears vertical, it slid to a halt just six yards away! Then the bear stood up on all four feet, remaining still with its two big pigeon-toed front paws pointing my way…and looking at me with an expression that appeared to be both surprise and embarrassment! And surprised was I, especially by the fact that it had stopped! The big bear waited motionless…as if not knowing what to do next…looking at me with a steady unblinking gaze. This was an uncommon blackbear, having a very dark chocolate brown coat of thick fur.

Sparkling dark eyes, wide and staring…were fixed on mine as its rounded blackish-brown ears remained perked straight up and forward! I looked steadily back…observing its big fuzzy face and head while reaching very slowly to my right-side pepperspray holster. Slowly, I pulled it out, with thumb flipped out the orange safety wedge…then in steady slow-motion moved it to the centre of my chest with nozzle pointing at the bear. Then, after a few still moments, while continuing to watch its eyes and ears…raising from my crouch I very slowly stood up while still facing the bear. After more moments of steady mutual watching, I noticed my left hand still holding tightly onto the mushroom. Releasing my grip, it dropped, bounced and rolled to a stop…while the bear took little notice, having its eyes locked onto mine. Again in slow-motion, I moved my left hand onto the pepper spraygun, now holding it with both hands. I stood motionless and silent: the best strategy in this sort of circumstance!

The big bear's steady unblinking eyes continued to completely focus on mine as I watched for any hint of change from its eyes, ears, lips. Long moments passed while we, as if frozen still, stood in silence and intense mutual observation. The shine in its eyes and strong steadfast gaze

— almost piercing — were certainly of an intelligent being…scrutinizing me as purposely as I did it! Even so, I felt no fear, strangely — but was instead acutely alert!

This bear's head was unusually large, with a very fuzzy face and thick neck ruff that was much like a grizzly's. Its rounded body was coated with deep, softly glowing fur and hair of dark brown tones to almost black. I could see that this big beauty was most likely the dominant bear of these mountains!

This was the first time a bear had charged, although I had met over the years several other bears at close range. I was at first puzzled by its having stopped. And wondered why it had charged to begin with! I knew it was after the deer but the deer was gone. Then I realized why this bear had come at me. Now it was showing no aggression…so obviously I was not its target. The bear's mind was focussed on its prey — the wounded deer! But where was the deer? The bear found itself in an awkward circumstance. So now it was waiting to see if I would be a threat to itself, or not!

The best way I knew to respond, to communicate with it, was by remaining neutral. This would be understood by the bear as nonthreatening, nonaggressive and therefore no need to fight me in self-defence: no need to attack! So…standing still, I silently but alertly waited for it to make the first move. All the while I held my position with the pepper spraygun ready, right thumb on the trigger.

After a long thirty-or-so seconds, the big fearless bear made a decision. Very slowly and deliberately…actually in slow-motion…its head turned left, then holding it in that ninety-degree position the bruin watched me from the corner of a sparkling right eye while keeping alert ears upright, listening. With this gesture, the nerve and muscle tension in my body relaxed slightly and a feeling of ease began trickling in. For about fifteen seconds the bear steadily held this head-and-neck position towards me, showing the right side of its neck — the jugular vein area!

The meaning of this surprising body-gesture came quickly to me! It was the animal's natural manner of communication, of silent speech. This nonvocal — also nonaggressive but serious — expression was saying something like: "If you want to fight, here is my jugular vein. If you dare, come and try me. If not, stay where you are." And it waited for a reply. Of course, my reply was a neutral nonresponse! The bear was testing me and I gave it the right answer by remaining still and silent!

After that body-gesture communication it again moved in slow-motion, deliberately short-stepping the two front paws, inch by inch, several steps to its left while rotating hind feet in the same manner until its butt-end faced me! Then it just stood still in this position. All the while the bear's ears remained straight up and forward, listening for any hint of motion from me. This was another test…another body-gesture communication. It stood thus with big butt facing me for another fifteen seconds or so…waiting for my reply…if I would. Again my response was neutrality — no motion, no sound! The bear accepted my nonaggression, responding likewise. After this waiting period of long silence and stillness…it appeared to suddenly relax and then calmly, slowly padded away uphill the same direction it had come…without looking back at me. At about fifteen yards distant the bruin stopped to sniff the air.

By now, I too, was quite relaxed and feeling very happy about meeting this large chocolate bear at such close range, yet not being attacked…even though it had the advantage and the power over me!

Catching the scent of deer puke, the bear turned sideways, looked back at me awhile then leisurely padded over to the little hemlock flat where the deer had very recently lain down.

There, it sniffed the ground where the buck had thrown-up. Raising its head, the lower jaw dropped slightly as the bear tested air currents…nostrils expanding and twitching. Looking back down at me a few moments then lifting and turning its head slowly from side to side, the big bruin kept testing the air with snout pointing in different directions. For about three minutes it tried to ascertain where the deer went and while doing so, periodically looked back at me…as if somewhat puzzled. Having a long look at it now, I estimated this powerful looking bear to weigh at least four hundred pounds.

By now I had moved gradually to the same big treetrunk that I hid behind when first hearing the buck coming downslope. There, now just ten yards away, with pepperspray still ready in my right hand I stood in full view of the bear with left shoulder leaning against the tree… watching. Then finally, it started padding slowly upslope along the exact line that the deer had descended…but in a zigzag pattern while taking two or three steps each time and with snout held high and lower jaw slightly open, stopping at each turn to check for airborne scent. I watched the big bruin's every step and stop as it padded higher and higher. It had now lost all interest in me.

White and grey mist drifting in between trees gradually faded the bear's dark form…as it became smaller and smaller with increasing distance. Big treetrunks and low brush blocked it from view now and then. At about forty yards up, almost to the truck, its pale grey form curled left and started back down towards the little tumbling creek…in the direction the buck had gone just five or so minutes ago. The bear was again back on track!

Now it was time for me to leave! In a hurry I stepped back to the bags and slipped on the button-backpack. Picking up the mushroom that I had dropped, I put it into a flagbag then grabbed the two plastic bags and paced quickly to the clearcut edge. There I turned upslope towards the truck. But all the while I held the pepper spraygun just in case the bear had a change of mind. Soon back safely, I placed the backpack and bags into the truckbox then got ready to head down the mountain.

Now two emotions were flowing within me: sadness for the deer and happiness for the bear. I sat behind the steering wheel looking at thin drifting fog, the heavily treed valley and high snowy peaks…thinking about what I had just experienced and feeling the inner turmoil of adrenalin-energy and emotions. I thought this deer was probably an important last meal before the bear went into hibernation higher up in a hollow tree or among boulder scree of some nearby mountain peak. I thought about the beauty and harshness of Nature, of all life on this planet, of life and death, of how life ends for one so that another life or other lives may continue. Such be the natural facts of our earthly existence for both animal and the half-animal human. And I thought…there must be more meaning to it all than this. But what and how?

I thought about how this dangerous meeting had occurred. My mistake was not leaving right away, after the buck had disappeared into the huckleberry brush below! Unknown to me the bear was upslope to northeast not far away and out of sight, following the scent trail but at a distance of about twenty yards downwind from it. As yet unaware of me the bear was quietly padding down along the other side of a little gravel and clay glacial finger that ran up and down the slope…hidden from my line of vision. It had deer in mind — as oblivious of me as I was of it!

While down on my knees pulling out a big pine mushroom flag, the bear must have detected on the northward drifting breeze the strong smell of deer's vomit. So…looking southward over the little hump, it could see low to the ground a slight motion and a white flashing. From that distance of about thirty yards and in the dim forest light, it assumed the flashing white to be coming from its deer! Could it think anything else? But this was the bear's mistake. It began a charge...not knowing that it was merely seeing a big pine mushroom's top being swished over by a human hand!

But the bear on approaching closer and seeing more clearly realized that this target was human — not a wounded deer! At that moment I jerked my head up to see the big bruin attempting to stop...sliding on the ground straight towards me! If this big bear had its mind set on me, it would have had me: there was too little time to get the pepperspray out to defend myself. Lucky for me, its mind was set on the three-point buck!

With such thoughts and attendant strong emotions rushing about, I fired up the truck and drove slowly down, cutting my day of mushrooming short. Lower, at the logging road's fork I was surprised that the second hunter had already returned and the two were busily breaking camp. Wanting to keep this rare event a secret, I just drove by them with a wave and a smile. I thought the bear needed that deer far more than did those overfed bigcity boys.

Although my smile was genuine it was actually the expression of great cheer inside because of this personal, face to face meeting with a powerful wild animal whose behaviour was surprizingly benign. With this, my appreciation of bears much increased! Here was an uncommon experience that taught me more than one lesson; it was to me of great educational value, especially about bears' silent language of gestures. The behaviour of this big wild beauty was one more example of how bears most often respect human space far more than people respect theirs...and also of how intelligent this animal actually is!

AGILITY AND GRACE

Slender beams of bright morning sunshine were lighting up the yellowgreen canopy of tall willow and small poplar…while starlike openings of robin's egg blue in the boughs above were all that I could see of the Cariboo sky. Straight ahead was a geometric maze of drab greybrown and grey crisscrossing, arching branches. These I ducked under, dodged or pushed through… moving westward in the shade of thick woods while following beside a long narrow brownish pond. Visibility here was too restricted for comfort so I remained alert.

At a mere one hundred yards in, greeting me were the loud snapping sounds of dry twigs, branches and large ground-snags breaking! Only a large animal could break multiple branches and of that size. And the unknown welcomer sounded to be just thirty yards ahead! I stopped to listen. It was moving away…fortunately! Well, a new pepperspray was belted on my right hip, so no worry. "Probably a moose," I thought, "but it could also be a bear."

Since visibility was so limited, I turned back to a narrow point where crossing was easy to the pond's other more open side. Then proceeding back to the west along its willow-treed northern edge, after some distance there appeared a mother Canadian goose with four fluffy grey goslings still too young to fly, paddling away. Standing still so they would not panic…I watched, enjoying their lively presence. She led them away in a hurry, all paddling single-file…she groaning and rotating her head, they peeping a high sandpapery tone. The goslings' eyes shone in the sunshine and with a special sparkle that all young animals have, they were obviously enjoying to the fullest their little all-new watery world! As this little family paddled away out of sight my first thought was to wonder why she had so few young.

I waited a few minutes to give the geese their privacy then moved in the same direction under willow, aspen and lodgepine trees. From across the longpond once again came sharp snaps and crackles of breaking branches but this time farther away in more open, low-growing brush and willow. The animal was slowly moving to the southwest. The sharp tone of larger branch-breaks told me that it was probably a moose, not a bear since a bear's soft paw would give a more muffled sound. Open hooves of a moose would usually render a clear sharp sound. Now certain that it was a moose, I had little fear and kept moving carefully, slowly westward under high willow trees…even though knowing that moose can be dangerous at times.

This pond was very long…it seemed to never end. Pushing through a brushy willow clump I arrived at one point where a lot of grey and white goose down was floating motionless on the still surface. At the pond's other side more goose down decorated the mud and grass. And a few yards farther in under the trees, little clumps of white and grey fluff almost completely covered a small shaded mound of damp dirt.

Curious about this seemingly excessive down I started looking for a narrowing where I could cross back over to the south side. Ahead the pond was now beginning to widen out, trees quit and swamp brush was all that grew. It appeared to be connected to a lake so soon I would have to change course, anyway. Luckily, not far along the pond narrowed somewhat into a little pinch and lying across was an old branchy willow snag. This small natural bridge was precarious but I trusted my balance…and decided to risk the crossing.

Manoeuvring slowly across this bouncy bridge — without falling in — I proceeded back eastward under silent willow and rustling, softly clicking aspen trees. Again some distance away to the southwest were more sporadic shuffling sounds of my unseen moose as it moved through the brush. And far off to northwest, croaking yodels began…as two or three sandhill cranes called out to each other. Soon nearing the decorated dirt mound, more and more white and grey fluff became visible near and on it. The ground here was shiny and smoothened with little indentations, as if having been frequently tread upon. Crouching down for a closer look: there were both old and recent scuffmarks and claw scratches in the damp earth alongside smooth packed-down, unrecognizable paw-prints. These indistinct tracks were too small for a bear or cougar.

Besides gosling fluff, the animal had left excrement of a type I did not recognize, on and near the dirt mound. Ground had been tramped over and over by a medium-sized animal that was definitely carnivorous. Now I knew why there were only four goslings!

Pacing about, I searched for a clearly defined footprint…but found none. Even so, the general form was discernible from pad depressions which were bear-like but more oval and were larger than a fisher's. An eerie feeling now crept into and enveloped my body.

"This animal cannot be far away," I thought, following its pathway towards a large thick-boughed spruce tree that grew on the edge of a low clay and dirt natural cutbank. There, an odd dark shape caught my attention. I stopped…looking at it from the side. Only ten yards away, half-hidden by the tree's large exposed roots was an oval-shaped hole excavated into the bank's bottom edge!

Small spruce roots dangled down from the top of this shady den entrance, which was about twenty inches wide by fifteen inches high. It was too small for a wolf, probably too large for a fox or bobcat…but about right for a lynx, badger or wolverine. I took two steps closer. Near this entranceway were tracks clearly formed in the mud: front paws wider than long, ovalish, with five toes and slightly visible claws. They were much like a cub bear's. That information ruled out lynx and badger, leaving just one possibility!

Instantly adrenalin ran through my arteries! In all probability, here I was six feet from a wolverine's den! My body bristled with lightning-like energy. Now I wondered, "Is anyone home? How safe is it to be here?"

Standing still with senses extremely alert, I listened and looked! A few tiny flies hovered and circled at the silent black oval hole. Everything was quiet but for a wee yellow-spotted warbler singing from a distant tree. Not wanting to provoke trouble I paced back towards the pond. So much grey gosling down covered the water's edge and the ground, it seemed enough for three or four birds at least.

The eerie feeling persisted as I kept looking around into the low brush and up into the big bushy spruce tree. I knew what agile tree-climbers wolverines are and as graceful in trees as pine marten and squirrels! Home or not, I thought it best to leave. But passing by the den, curiosity overcame me. I stopped directly in front six feet away and bent forward, hands on knees…peering into the shady darkness beyond the little hanging rootlets.

That same moment — one loud medium-deep throaty growl erupted from inside! Veering to the left I jerked back up and sidestepped while keeping a hard steady look at the black hole for whatever may appear! This strange growl was unfamiliar, one that I had not heard before: neither cat, dog nor bear. Nor was it the voice of a badger, which I knew. And the sound seemed too deep for an animal that would fit into a den entrance this small.

Well, this was my answer! Not wanting to provoke the defensive animal more I kept a steady pace away, watching the den-hole as I quickly glanced ahead to dodge branches and brush! Fortunate I was that the wolverine stayed home — not feeling threatened enough to come out after me! Knowing the wolverine's reputation for agility and of fearing nothing, fearing not even wolves or a grizzly — the sooner I distanced myself, the better!

Following the pond eastward under tall wild willow trees back towards the gravel road, I was extremely excited and feeling pleased about hearing this most unusual vocalization. I was certain that I had just been looked at…and growled at — by a wolverine! Although I never saw it, coming so close to this rarely seen wild Canadian animal was certainly special. Feeling elated, as I pushed through more thick brush…I began wishing it had shown itself. Even so, I sensed that this was probably a mother wolverine with small cubs…the reason it was in the den on such a sunny warm day!

After a short but quick and noisy walk I was back at the gravel road and my truck. By now hungry, I sat inside to keep a small cloud of mosquitoes at bay…and wolfed-down a quick lunch. Still charged up as I was, the wolverine and its deep growl dominated my mind. I just sat quietly for some time enjoying the energy, the audible memory and…resting my legs. Then just as I was ready to drive away, a young cow moose stepped from among tall willows out onto the road just twenty yards ahead.

Whether it was the branch-crackler or another moose I did not know but thought this was probably a different one. Looking to be two-and-a-half years old, it stood at the roadside gazing steadily at me. Apparently on its own for the first time this moose seemed more curious than afraid! Then calmly walking away along the gravel road a few steps, stopping and starting again, it was in no hurry. Reaching its head up, the moose continually nibbled off willow twigs and leaves. With each movement its dark blackish hair glistened in the bright sunlight, shining silvery, highlighted with touches of blonde and white on the neck and back. Soon though, stepping behind thick spruce and willow…the animal went its way.

At first glance, seeming an odd-looking creature this tall animal had large soft drooping nostrils, very large rotating ears, overly-long thin but graceful legs and almost no tail. All of these features I could see were appropriate to the moose: having lived, played and long-evolved in this four-seasoned northern climate and pond-filled ecosystem. Perfectly designed it was… for wet woodlands where the ground was soft most of the year while during winter, frozen and deep with snow. This young moose was a beauty in itself, just as graceful in its way as were the Canadian goose, her goslings and the fearless agile wolverine! Here, in this wild forest they all belonged. And I was merely a privileged visitor.

FULL AND SATISFIED

Although the day was ebbing away, I slipped two pepperspray holsters onto my leather belt then donned a small green backpack and stepped into the fir and pine forest. From the distance this little wooded area looked to have good potential for pine mushrooms, so I wanted to do a quick scout. Pushing my way through thick yellow-leaved willow and hardhack bushes to openish ground then skirting by three very large old Douglas fir trees, I could now see how rugged this terrain was. But neither the steep mossy rockbluffs nor small brushy swamp dips were to deter my desperate resolve to make some money!

This was the sort of ground that I did not like — visibility being so limited — where one could meet a large animal at close range to the surprise of both! Moving slowly and cautiously almost straight up...when nearing the top of the first granite ridge I put my hand onto one pepperspray holster. Then for best visibility, walking along the top edge under small lodgepine trees I checked moss and lichen-covered ground as far as the ridge's north end. There it dropped off almost vertically...down into a little roaring river that frothed a creamy yellow whitewater far below. Then down across the next swampy dip and up onto its parallel ridge, I reversed direction following southward the full length. The ground looked good but so far no hint of mushrooms. This ridge also abruptly stopped at a fifty-foot vertical dropoff.

At this clifftop, the loud roar of swiftmoving whitewater echoed up along grey granite cliffs. The canyon's walls were beautifully patterned with lichen growing as triangles in various shades of grey, crisscrossed by irregular, blotchy lines of yellow and black lichen. I stood awhile enjoying the warm sunshine which was just about to cease, with the brilliant orange-red Sun dipping low over a deep blue southwestern mountain. Then continuing this zigzag pattern, I walked two more ridges. The forest air was delicious with scents of pitch and live pinetree needles. From some trees, pitch had oozed through bark here and there...the thick liquid trickling down in long thin golden yellow streaks that terminated as wee shining teardrops.

At the bases of several trees, large dry honey-amber and bright yellow blobs had slowly grown over the years. Breaking off a little piece I put it on top of my tongue savouring the strong, yet pleasant resinous flavour. But I could not linger long. Now the Sun had just moved below the darkening blue mountain...evening would be soon-coming. I quickened my pace. Finally, along one ridge a few small pine mushrooms appeared...but were too old and maggot-eaten. Maybe now I was nearing a patch?

Just then in the near distance below I could hear the sound of brush rustling. So...I was not alone! Company of some sort was just ahead! Could it be just another mushroom picker? But I had a poor day in other areas, so was not to be deterred from this possibility. Besides, I had two pepper sprayguns for self-defence. Wandering back and forth, gradually moving lower, closer to the river and to the last ridge where it levelled slightly into a gentle mossy slope…I refused to give up. The river's roar was now much more audible — dominating the senses.

Again, a faint rustling of brush below caught my attention! Looking downslope…its cause was yet beyond sight. But here, just at the base of the granite ridge and beneath a bushy hemlock tree was a patch of ripped up, thick moss; it had been recently and considerably churned up over a three-yard diameter. Moss and creamy white chunks of broken pine mushrooms were strewn about. And stem bottoms showed large toothmarks where they had been snipped off by some animal! The brush-rustler was definitely not human!

Such I had seen before where deer, elk and bears had eaten mushrooms; these moss-rips, selective and not too encompassing, looked more like the eating-style of a deer. Bears would usually rip the moss in a more blatant way than deer. Also, the toothmarks on stem bottoms were deer-like. That eased me slightly. Even so, a bear's front-centre toothmarks would look much the same, so I was not completely sure who my woodsy companion was.

Removing the backpack, then down onto hands and knees — while keeping a watch downslope — I checked the ground by patting moss gently, feeling for rounded bumps of mushrooms hiding underneath. My reward was one button and a couple of open mushrooms that the animal had missed. Quickly replacing the largest divots of moss left by the brush-rustler, I then longstepped downward to the next nearest ripped spot. I visually scanned the slope below. The animal was still out of sight beyond the slope's curve.

Here, much like the first spot several mushrooms had been partly or completely eaten. Again patting the moss while replacing divots, this ground produced two more nice solid buttons. Looking around, more rip-ups and white bits could be seen here and there in the near distance on the open mossy slope, both above and below. There had been a lot of big open pine mushrooms! Whatever the animal…it was having a real feast!

As I checked moss-ripped spots, each time stuffing two or three mushrooms into the backpack bag…sporadic rustling of brush below mingled with the continuous din echoing from the canyon. Yet constantly looking up and around, I saw nothing but trees and brush on the curving horizon. As I worked downward the slope steepened. This whole area of north-south ridges was shaped like a short peninsula defined by vertical and nearly-vertical dropoffs at the north and south ends. Now I could see that this lowest part too, ended abruptly as a high grey cliff dropping straight down into the noisy rapids far below!

My unknown animal companion was somewhere down there close to the dropoff edge…so obviously could not escape downward; it would of necessity have to come back towards me. I thought to not go any lower. I knew approximately where it was but did not know if the animal had detected my scent yet. I suspected it probably had not heard me. Even so, I kept looking for the animal, although feeling fairly safe. Here, with trees far apart one could see a good distance.

I continued picking up mushroom scraps left by the animal. It had found and eaten several open mushrooms from every spot on this mossy green slope but did leave a few for me. By now I realized this could not be a deer: having eaten just too many large open flags and in some spots churned over the moss far more than a deer would! There was no hint on the ground of elk here. I had to vacate as soon as possible, suspecting it be a bear. But the prospect of gleaning a few more needed dollars kept me!

Now the southern sky had turned a pale copper colour, with evening rapidly approaching. Dips and hollows in the forest across the river gorge were turning a deep blue-black. And I had tensed somewhat with apprehension. Wanting to leave and wanting to stay — these thoughts and feelings fought within! But I was held by the mushrooms which were now showing in fair numbers! I looked frequently up and around while moving on hands and knees, checking the ground.

Then from the south as I knelt with head down — a loud swishing of branches and leaves brought my eyes instantly up! There it was! Just fifteen yards away — a blackbear was padding slowly broadside with its head cocked sharply sideways, watching me. It was endeavouring to pass quietly along the southern edge of the clifftop. The bear had been tiptoeing past me!

When I looked up, it stopped…and continued its quiet steady gaze. With right hand I reached slowly for one pepperspray, lifted it from the holster to my chest and with thumb flipped out the orange safety-wedge while pointing the nozzle at the bear. I did this as a precaution — knowing how lightning-fast bears are when they attack and that when they do, sometimes give no specific indication of their intention. Even so, now seeing the bear, my apprehension subsided…knowing what it was and where it was!

But I remained alert, silent and still. Our mutual staring, observing and assessing continued for long moments. The bear showed no expression of ill-will…also keeping silent and still. Its ears were erect and focussed on me as intently as its unblinking eyes. But erect ears, I knew did not necessarily mean a benign attitude: a bear will attack with ears either flat back, erect or somewhere in between. Ear position, I had learned before was an ambiguous gesture. And I was happy to see that its belly hung down in a deep curve, full of pine mushrooms…no doubt with a touch of added protein, minerals and vitamins in form of fly and beetle eggs and larvae that were in the mushrooms!

So I knew now that this bear was unlikely to become aggressive…having just finished with a very big feed and also seeing that I was no threat. Not large, it looked to be about one hundred seventy-five pounds. As was the case with most bears that I have met in woods over the years, this one was aware of me well before I saw or heard it! The bear had walked up from below. When seeing me so busy with the moss and unaware of it…the little bear just tried to pass by; which it would have unnoticed if the tough-stemmed bushes were not there to alert me! Such be the usual benign behaviour of a bear: very accepting of human presence and if possible avoiding close contact. If bears were normally vicious by nature, this one would have had me and so could have several others in previous years!

After about two minutes of mutual observation this content-looking bear lost interest, slowly turned its head away then continued upslope to southeast, padding silently around the little pine-treed granite ridge and out of sight. Now it was time for me to move! I picked up my backpack which was now almost full of mushrooms, slipped it on, then started a quick pace back up along the forest's northernmost edge. This route was the farthest possible from where the bear had exited.

Twilight had surreptitiously arrived but was now quickly fading away…as now everything was almost visibly darkening in the silent forest all around. Suspended above the high southern mountains and across the dark grey sky were little scattered billowy clouds of pink, copper and mauve. Trees all around me were now ghostly grey-black silhouettes and the forest shadows almost black. Visibility was now very poor in this dark twilight and in the dips there were thick bushy parts to pass through yet! Apprehension again tensed my body. I held the pepperspray in hand as I skirted past or climbed over each rocky ridge.

Under this circumstance I thought it best to let the bear know where I was, to avoid any chance of a nose-to-nose meeting…so yelled out frequently to the bear as I went, as loudly and deeply as I could: "Hey! I'm over here! You stay over there! Okay?! I'm going this way…you go that way!"

Crashing through the brush as fast and noisily as possible, racing against the fast-approaching night, I stopped very brief moments to listen. But of course…in fifteen minutes or so I was back safely at the truck — just in time — as the woods had blackened even more and visibility was almost nil! Bear or not, walking out of a forest in the dark is extremely hazardous, so to be avoided whenever possible.

Now the sky had turned even darker grey. A few bright white lights were beginning to sparkle down through wide sky openings between the small greyblack and mauveblack cumulous clouds. Starlight from countless aeons past had arrived…also just in time…for this human to see, enjoy and appreciate. I wondered what the bear thought, if anything, of the starlight shining over its vast open, mountainous home. And I felt very cheered meeting this benign young bear…also happy that it had beaten me to the mushrooms which were more important to it than to me!

Seldom Seen or Heard

One extensive lowland forest along British Columbia's saltwater coast was populated by a mere handful of people and a small herd of deer, mostly does with their fawns and yearlings. Predominantly mixed forest but with three little hayfields, it also had a 'no hunting' designation. Treed with second and third-growth fir, balsam, hemlock, maple, alder, wild cherry, arbutus, dogwood, hawthorn, sitka spruce, yew and red cedar...through this special forest ran four crystal-clear creeks. This sea-level ecosystem was a unique meeting point of Nature's wilderness and human doings where both co-existed in relative harmony.

Having been clearcut first from the 1890s to 1920s with small blocks selectively logged at various times subsequently the trees, shrubs, wildflowers and herbs were in great variety and of various ages. Huge old partly rotten stumps loomed up under the forest canopy with their beautifully curved flares and roots thick with moss and licorice ferns. Some of these tall flaring stumps were topped with young hemlock trees or clumps of huckleberry and salmonberry bushes, now just beginning to bud...all looking quite beautiful. On the ground too, every square inch was occupied by a plant of some sort, varying with the sunshine and shade mix: shalal, red huckleberry, redflowering currant, moss, bleedinghearts, pink ladyslipper orchids, trilliums, pink and white fawn lilies, wild ginger, sarsaparilla, grass and other herbaceous plants. The forest floor was now quickly greening with these plants. And spiralling up fir, balsam and maple trunks here and there were the woody vines of wild orange honeysuckle...climbing right into treetops thirty to forty feet up.

Such habitat was perfect year-round living space for deer, grouse, squirrels, voles, wrens, chickadees, jays and other wildlife. During my first winter residing in this woodsy paradise, some pleasant exploratory walks were enjoyed along a lengthy wild saltwater beach that bordered the forest. About one-quarter mile along were seven large Douglas fir and amabilis trees, three hundred to five hundred-plus years old, that were left standing by the first loggers probably as seed-trees. One fir with a six-foot diameter trunk had a large eagles' nest built near the top.

One early spring day, out walking the beach at this point I ducked under thick seaside brush of oceanspray and snowberry to enter the shady forest. On the ground between shalal bushes lay a large old eagle's wingfeather...and hungup high in hawthorn branches, a more recent white tailfeather. These and a few little mottled feathers were clear indication of a nest recently or presently occupied.

I walked slowly towards the first big fir tree. Mahonia brush and shalal leaves rustled softly against my bluejean pantlegs. Approaching the huge treetrunk, fixing my line of vision onto its thick deeply-grooved bark, I mentally absorbed its varied and almost-animate patterns, its soft rust, grey and cream colours and deep texture: even tree bark has a unique beauty that can be quietly enjoyed. Moments later I stood at the ancient tree's base. An odd surprise was there on the ground completely encircling the tree; this raised both my interest and awareness to keen! Here, broken into almost perfectly round tincan shapes were many solid pieces neatly piled, composed of pale brown hair and powdered white bone. A dozen piles were deposited all around the big treetrunk…with each representing probably a week or more. Each little tincan-chunk was about one-and-a-half to two inches in diameter.

These small heaps were the fresh and older scat of a large adult cougar! That the animal had spent a good part of the winter in this forest was certain…and I felt it was most likely still here! Suddenly, an uneasiness pervaded my mind and body since I had nothing with me for self-defence! But interesting it was to see how the big cat chose one little place to leave its droppings. It had been feeding on the local deer of course, and spent much of its winter leisure time under the thick branchy umbrella of this largest tree of the seven. This fir tree was a good hiding place for the big cougar, where it would be protected somewhat from rain, snow and wind…while also secluded enough from people. I was lucky that the cougar was not home when I arrived at its hiding place! But this discovery now ended my day's exploration…I turned and walked quickly homeward…happy all the while for this rare discovery.

The following autumn I had a small bonfire going, burning scrap wood and branches at the edge of the property where tall grass ended and forest began. Nearby were two large old lichen-coated plum trees fairly loaded with fruit and ready to pick. It was early evening with an ever-shifting sky of orange, pink, mauve and pale green playing above the steep, deep blue and maroon westward mountains. Hardly a breeze blew, giving the forest an almost touchable calmness. I stood by the fire enveloped within this soothing, peaceful space…and staring at its bright orange-pink coals.

Within this all-encompassing silence the fire's soft hissing, squeaking and sudden little popping sounds were to me a pleasant natural music. For about an hour I fed the flame bit by bit until no scrap of wood remained, and in between, warming my hands over the fire. As it diminished I crouched closer, watching the brilliant pale orange embers and tiny pure blue flames flickering…while off-and-on sunk mentally into reveries of the past. At undetermined periods, a loud pop would bring me back to the moment, to the present place and time for a short while…until drifting again into calmness and peaceful thought. Then at some point an uncommon but familiar feeling came to the fore…this time holding my attention.

Now the silence had strangely lost its peacefulness. The forest, the air and space all around seemed just too quiet! Inexplicably, a touch of fear ran through my body. That rare sensation came…of being watched: that odd, slightly paranoid feeling sometimes called the sixth-sense. It was as if subconsciously my awareness knew something that I was consciously unaware of. But this sort of experience I was familiar with, having had it several times over previous years.

I became very uneasy. Standing up, I looked around and into the woods…seeing nothing unusual. Even so, I mentally fought against this odd sensation while poking the dying, sizzling coals with a long green maple stick. A few quiet minutes passed. I calmed somewhat. Then one very loud high-pitched scream shattered the silence! From twenty yards distant just behind a clump of tall blond grass and sapling fir trees, this was a sound that I knew!

Although almost identical to the scream of a teenaged girl…this was not human…but the scream of a cougar! Looking hard towards the grass and little evergreen trees, nothing moved, nothing materialized. The big cat kept low and out of sight. It had been there in a crouch watching me for some time unknown!

I guessed the cougar was either afraid of the fire or upset by my presence in a place where deer frequented. Now slowly walking sideways to the safety of the nearby shed, I watched and listened. Standing in the doorway I wished the cat would show itself. I waited and waited... charged with excited energy and some apprehension! But the big feline did not appear.

A minute later though, it screamed once more from about fifty yards farther into the woods! That was the cougar's last communication to me. A bit disappointed...I had not been fortunate enough to see it. Even so, I was happy to have this experience just as it was! People had mentioned that a female cougar would at times call that way for a mate. But this seemed to me an odd moment for that! It had no doubt been watching me, probably longer than the sixth-sense indicated...as I stood or knelt obliviously with my stoking-stick, calmly watching the beautiful glowing orange and blue fire. Maybe deer that I was unaware of were nearby using me as a shield?

With the cougar going deeper into rapidly darkening woods I walked back to the fire, flipped embers towards its centre, then kicking dirt up, circled the glowing coals making a small fireguard. The western sky had dimmed to bluegrey while mountains had turned deep blue-black. Twilight was vanishing fast, as greyblack shadows overtook the sleepy forest. I thought of my hungry cougar padding slowly, silently, between trees somewhere in there where I could not see; yet its vision was no less than before with its natural night-vision adjusting to the coming of darkness. And now five little blacktail deer stepped from hiding under tall thick fringe brush...then out into the open hayfield only about thirty yards away. So...I had been between the cougar and them...in its way! Well, the deer were safe for awhile and could now graze in peace this evening.

Winter passed with no further contact. Then one day the following spring I was driving along a gravel sideroad towards the highway. Large old mossy-trunked broadleaf maple trees arched over, high above. Their branchtips were brightly yellowed with little drooping clusters of bloom among tiny pale green leaflets that had barely started to sprout. A few early-arrived hummingbirds hovered and darted about, feeding on nectar and pollen from these minute yellow-green blossoms which were the first and only wild bloom at this early springtime.

Where this sideroad met the highway I stopped the truck a moment, then turned left. Here the highway was built up about eight feet above normal ground level. Clumps of brushy shalal and upward arching swordfern grew below in the right-of-way. Maple, dogwood, spruce, cedar and hemlock trees lined the forest edge. I shifted into second gear then just into third, slowly accelerating to about thirty miles per hour. A hint of something moving towards me from the left side entered my vision.

A rusty-brown streak flashed up from below the gravel shoulder! Next instant, it became the stretched-out form of a cougar flying through the air! That same moment my heart tensed as I jammed on the brakes — seeing the near-collision course it was on with my truck's front end!

Front paws landing on the centreline, then big rabbit-like rear feet touching pavement on each side of them, it hopped one long-jump into the air towards the rightside gravel shoulder! Long black-tipped tail followed almost straight out as the big cat glide in midair directly across in front...a seemingly very long split-second! I watched its beautifully marked youthful face: solid white muzzle, thick white whiskers, rusty nose, short black moustache, rounded erect ears and sparkling amber eyes that looked straight ahead...yet simultaneously watched from eye-corners the big blue machine rapidly approaching!

The truck slowed as I jammed hard onto the brake pedal! The big cat's forepaws hit gravel as it disappeared from view beneath the truck's hood!

I was likewise in grief, thinking and wishing: "Don't hit it! Don't hit it!"

Desperately, I waited for — expected — a bump and a thump! A split-second later emotional and physical ease shot through me, as glancing sideways…the cougar reappeared at the gravel shoulder leaping away over shalal and swordferns!

The big beauty was so close to the front bumper its tail may have been hit by it. But I was extremely relieved as I looked back…watching the auburn-red cougar bound twice more to treeline then run in a low crouch between fir and dogwood trees and away! This all happened in about three short seconds of time. Yet the experience — and the memory — seemed more like three minutes…as if it all happened in slow-motion!

Luckily, no other traffic was on the highway at that moment. As the truck came to a stop I pulled onto the gravel shoulder, grabbed my camera, which I happened to have…then ran back hoping the sleek feline beauty were yet visible somewhere in the semi-open forest. But no, it was long-gone. This was the first time I had seen an auburn cougar, the dark reddish colour variation that is unique to Vancouver Island! I was happy to the point of elation!

Walking back to the truck as my hands were shaking from adrenalin, I thought: "Oh well…if I had gotten a picture it would be too blurry anyway." And I wondered if this cat was the one that screamed at me one evening last fall.

This beautiful young cougar, two or three years old, was a juvenile female not yet fully grown. It was obviously youthfully naive, not yet fully comprehending the highway and motor vehicles…those noisy smelly things that shine and move along it. But the look in its sparkling eyes and on its face seemed to indicate a lesson learned about the danger of roads: to be more cautious next time!

More months passed by as Earth inexorably rotated and revolved around the life-giving Sun. Another autumn was now in the wind. I arrived home at about midnight and from the headlights could see five or six deer grazing in the hayfield next to the house where they often were. Having to unload a few tools at the back shed about thirty yards from the house, I drove directly there between a row of fruit trees and thick thimbleberry brush, stopping, then shutting off the lights and motor.

The night was calm and quiet. Everything on the ground was pitch-black: brush, trees and buildings were outlined against a clear grey sky that was alight with a billion or so stars. Black forms of big balsam, maple, cedar and spruce trees stood motionless under the silent twinkling sky. A distant high-pitched call from the muddy brackish bay…that of a long-legged shorebird, joined the jingle of my keys… tiny sounds of life amid this great silence and vastness of Space.

Stepping out with keys in hand but no flashlight, I fumbled and felt in darkness for the door's lock and handle. Finally opening the large metal roll-up door, I switched on the building's lights. There at my feet stood a bright-eyed, reddish brown and white miniature Sheltie dog… with bushy rusty-brown tail wagging in cheerful excitement! An unexpected surprise greeting this was by a sweet friendly family dog! During my absence someone had been here, locked her inside and left.

Putting away my tools, I closed the big door then picked up the dog and carried her to a small end-door, thinking to watch the deer from there. With dog in arms, I switched off the lights then opened the door. For a few moments I counted silhouettes of seven deer, all does and fawns, standing in the open field but close to the house. Beyond them as if touching the stars were black outlines of two very large cottonwood trees, a row of large grand fir, one big Sitka spruce and to northwest the high round-topped rocky mountain.

Then I stepped out, closing the door. With dog in arms, I stood a few moments in the dark near a plum tree and row of apple trees…watching deer silhouettes and enjoying the cool still air, the silent darkness and a brilliant starry sky. Turning right, I took one step back along the shed wall towards the truck. Just then near the ground close behind and slightly left — burst forth a loud, very deep, rolling cat-like growl! This big throaty growl ended with a short indrawn, raspy breath! It came from only a few paces away at ground level under a leaning apple tree! Simultaneously, a bolt of electricity seemed to shoot through my body! I had never heard this sound before but instantly recognized it as that of a cougar — no doubt a large adult!

Glancing back to the left, I just kept walking…but could not see the big cat in the solid blackness of grassy ground and thick brush beside the leaning tree. All I could do now was keep longstepping steadily towards the truck! A strange tingling sensation ran up along my spine and back. Split-seconds seemed to last and last…as I waited to be jumped from behind! This strong thought and sensation pervaded…persisted…for the long ten-yard walk back to the truck! But the big cat was kind. It left us alone!

Safely back at the truck, I placed the dog inside then stepped in myself. I wondered: "Now, how am I going to see this cat with the truck facing away?" Slipping the ignition key into place, not thinking of just switching the key on and putting the gear into reverse to get the backup lights on, which was my only real chance…instead, I started the truck and turned around. With headlights on high I searched for the animal in the brush, trees and grass but saw nothing. Of course, the big cougar had moved away out of sight under the thimbleberry bushes. I felt slightly disappointed for not seeing this cougar but was far more pleased with just having such an unusual and rare meeting!

After a few minutes I gave up looking and drove slowly back to the house. The deer were alert but still grazing at the far side of the grassy field. Thoughts raced through my excited mind. Now, I understood! The big cat had been stalking them…crouching low in thimbleberry brush and tall grass that grew beside the row of apple, plum and cherry trees. From there it had been silently watching the deer as they grazed…waiting patiently. Then I arrived, driving right past, not noticing it hidden under big thimbleberry leaves. The cougar held its position undeterred by the truck — so concentrated it was on the deer!

While I was in the shed the big cougar moved out beneath the leaning apple tree, still focussed on deer and unperturbed by my presence…continuing to stalk them. No doubt this was a hungry carnivore! But then I stepped out of the shed into its line of attack…something the big cat had not expected. I had suddenly interfered with the cougar's strategy! Hence came the jolting, spine-tingling, very deep growl!

This loud powerful growl must have erupted partly in protest and partly as a warning to me for coming so close! But with its mind set on deer…attacking me just then did not fit the big cat's plan. Interesting also was the fact that the herd of deer never moved from their grazing spot — even after hearing the cougar! How far it had retreated into the forest I did not know, but this big wild feline would now have to endure hunger a bit longer. While conversely the deer were feeding well, out in an open hayfield under a star-filled sky…enjoying life for the time being at least.

Autumn gradually transformed into winter. Snow began to fall and by January temperatures were excessively cold so the snow remained, whereas most winters in this area it would have melted away. More than two feet had built up. This snow and extreme freezing lingered on and on…making life very hard on the small blacktail deer. By February local people were finding dead deer lying here and there in the surrounding woods.

One day in March I found at the hayfield's edge, the body of one poor little yearling deer curled up under a clump of overhanging swordfern…as if it were just sleeping. It had lain down in this foetal curl and fell asleep, never to awaken again. Strangely, this little deer was still full-bodied with a thick winter coat of fur, looking healthy. It had not been shot; no blood was visible. There were apparently no broken bones so it had not been hit by a car.

By now the snow had melted away but nights were still freezing. How this little deer died was an enigma to me but thought the probable primary cause was exposure: the temperature must have been too cold, too long for these little deer to endure. This one looked well-fed so it had not starved.

A couple of days before while I was socializing at the local coffee shop four miles away, one friendly acquaintance told me of a very brief recent encounter in his backyard. He arrived home in the dark and had just left his van when a lightning-quick shadowy image passed by him a mere five yards away. It was a medium-sized animal, long and low to the ground. He thought it could have been a juvenile cougar but was not certain, thinking one would never come that close. I told him that yes, the big cats will come…especially at night! He also informed me that someone else had seen a cougar crossing the highway half-a-mile away a few days previously. We both thought it was probably the same cougar and hungry enough to stalk pet dogs and cats at night.

Knowing these woods quite well, I had a good idea of where it would likely be lying low during the day but never told him or anyone else, also knowing how paranoid most people are about cougars. So this deer that I had found dead on the property, I thought would make a good offering to the desperate young cat. Next day I lifted the stiff, lifeless little body into the truckbox then drove up a gravel sideroad to a bit of forest that would be the cougar's probable hideout. Stopping near that spot, I carried the fifty-pound deer into a small five year-old clearcut to about forty yards off the road. Leaving it there among shalal and brown died-back bracken ferns, this little offering was beyond human visibility from the road.

Four days later I drove back to check, bringing my camera…hoping for a chance photograph. I waded slowly through low brush of green shalal, red and green mahonia and rusty brown bracken ferns. Approaching the spot cautiously…I was mildly disappointed. There was no big cat in sight but otherwise, yes…I was happy to see that the body of my poor little deer was gone! It had been definitely carried away by the cougar! This food offering no doubt brought some happiness to one hungry carnivore…I felt very good about that!

Now this deer's death had served a useful purpose in helping one young cougar to survive. Hesitating a few minutes, I peered into the standing timber fifty yards away where I thought the cat was. All was calm and silent…but I could feel again that sixth-sense…that odd sensation of being watched. But now I knew it was a futile wish to see this cougar…so reluctantly walked away from the spot, both cheered and sad: acutely aware of the natural reality of life and death. "How strange," I thought…"that such beauty and complexity of being always ends in death."

These five very interesting, even exciting contacts with our elusive, misunderstood cougar occurred over a period of two years in beautiful, mostly wild terrain that was ideal living-space for both deer and cougars. Deer were there year-round while to the big camera-shy cats, it was more a winter residence that overlapped with autumn and spring. I felt most fortunate and privileged to be living for awhile in such unique natural paradise — so alive — where human beings had not yet taken away the wildlife's crucial life-habitat.

How long this special forest would remain intact and alive though, was dependent on human plans: management or mismanagement, kindness or selfishness. The fate of this crucial habitat would be decided locally by people's personal plans and nearby municipal strategies, along with political and commercial schemes in more distant Victoria and far away Ottawa...by those who have almost no experience with Nature...therefore very little comprehension of its immeasurably great importance!

Eastern British Columbia
and
Western Alberta

TRACKS IN THE SNOW

Warm April sunshine had melted back the snow into mottled curving patches, now only in the broad valley's shady dips and under northslope forest. And on southern slopes of this high Rocky Mountain pass, winter was retreating far above the hamlet of Lucerne. I had just recently moved here, into the eastern end of an old wooden CN Railway shack. My end of this long narrow building had only one window and was intruded by the single entrance-door. Only fifteen yards from the mainline tracks, the shack would shake in unison with each passing train. Its faulty door latch would randomly lose grip letting the door swing open during passage on average about one in five trains. Such be my new residence and happy I was starting a new job!

Just into my second week of work as a train-order operator, now off duty, I was asleep. My small narrow cot was against a dark wall, cramped by the only door and I slept with my head next to it. Outside, winter gave a late overnight showing as snowflakes quietly drifted to the ground…slowly piling up to about two inches. Several trains went by this night, which I would hear and feel in the background of my slumberworld as the cabin and its contents shook and swayed harmoniously with each train.

In the twilight of early morning another train rumbled by. Railjoints clicked rhythmically as heavy steel wheels rolled over them. The walls shook, my bed swayed and the doorlatch let loose…unknown to me, lying so blissfully asleep. The door swung open. Cold air drifted in.

After some unknown time this wintery draught pulled me from my dreams back to earth. I got up to close the door. Outside everything looked so clean and fresh, all covered in new snow! Stepping forward, I took a slow deep breath of cold delicious-smelling mountain air. And just outside the door, stamped into the new snow were large tracks of local wild mountain residents. Surprised and excited, I looked closer! Three sets of big cat tracks passed by the doorway and only one yard from my wall…paralleling the cabin just outside of where I had been sleeping!

The largest paw was about five inches in diameter and two smaller about three inches — those of a mother cougar with two juvenile kittens! They were on the prowl and no doubt hungry. These tracks were very distinct with no snowflakes inside them. The big cats passed by after snowfall had stopped just an hour or so ago! And they may have been only minutes away. I was certainly glad and eased that the door latch was not released by an earlier passing train!

This cougar family was out for a nighttime hunt…passing through Lucerne with dogmeat in mind. For them a dog would be an easy catch. Cougars seem to prefer dogmeat, especially when their staple food animals are scarce. They eat coyotes too, but have to work harder to catch one. Four pet dogs and cats were top priority to the big felines, since thirteen railway employees with their families and pets lived here. They had lost two dogs to cougars over the winter so now kept the survivors inside overnight. Here, the wilds came right to one's door: humanity and wildlife were living together, albeit semiharmoniously.

Later this spring when snowline had retreated higher, I went hiking along one trail up the prominent mountain above. Young and naive, my only self-defence was a little dull hunting knife with four-and-a-half inch blade; I thought that if danger arrived I could just climb a tree to safety! But this day was perfect for a mountain walk, with a cloudless blue sky above. Hardly a breeze, all trees were silent except for trembling aspen which softly rustled only now and then.

It was a long hard climb...working up a sweat, I often stopped to puff and pant for oxygen. But once higher, looking between pine, birch and poplar trees was complete visual pleasure...as distant snow and glacier-capped dark blue mountains filled the whole southern horizon from east to west. And below them the heavily treed valley was a patchwork of living green in deep, medium and pale shades gracefully curving downward along gentle slopes and ridges. At the bottom, fanning onto narrow flats the forest thinned into limegreen and pale tan meadows among wee patches of dark spruce, pinetrees and dots of brilliant white snow.

Finally, after maybe an hour of stop-and-go, I reached the subalpine forest of small lodgepine and whitebark pine where patches of meadow yet to sprout green were encircled by large wavey patches of sparkly crystalline snow. At one little yellow-spotted subalpine meadow I sat down on a dry lichen-covered boulder. Tiny rivulets of crystal-clear snowmelt quietly trickled by... over moss and pale ochre grass, past deep yellow curling blooms of snowlilies. Almost-invisible water droplets and thinlined trickles sparkled brilliantly beside spingtime's first flowers...all standing still, silent and glowing yellow in the sunlight...looking very perfect, as if emanations from the pure essence of the Universe.

For some unknown time I just relaxed...silently experiencing this little natural paradise. The Sun's warm rays penetrated my face, ears and hands as I breathed in the cold, pine-scented mountain air...feeling as if I were enveloped within a threshold of nonphysical reality: peaceful beyond words, beyond concepts, beyond feelings. At this altitude the silence was a most powerful phenomenon...it dominated everything!

Silence was so all-pervasive that for the very first time I could hear my heart beating in my chest and blood flowing through my ears! All external visual, tactile and olfactory sensa were modified and softened in a most unusual way that is really conceptually indescribable. This most unusual experience was the first such that had ever come to me; it spontaneously effected a positive psychological change...there was a clear calmness inside. Something deep and profound seemed to emanate from the vast stillness of forest, mountains and sky.

After some unknown minutes completely absorbed by this unusually positive something... my heartbeat and physical reality, the hot sunshine, brought me back: a happy human sitting on a rock, high in the Rockies. Looking about, I could see the trail leading into shallow snow of about six inches. I decided to continue onward into the snow since here the ridge had levelled to almost flat...easy walking. But within minutes it deepened to about eighteen inches. The soft wet snow was glaringly bright with reflected sunshine. Plodding through it along the now-indistinct trail, I mentally debated on when to stop and turn around. Soon I would have to turn back. Then at a point where the pine-treed ridge began gently sloping to the northeast, a row of deep shadowy depressions appeared just ahead crossing the trail in a straight line.

Could it be a moose? I quickly paced to the large, clearly separated tracks. Bending over to look down into them: bear tracks! Very large prints with distinctively long claws...this was certainly a grizzly! Instantly a jolt of electric energy ran through my spine and nerves then adrenalin entered my arteries. A tingling sensation came to my upper back and neck!

Looking up and around...no animal was in sight. Pinetrees were all too small to climb. The bear's tracks led downslope to the southeast. I knelt down to measure the length of one larger depression using my right hand and arm. It ran from my elbow to middle of the palm in length! "This bear is huge!" I thought.

Its claws and pads were clearly impressed as packed snow, showing no slip. By considering the snowmelt and general track appearance, I could see that this bear was here probably not less than eight hours and no more than twenty-four hours ago. My fear and sense of urgency increased, even so! The grizzly was no doubt hungry: just recently out of its hibernation den!

Standing up, I listened and looked hard in all directions just a few moments — then turned back down the trail, longstepping as fast as I could! Although the bear's tracks were angling downslope towards the Alberta border and Jasper Park, it may not have kept that way. I scooted past the little magical patch of yellow lilies, merely glancing at them. Keeping up the pace, jogging at times…in about ten minutes I was back under larger poplar and spruce trees — climbable ones — so felt better about that! I kept a keen eye and ear ahead and especially to the east knowing the bear was most likely in that area.

The walk down was relatively easy and quick, although not pleasant with discovery as it had been going up. Another thirty minutes or so and I was back down almost to the trail's end. Now walking along a glacial clay hump just above the little hamlet, I was forty yards from the railway tracks. Down in a dip to my right, filtering through a clump of brush came the sound of ripping dry bark…squeaking and snapping…only ten yards away! This was the high-pitched squeal of sharp claws heavily raking and knitting on a treetrunk!

Large paws were alternately sliding down, claws slicing the bark and at short intervals grabbing and pulling at it. No doubt this was a cougar! Knowing it was unaware of me, I tiptoed by…in a hurry! By the time it sensed my presence, I would be safely by and almost back home. I jogged across the rails and stood by my cabin door looking back. From this safety…I watched for quite some time hoping to see it venture out. But it never did. The big cat was northward across the rails and into the woods only about seventy yards from my cabin.

Next day, I walked over the rails and into the shady dip to satisfy my interest and confirm my assumptions. The cougar's scratching-tree was a twelve-inch diameter aspen with fresh and old clawlines running from about eight feet high, down almost to the base. Much bark was removed to sapwood on the trunk's north side and was lined with many very thin vertical clawcuts. These were definitely made by at least one cougar. I thought this tree must be a signal post and boundary marker.

Summer passed into autumn with little indication of the big cats nearby other than a set of fresh tracks one day, sunk into a sandbar beside one nameless creek. Now it was a dark cold mid-November night. I was at work in Lucerne Station. I had copied some train orders which were cleared by the Kamloops dispatcher. I then hooped-up these orders for a westbound freight train that had just left Jasper.

The train-order board was on yellow with semaphore arm pointing upward at a forty-five degree angle, meaning that the traincrew would not have to stop for orders but could take them on-the-fly at medium speed — fifteen to twenty miles per hour. I sat back waiting in the sturdy old captain's chair. Most comfortable it was, having a cushioned seat, curving wooden back and wide armrests.

Directly in front just outside the window a light powdery snowfall quietly tumbled down in curving zigzags, gently floating slowly to the ground…where eight inches already lay. Tiny flakes sparkled on and off reflecting light from the station's brightly shining gas-mantle lamp. Hanging from the ceiling above and behind me, it hissed steadily, softly. On the wall in front a beautiful old oak pendulum-clock ticked its steady lowpitched sound…as the large shining brass-yellow pendulum swung silently from side to side. Although now an antique, it kept perfectly accurate railway time, being designed and made for consistency and safety.

It now read a few minutes past nought-two-hundred. In other words, the time was just after two o'clock in the morning. But now the old clock's steady but pleasant click-clock, as if it be gentle music, lulled me into the twilight edge of the dream-realm: half awake, half asleep.

Outside, little wind blew. Falling snow made the calm quiet forest all around seem even more silent, bestowing a sense of peace: as if this wee village, the lake below and mountains above were all in a comfortable cocoon. In darkness directly across the rails at a small bay, I knew that whistling swans were sleeping, heads tucked under wings. They seemed late migrating. Inside, the little station was warm and cozy but outside…very cold!

This momentary pleasantness I much appreciated while not letting it deceive me into thinking that it would last. I thought about how everything in life is in constant motion, ever-changing… similar to the old oak clock's pendulum and hands: that life is certainly a dynamic phenomenon by its very nature. The clock indicated a mathematical measurement of the Universe' and Life's motion, besides day to day mundane time. Like its click-clock sound, my awareness oscillated between philosophical thought and semi-sleep for some unknown time.

Then just behind the station, one very loud high-pitched sound pierced the cold darkness outside…and my ears! Bringing me in a flash back to alert — this was a familiar wild sound. It continued on, breaking the frozen night air with continuous high to medium-pitched crescendo-diminuendoes along with yodels and short coarse barks. Remaining very close to one back window, the coyote continued to vocalize over and over! Picking up my large flashlamp, I shone it through the back window at the noisy coyote. Immediately it moved into darkness towards the station's east end, out of sight.

Walking quickly to that window and shining the lamp's spotlight beam across the snow I found the coyote, a large adult standing ten yards away in the open snow-laden grass flat. Almost at this same instant a tan-coloured flash of blurred motion dashed into the lightbeam from the station's southeast corner! Simultaneously the coyote bolted away — kicking powdery snow into sparkling white clouds! One large cougar leaped and hopped just two yards behind! The coyote zigzagged in quick left-right-left-right movements as the big cat bound along, zigzagging right behind…but looking a bit clumsy in comparison!

Off they went into a stand of sapling pine trees, the coyote zipping sideways at each tree using them as a shield! Then — as suddenly — they vanished into the trees and night's deep blue-blackness! Having brushed against snowladen pineboughs, the animals left in their wake little clouds of swirling powder snow that glistened and sparkled minutely as it settled ever-so-slowly to the ground.

I just stood as if frozen…with nose pressed against the ice-cold window, staring out and wishing this three seconds would have lasted longer. Mentally, these vivid moments kept replaying on my inner screen. This astonishing brief event, I would never forget! As the animals dashed away from view, it was obvious that the coyote was in full control of the run. Only if it slipped would the cougar have caught up. The thickly growing pine trees were a perfect rear-guard for the coyote. Although very short and quick, this wild chase was all visually strong and clear.

After a minute or so…I returned to the captain's chair, heart still pounding fast with excitement and most happy to have finally seen one of the local big cats! This coyote seemed to be leading the cougar, I thought probably away from young family members that were somewhere in the opposite direction, westerly. Then I realized how lucky I was not to have stepped out the station's front door a minute or so earlier — where the big carnivore had been crouching less than five yards away!

A few weeks later winter had settled in with permanent freezing day and night. About one foot of powder snow had now fallen to the ground bringing a different beauty to the forest, lake and mountains. Everything became softer, more rounded and now coloured in pastel shades of white, cream, grey, greenish-grey and blue. One sunny day, taking my camera, I went for an early afternoon drive in my 1953 Ford ranchwagon in search of whatever might appear in this lovely land where other than Lucerne, no people lived for many miles in all directions.

Chugging along slowly on the narrow winding snowpacked road, three of my little friends, squirrels, were above in pinetrees still picking cones. Sitting or climbing up and down...they shook snowflake powder from the snowy boughs. Clouds of tiny white sparkling crystals drifted and slowly dropped in the cold still air. Flashing on and off, flat snowflakes reflected sunlight intermittently as wee points of the purest brilliant silver, yellow, red, green or blue...as if light from a realm beyond!

I crossed a low wooden bridge where frozen edges of the lake were covered with large feathery and rare leaflike frost crystals, all very beautiful in white, pale grey and colourless clear. Then at the little-used new highway, I turned westward driving at a leisurely pace while watching for wildlife and animal tracks in the snow. Shortly, I was paralleling downstream the transparent pale green river that here was more like a creek...shallow and with clear bubbly ice beginning to grow alongshore and around small speckled grey or brown rounded boulders. Across the river visibility was good with large open flats, little clumps of dark spruce and leafless grey aspen and poplar groves, all gracefully draped with hanging snow.

On that side I noticed a set of tracks stamped in the snow angling either towards the river or away from it, depending on which way the animal had been walking. From this distance I could not tell what sort of tracks they were. There was no sign of any on the highway side. "Probably moose tracks," I thought. But being naturally curious I decided to stop for a closer look. Maybe I could get a photo or two. Driving to a wide spot nearby, I parked, slung my camera strap over shoulder and even though wearing feltlined snowboots, went down to the river anyway.

Pure ice-cold water gurgled and blubbed quickly past the beautifully ice-ringed projecting rounded rocks. Larger ones were slippery steppingstones, so I carefully stepped and jumped across this precarious natural bridge...one boot zipping into water at one point! Now I had one wet foot and one dry. Once across, I went directly northward hoping to intersect the animal tracks. At this point I was a bit downstream from them. But no, they had not gone this far downstream. About thirty yards from the river I turned and moved upstream through a foot of snow.

Nearing a thick clump of small spruce trees that grew ten yards from the river, the tracks came into view, angling towards this treeclump. Moving closer, I could see open snow all around the thicket. This single set of tracks was on one side only...the animal had either left or entered it. As I approached closer, it became obvious by the track pattern that these were not moose but either bear or cougar! Now more than the cold breeze had me energized! Was it still there inside the thicket?

Quickly stepping to them...I knelt down for a closer look. An electric shock jolted my body! Long-clawed bear tracks about six inches wide were set clearly into the snow — and very recently — pointing to the silent little island of trees! These imprints were as fresh as mine! Adrenalin coursed through arteries as my heart pounded hard and fast! A good-sized grizzly was only twenty yards distant! Turning my head only slightly, I looked hard…with eyes sharply right to the point where the bear had entered. Slowly, I stood up…quietly listening. No frozen mist could be seen issuing from the spruce clump. All I could hear was riverwater tumbling and trickling by.

Not knowing if the bear was lying asleep or standing awake and aware of me, I forgot about wanting a photograph and hastily stepped away as quietly as possible…angling towards the river upstream from the little spruce thicket! I was glad the snow was fresh and quiet-walking, unlike older packed snow that would crunch noisily with every step. Having no self-defence, the less time I was here, the better. With camera under-arm, I started a jog to riverside while glancing back at the bear's hiding place! Such a thick treeclump, I thought the bear had probably not seen although may have smelled or heard me.

At the river, ignoring the steppingstones I kept jogging most of the way across regardless of loud splashing and careless of getting cold wet feet and legs. Again, I glanced back over my right shoulder, hoping to not see the bear…no bear visible! Once across I clambered awkwardly up the steep bank on all-fours, slipping and sliding to the highway above. I was lucky! All remained silent and still except for the little river's shishing and swirling crystal-clear green water.

Walking along roadside downstream towards the old ranchwagon, now my breathing slowed and hands shook less. I could not help smiling…as I looked across river at the grizzly's hiding place. I hoped that no one else driving by would notice its tracks, especially someone bent on poaching. Soon back at the ranchwagon, I took off my waterlogged snowboots and socks then fired it up to warm my cold feet and legs.

Sitting in this comfort and having got not one photo, I thought about the stupidity of what I just did. Even so, having lived through it, I was exhilarated! Here was a rare experience that few people would ever have — a little taste of the western Canadian wilderness. This was one more identity-forming wild event for a naive young man who loved Nature…regardless of the general social taboo about that positive attitude.

Again looking across at the bear's treeclump hiding place, I wondered why it had not yet denned somewhere higher. Since winter was just beginning, I assumed the big bruin to be probably on its way to a specific denning place and had just stopped for a rest. But this little grove of spruce I thought may have been its actual wintering place; the thick tangle of branches when covered by a foot or so of snow would certainly keep out harsh winter wind while likewise forming a cool quiet cocoon for the bear's long sleep. Whatever may be, I wished that a good snowfall would soon hide its tracks! Well, that night my wish came true…as another foot of snowfall prevented detection of my unseen grizzly.

Brown Lake Blue Lake

Springtime had arrived in the Rockies with warm sunshine bringing new life to the woods. Now a calm early afternoon, the time was perfect for exploring my wild neighbourhood: walking with Nature was always a favourite pastime. My first destination was a little dark brown lake that I knew only from a distance. Walking along the winding gravel road for a short while, at one point I ducked through thick buffalo-brush and small poplar trees then walked towards the lake under a motionless canopy of shady pine and spruce forest. So quiet, all that I could hear was the crunching of old dry twigs and branches under my boots.

After a short while in dark shade, dodging around treetrunks and snaggly dead limbs, a brighter part of the forest ahead indicated the lake's position. A minute later I broke through a tangle of willow brush, stepping out into sunshine at the lakeshore. Walking along a wide silty sandflat at the shallow eastern end, tiny ripples were everywhere in the tea-coloured water close to shore. Farther out the lake was a flat mirror reflecting blue sky and inverted dark green treetops. With hardly any breeze, these rapidly moving wavelets could be caused only by some form of life! Walking to the lake's very shallow edge, I crouched down to see countless tiny glistening black ovals, all swarmed together with black tails flagellating while golden-ringed eyes looked out at their little muddy world and no doubt the big blue sky directly above.

Tadpoles in the thousands were fully enjoying this shallow warm water and probably the Sun's rays too, which penetrated the murky rusty brown shore right to the bottom. On this shimmering surface, wee bright flashes of sunlight reflected half-randomly with soft skyblue, touches of cloudwhite and leafygreen. Just below the watery mirror an immense number of them were nibbling, grazing on minute algae…blackening the shallows from the quarter-inch-deep shoreline out to ten yards distant, a one-foot depth, and along the whole eastend beach for about fifty yards length! I knelt for several minutes at the silty water's edge enjoying these little embryonic creatures that were soon to become baby toads.

Along with them, I too, was appreciating the warm sunshine on my face and hands while watching their silent, cheerful liveliness…and gazing along this little unexplored wild beach. In the tall beachgrass ten yards away stood a large old stump with twisted grey roots. While regarding the beautiful curls and swirls of their wavey root patterns, a quick flash of white and rustybrown appeared at the stump's base. Over there was more life…a small animal hiding within the shadows! Remaining in my crouch, I watched and waited. It wasn't long until a little triangular face with brown nose and low squarish ears appeared in the dim light between two roots. Its sparkling brown eyes were looking steadily back at me: an adult weasel was more keenly observing me than I was it!

Moments later another face appeared from within the shadows…then another and another. But these were tiny and each with pale blue eyes. Three baby weasel faces peered out from just behind their mother! Looking out at the world from the safety of their snaggly grey stump, they were quick with the energy of youth — bobbing in and out of sight. But in a short while mother weasel climbed cautiously out onto one large root. Her darker-coated wee ones soon followed. Within a minute there were five baby weasels chasing and jumping from root to root around their mother and oblivious of my presence, it seemed. But she closely watched me…while now and then staring at the rippling black mass at water's edge.

She seemed quite fearless, probably due to my silence and stillness. Non-aggression towards wild animals often reduces or negates their initial fear, I had observed many times. The black-tipped tail was as long as her body and like an identification tag told me that she was a longtailed weasel. Hopping off the root, she bound towards the lake's silty edge. There, she stared steadily at the rippling black mass of tadpoles. Then her five babies, one by one scooted and jumped in lightning-fast spasmodic movements along the sand to her! It appeared that she was giving them a lesson about one food source…but they were more interested in play! Even so, they did glance at the rippling water…between longer bouts of jumping and wrestling!

I assumed she had probably been feeding tadpoles and toads to her wee ones. Her nearby stump was a perfect nest site, an intelligent choice: safe and close to food. Also nearby at the lake's southern side was an extensive grassy area inhabited by voles and mice, which too, she no doubt frequented. After a couple of minutes standing next to the shimmering tadpoles, she led the little troop — leaping and zipping along beside and behind — back to safety under their stump. I was quite humoured by their antics and thoroughly enjoying these few minutes with this family of seldom-seen little carnivores!

Standing up, I walked along the grassy sandbeach past their stump. Three babies came out, testing their skills on the upturned roots, running and jumping playfully. Like their mother, they showed no fear yet maintained awareness of my presence. I could not help liking immensely the tiny slim carnivores as they played that innocent play which is common to baby animals of so many species. Unknown to them, these lively little animals were inducing a peaceful happiness within one lone human. Looking back, I gave them a silent, "Goodbye…" in thought as they watched through shining pale blue eyes.

Now at the lake's south side, from up on the grassy bench I could see a beavers' lodge at the far western end. Arcing through this vole-and-mouse meadow just above lakeside then down into a damp shaded dip under spruce and poplar trees and up onto a well-trodden dirt bank, I arrived at the lodge. It was built into this dirt bank, mostly of interwoven old grey sticks. But a few rustybrown and tan, recently chewed branches told me that it was now occupied by beavers. I decided to sit down at the top edge of the lodge and wait. Maybe soon one resident would venture out.

At this end the lake was deep, almost black and as smooth as glass. And sure enough, within minutes two small brown animals did appear paddling away from the lodge, making little waves and watery blooping sounds with their rotating tails. Long and thin, their greyblack tails circled around and around, at times flipping out of the water, propelling them forward. These sweet little furry animals looked like miniature beavers on front but with long propellers rotating at their backends! Funny little beings that I had to smile at: they were muskrats! Swimming away close to the lakeside in fairly deep water then rounding a low muddy point, they gradually moved out of sight behind clumps of deep green bulrushes. Their trailing ripples moved out in a long vee-pattern, slowly, silently fading away farther out on the lake's flat-calm surface.

Here, animal behaviour and interdependence that I had not previously known was presented to me. Muskrats would take advantage of a beaverlodge by moving into a higher level, living safely within the stick-and-mud pile. Also beavers were benign, calmly accepting muskrats as good co-tenants and neighbours; as competitors for food they were no threat to each other.

Sitting quietly atop the beavers' lodge I waited for whatever next event, if any, would unfold in this little bit of wild space and time. After some unknown long duration I noticed in the middle of the lake almost flat with the surface, the dark head of a beaver…with large waves moving out in a vee from behind it. Swimming directly towards the lodge, it seemed to have not yet seen me. I sat perfectly still watching and wondering when the beaver would notice. At twenty yards out it slowed, then — in a lightning-quick flash, a big splash and loud tail-smack — it dove under!

The sound soon dissipated. Circular waves slowly, silently moved towards shore. Bubbles and white foam lingered awhile on the blackish-brown lake surface…popping one by one as their elements returned to lake and sky. My beaver never resurfaced and dark deep water at the lodge entrance prevented me from seeing it swimming below. I kept waiting and waiting…eventually just one muskrat returned, swimming directly to its water-level compartment. By now tiring of this area and impatient with the beavers-in-hiding, I decided to explore another nearby lake.

It was about two hundred yards distant through a stand of poplar, willow and lodgepine. But hidden in this forest close to the beaverlodge was an interesting surprise: remnants of an old townsite, evidenced by low rectangular dirt outlines, concrete building-footings, broken clay jugs, rusty metal and broken glass that was coloured turquoise blue and pink. All of this indicated a settlement of 1890s to 1920s.

Here too, among rusty old cans were two pieces of a wolf skull that fit neatly together; it had been sawn in half, lengthwise. One half had a perfectly circular hole in the forehead the size of a 30-30 bullet. I assumed that a trapper lived here then and had used the wolf's brain matter for tanning, maybe for its own skin. Now wolves had been almost absent from this part of the Rockies for many years!

Where buildings once stood just a lot of wood ash remained. The village had either burnt down or was later set afire intentionally, destroying a little piece of our early western Canadian history. My enquiry later of railway employees gained little other than there had been two vying railways here at turn of the century: Canadian Northern Railway and Grand Trunk Pacific. Apparently one railway ran along the valley's north side and the other along the south but which-was-which, no one knew. And what happened to them, no one knew.

After exploring this enigmatic townsite awhile my thoughts returned to the next lake. With the old wolf-skull halves in my little yellow backpack as interesting and valued keepsakes, I turned northward pushing through thick sapling lodgepine trees. This section of tightly-growing trees was the sort that brought visibility to almost nil, which if possible I would usually avoid entering. But the little forest opened slightly and I was soon standing on shore of the second lake among stunted but pleasantly aromatic spruce trees.

This one was much larger — a real lake with crystal-clear turquoise blue water! Sunlight sparkled brilliant silver-white from tiny bluegrey wavelets here and there farther out, wherever gusts of breeze touched the surface. A throaty yodel resounded along the water as a lone loon called from far across the lake! Although I knew this message was not meant for me, it felt friendly, welcoming…reminding me that I was not alone in this vast mountainous forest where silence dominated everything! The loon's presence brought a feeling of cheer, comfort and pleasure…even though it was barely visible at the far side as a wee black-and-white speck.

I followed westward a narrow animal trail that ran along lakeside just above highwater, under the little black lichen-draped spruce and tamarack trees. Thick mossy ground was packed down into a path about six inches wide, looking to be made by pine marten and mink. This trail led to a short gravelly southwesterly spit that protected a muddy bay and another beaverlodge! This lodge was quite old, having dry grey grass, pink-budding wildrose and little green-leaved willow shrubs growing on top.

A perfect place to stop for a rest, relaxation and enjoyment, I sat under the largest spruce tree using its fourteen inch diameter trunk both as a back-rest and rear-guard…even though the bark was a bit pitchy! Thus waiting quietly for any local resident to appear, the visual beauty of living Nature was spread out in front of me…as if I had entered a perfect piece of paradise. A large mountain to the north reflected from a shimmering lakesurface as if composed of a billion dots, ovals and curves in ever changing white, grey, brown and green…while the seven-peaked rocky mountain itself stood still and solid against the infinite, open blue sky.

Dark bluegreen spruce boughs hung down in front and above with greenblack beard-lichen hanging from them. Atop and next to the beaverlodge, little wildrose bushes expressed themselves with dark pink, five-petalled wavey blossoms and deep red twisting buds. These were just beginning to show their beauty and offer nectar and pollen to local bees, flies and butterflies. All of this I could enjoy because mosquito season had not yet arrived! Soon my body and mind became charged with a peaceful, yet vibrant energy and attitude.

After five minutes or so of earthly time, muted sounds of a medium-high pitch began filtering through the flowery mud-and-stick roof of the beaverlodge. First one, then two childlike voices could be heard: "M-m-m-Ma-aa-aa…M-m-m-oo-oo-oo…M-m-m-Ma-aa-aa." Sounding almost human, these little vocalizings quickly became more and more persistent and louder! Soon I could not discern if there were three or four separate voices, all increasing in volume as if vying for attention.

For the first time I was hearing the sounds of beaver kits! A most enjoyable experience…I smiled with pleasure at their cheerful chatter and squeals. Unknown to them and without effort, these wee beavers just from their mere being had the power to induce happiness within the solitary human. Their sounds became quite loud at times so I began wishing they would keep quiet: if any large carnivore such as a grizzly were nearby, they would not be safe! After a few minutes though, they did calm their voices into little murmurs then gradually to complete silence. Now…all was tranquil within the lodge.

The mud-bottomed shallow water at front of this lodge was a crystal-clear pale turquoise, so the approach or departure of any adult beaver would be obvious. I waited and watched more than an hour for a parent to show. But none did. The beaver family all remained within, cozy in their shadowy home. By now though, afternoon had moved on into early evening so the time had arrived to leave this little bubble of earthly paradise. Standing up by the big old spruce tree, I gave my unseen beavers a mental, "Goodbye," then followed the marten and mink trail back towards home…satisfied and happy with a most pleasing day of discovery!

Bangs and Thumps

There were two parts to the lake, one higher than the other a foot or two and connected by a short narrow channel of clear fast-flowing water. Two spits of gravel and mud had pinched the lake from opposite sides after the last ice-age to form this uncommon phenomenon. Water flowed westward from the larger lake into the smaller. This was the usual but at highwater they were as if one lake. A long low wooden bridge weathered grey from age stretched across at this point, spanning about fifty yards.

At its centre directly above this rippling channel, the bridge was less than six feet high. It had been sturdily built on short hefty spruce log pilings and with solid plank decking of four-inch thick by ten-inch wide pieces. Here a few locals, railway employees, would sometimes catch whitefish even though they said were too boney and too small!

Having never seen a whitefish, I walked the narrow quarter-mile gravel and dirt road to this bridge, then lay down on the planks at its middle to peer down over the eastern edge. The cold water was so pure and crystal-clear! Through the steadily changing surface ripples caused by the current, greybrown sticks were visible on the bottom seeming to twist and bend in time with the current's wavey motion. Now and then, faint movements not coinciding with the water flow could be discerned.

As I gradually became accustomed to the drab grey and brown bottom colours, motion and shapes…fish emerged from invisibility…with their translucent tails rapidly swishing side to side, gillcovers moving in and out! And their black eye-pupils no doubt looked upward enough to detect my head jutting out at bridgeside and marked against the blue zenith, seeing more of me than I was of them. They were small fish, varying in length from about four to ten inches. At irregular intervals one would flash silvery as it flipped and tilted sideways — either chasing another or being chased itself! This seemed to be a favoured place for these pisces, since there were at least two dozen.

The next day I thought to try fishing so dug up a few earthworms, putting them with moist dirt into a tincan. Borrowing a short piece of fishing line and a hook, I fashioned a simple fishing pole from a long thin alder sapling, with tiny single hook for the whitefish's wee mouth. Everything ready, I walked along the narrow winding road where two squirrels chitchatted and chased each other up and down overhanging pine and spruce trees. Just beyond these little entertainers I came to a point where the gravel and dirt had been very recently scraped in a streak two to three feet wide, angling across the road. Something large had been dragged across!

A week before I was told that a railway section crew employee, a native indian, had shot with his 22-rifle a blackbear. It then ran away wounded into the woods by the lake. No one had seen it since. I had just moved here to work so was glad that people told me to watch out for it, since the bear could still be alive and dangerous!

I thought at first this wide drag mark must have been made by that bear. But then maybe it was some dead prey animal being dragged into hiding by another bear or cougar! I was not certain. If this be the wounded bear though, I could see that it must be partly paralyzed, unable to walk. Looking closer at these scuff-marks…their pattern indicated the direction it had gone. Whatever-it-was had been pulled from a shaded thick clump of small spruce by the lake, then up across the road into a more open area of tall poplar trees and scattered soapberry bushes.

Here the forest was open enough for good visibility so I took a chance and cautiously followed the scrapes and bent-over plants. Only about thirty yards off the road, there it was: lying on its side, back legs limp and straight out behind! The bear heard me coming, so was up on its elbows looking back at me when I first saw it. Watching me with unsteady fearful eyes, darting quickly from side to side, it looked so helpless…this was the first and only time I had seen a bear's eyes show fear. It was a depressing sight. My energy suddenly left and I felt about as limp as the bear's paralyzed legs looked. A heavy sadness swept into my body and mind.

A few moments after I came into view the blackbear began dragging itself away. Its front legs were functioning but was paralyzed from the waist down. A bullet had no doubt lodged in the spine. The bear stopped at the base of a fourteen-inch poplar tree, the nearest one to it. There it lay…pathetically looking back at me! For a few minutes I observed this unfortunate animal. There was no hope of recovery for it. I felt very unhappy.

Returning quickly to the little hamlet of Lucerne, I told a few people of the bear. Under this circumstance, it was decided that the only solution was to shoot the animal since otherwise it would die slowly of starvation, if not killed and eaten by a cougar or another bear before that. With the condition it was in, the bear was no threat to people. Taking my 30-30 rifle and a few bullets, I led four others back to the bear. It was still there at the same spot by the tree…looking back at us, then up the tree, then back at us again.

As we approached closer, it panicked — head turning quickly side to side, fear-filled eyes darting towards us and back at the poplar tree. Its two front paws clawed into the tree's base. Dragging its limp body and lifting itself up, the bear began climbing as fast as it could! The power of this bear was clearly evident from the speed that it was lifting its whole body — about two hundred fifty pounds — straight up, using the two front legs only!

As it glanced back at us the fear in its eyes was almost tangible. We stood silently watching. I felt very helpless, myself. I think we all felt sorry and sad for this poor animal.

When it was halfway up, about twenty-five feet…with forelegs tiring and body hanging down, it began grabbing branches with its teeth and using neck muscles to lift itself higher up the tree! Thus it climbed to a forty-foot height where the treetop thinned almost too narrow to hold its weight, the poplar's green leafy top arching slightly back. The bear could climb no higher.

Now near the treetop just holding on with front paws and back legs dangling, it looked straight up at the wide blue sky. The bear hung motionless…staring skyward. I handed the rifle to the section foreman; the bear had to be shot but I did not want to do it. Anyway, my eyes were teared, a credible excuse. We plugged our ears with fingers and hands as he aimed carefully at the bear's heart area and pulled the trigger — one very loud bang!

The shot hit its mark and the bear tightened. All of its body muscles tensed so much that their form was actually visible through the fur! With mouth tightly closed, glistening black lips curled back showing all of its clenched teeth. This grimace indicated intense pain but at least the bear was dying quickly. Still looking skyward…the bear's eyes slowly closed. At that moment I thought to the bear: "Goodbye…I wish there be a good life for you in the beyond."

About two seconds elapsed from the moment the bullet hit and this bear's life, its consciousness, left. Then the toes relaxed, claws slipping out of the treebark. At this...the head, shoulders and forelegs slowly toppled backwards. The body gained speed as it fell, arching over and landing on its back with a solid thud! We all stood speechless and in silence for some long moments.

A deep, tangible calmness surrounded this large animal...pervading the space around us in all directions for some time after it died. I thought and wished this poor bear's essence of mind be now floating away...into the deep, the blue sky that it had been climbing towards for safety. Indeed, the last thing it saw from the treetop was infinite, open blue above. And I was certain that this bear had a nonphysical component or conscious mind not too different from that of a human being!

Spring moved into summer and about two months later, I once again walked back to the bridge with fishing pole and a few earthworms in a tincan. As I approached the bridge, in the trees at the south end three or four squirrels were emphatically chirping their sharp danger call! Someone or something was there causing the excitement. I walked out to the middle of the bridge, watched and waited...expecting someone to appear, coming along the road. Since there was a small camping area just up the road towards the highway I thought the cause could be a camper out for a walk, enjoying Nature.

But no one appeared. The harsh squirrel-chirping continued and I noticed was mostly in one area on the west side of the road. The instigator was there in the poplar and spruce woods, either human or animal. Maybe it was an owl or hawk perched in a tree? After awhile since it was a fair distance away, about forty yards, I ignored the squirrels' warning calls, climbed over bridgeside and ducked under the bridge. Here the short swiftwater stream flowed and whitefish swam! Sitting down on the gravel, first attaching a lead sinker, I then baited the tiny single hook and placed it into the water, holding the pole steadily out as far as I could reach.

After about five minutes of fishing...I caught nothing. Whitefish did take the worm though, nibbling it off in wee bits. I didn't mind just feeding them, anyway! Squirrels continued with their sharp calls, but less now. Then a sound of someone walking began at the south end of the bridgedeck, faintly at first but getting louder and approaching slowly. This sound was just like heavy workboots thumping on the planks.

I was sure that someone on the bridge was walking across in my direction. This clunking pattern was so much like human footsteps coming closer, closer, louder and louder. As I sat in the pebbles listening, I contemplated a few moments of sending up a greeting: "Hullo, up there!" but for some reason unknown, held my tongue...saying nothing.

As the thumping came nearer it changed cadence and likewise became far too loud for mere bootsteps. The bridgedeck planks now began visibly vibrating and the clunks became a violently loud banging! The cause was definitely not human! Then it stopped at bridge-centre directly above the little swiftwater stream — pounding the deck! Sand, pebbles and dirt fell steadily from the cracks between planks and dropped into the stream. Putting down the pole I got up into a crouch — watching the heavy planks bend!

I thought this could only be a bear! Now I felt trapped and began to plan an escape route, should it come after me! Whichever side it came down I had one way to go: dive into the lake and swim underwater!

After about five seconds of this loud solid banging, the animal began moving again...pounding its way to directly above me — as the four-by-ten-inch crossdecking bounced and bent up and down! There, it stopped again as the banging continued steadily on the spot...incredibly loud!

Pebbles, dirt and sand fell onto my head and as I looked up, into my eyes. Sounding out: "Bang-bang! — Bang-bang! — Bang-bang!…" this powerful animal stood at the spot straight above sending its message for about ten seconds or so — pounding constantly! I kept silent and still… alert and waiting, crouched ready to run and dive either way. But at least now I knew where it was — less than two feet away directly above!

Then finally the stamping feet started moving again, continuing northward. The animal was now moving away! I felt a slight sense of ease…as it went, the pounding lessened somewhat. Even so, I remained alert for any pattern or direction change in the sound, not being certain of what the animal's motivation was. As distance increased my tenseness lessened and with this came a burst of indescribable ease and an almost overwhelming positive energy! The animal kept a steady pace…stamping steadily towards the bridge's north end, not quitting until it was close to the gravel road.

Now all was quiet. In a crouching walk I moved quietly to one piling on the west side. Leaning against it and peeking with my left eye along the piling's edge, at first I saw nothing. But a few seconds later the big bear appeared, walking slowly, calmly from bridge end then off the road and onto the rust-coloured stoney gravel beach. What an impressive-looking animal! It was huge for a blackbear…the largest I had ever seen! This big beast padded along in a superior manner not bothering at all to turn its head to look back, although the corner of its left eye seemed to be watching me! The glowing black beauty was now only thirty yards distant but I felt safe, now knowing it had no interest in me as a food item.

Following the gravelly lakeside awhile, the bear angled up under willow trees then into pine and poplar woods out of sight. This bear's calm, superior manner of movement, head and body expression told me that it was self-confident in the extreme and afraid of nothing! It would certainly be in a position of command in the Rocky Mountain society of blackbears. As I expected, it was a boar. Just seeing the big carnivorous omnivore for a few moments brought me to respect it as an animal of great power! And likewise, I had to admire this bear for not abusing that power when it had me trapped under the bridge: a quality that is not common even with human beings!

Now I was asking myself: "Why did this bear stop above me, stamping paws so hard?" I thought this must have been a warning to the human to give it some space. No doubt seeing me on the bridge when I first arrived the bear stopped, hidden in the bushes, waiting. Its having already planned to walk across the bridge…I was in the way. But it preferred to keep dry instead of swim. And being a superior bear, it had no fear of the lone human! Seeing me go under the bridge…after some minutes, it decided to walk the planned route. Since it did not regard me as a threat, the boar sent the message that it was coming…and likewise warning me to stay away…by stamping legs as it walked across. To me, this experience was most valuable: one lively lesson about bear behaviour! The bear's nonverbal communication was apparently saying: "If you respect my space, I will respect yours." But it may not have known that I felt caught and was itself unsure of what power I had. Even so…it was confident and courageous enough to challenge the human under the bridge by walking directly over!

As I watched it move into the forest, walking in a purposeful manner as if having a particular destination to reach, I thought the bear would probably check one or two garbage barrels behind cabins in the hamlet. Most of the local bears had tasted those barrels at least once. I quit fishing and waited five minutes or so before heading home, since the road back paralleled the bear's route.

The big wild visitor would be approaching from the west and my barrel was westernmost in

Lucerne. It was a very empty barrel so — at that time not thinking of creating a garbage bear — I got out a handsaw and cut in half lengthwise, a raw chicken: half for the bear and half to keep. Throwing its half into the barrel, I then waited inside my cabin watching from the west-end window.

Sure enough, within five minutes the regal-looking bear appeared atop a thinly treed, kinnikinick-carpetted hump just to the west. It approached steadily downward in a straight line with chest pushing over soapberry bushes, sapling poplar and birch trees. They bent like flimsy grass as if things of no significance to the bear! Its head high and shiny black nose moving slightly from side to side, down it came, padding slowly past the white outhouse and over to the rusty brown barrel. With one paw this silvery black beauty pulled over the barrel, put its big head inside and pulled out the chicken. There it lay down in high green grass, casually consuming the chicken within minutes. Then, after sniffing the barrel awhile, finding no more food the big bear stood up and paced away...in its awesomely powerful manner...back into the poplar woods, heading northwest.

I had wanted to know how tall it stood on fours. When the bear passed in front of the outhouse, I noted a point on the door: a knot in one board that lined up with its shoulder hump. So shortly after it had departed for the wilderness, I went over and stood at the outhouse door. That knot was level with my solar plexus which is fifty-one inches high! Accepting that height when down on fours, was difficult. How could a blackbear be this large? Yet it looked to weigh between four hundred and five hundred pounds.

I thought: "Is it possible for a blackbear and grizzly to cross-breed?" Maybe this was just such a cross...although grizzlies and blackbears rarely socialize in a peaceful way.

After getting the bear's height I walked to the garbage barrel, stood it back up and looked at a big area of flattened grass where it had lain down for a relaxed but quick feed. Looking into the shady forest where the bear went, I thought to it: "Goodbye...and thankyou!" Meeting this big boar was an experience that I will never forget! A good firsthand education about bear behaviour, it taught me that bears are not usually out to get a human...and that they — more often than not — respect a human's space as long as the human respects theirs. I was hoping to see this most impressive blackbear again sometime...but it did not return.

BESIDE A WHITEWATER CREEK

Looking for something nice to shoot with my 35 mm camera, I was following the creek's west side slowly upstream. This little whitewater creek flowed southward at a rapid rate: water, rocks and air combined to generate a loud, steady sh-sh-shishhh…that rendered any other sounds inaudible. I could see on the distant bluegreen forested slopes above, hints of a rocky gorge which seemed quite worth seeing up close. Crossing an open brown-grass meadow and low leafless bushes, then the railway tracks, I came to an inconspicuous seldom-used animal trail running along the bank parallel to the creek.

Enveloped by loud whitewater sound — for safety's sake, I had to remain visually alert! Being human, with very little sense of smell, I could not depend on it either. I paced along the animal trail, enjoying a pleasant cold breeze that wafted up from the creek's icy snowmelt water. With the sky a cloudless blue, warm sunshine was quickening the natural pulse of the forest which I was just entering; life-generating rays were touching bark and shiny brown or green buds of poplar, willow and birch trees now heavily spotted with wee yellow and yellowgreen leaves.

Approaching closer to the little canyon, I could see that it was a narrow pinch in the grey rocky mountainside, with jackpine trees on each side hiding the creek from view. Now into thicker forest, I noted as I went trees which were climbable…if perchance I had to escape from something not-so-friendly! I had almost no self-defence, since my six-inch-short hunting knife would be quite useless against a large carnivore. Closer to the creekside I came to an open gravelly flat with a few saplings of pine and poplar growing randomly here and there. At this point alongside the creek was a naturally formed, rounded pile of small grey and brown boulders, about three feet high. And here, the rushing whitewater sound so dominated that even visual perception seemed muted! I paced towards the rockpile…thinking to step up onto it.

Just two paces away, there began a sequence of deep loud thumping! Directly ahead and across the pile — a huge brownish-black object of indistinct form loomed upward! That instant, I wheeled around clockwise — dashing across the gravel flat then back along the trail to the nearest large tree: a thick branchy spruce! Glancing back just before reaching the tree, I saw a cow moose trotting in stilt-like run — going in the opposite direction! I stopped to watch.

What a relief! Then she stopped and turned around to stand behind one very thin sapling pine tree…with head high and big ears up, looking back at me! I felt safe now beside my tree. And she looked quite humorous, safely standing behind her two-inch sapling! I almost laughed…but just smiled. Heart pounding from adrenalin, I tried to steady my hands for a photograph but of course that was impossible. I took one photo anyway, knowing it would be blurry but better than none. She quietly stared for maybe ten seconds then trotted away on her long stilt legs heading upstream past a thick clump of tall spruce trees and out of sight. The unique leg movement of this jogging moose was really fascinating!

Now I felt quite amused by this sudden mutual departure from that little boulder pile! Pondering on what to do next as I stood beside my safety tree, a medium-high-pitched sound began emanating from amid the loud shishing whitewater in the direction of the rockpile...a little voice! Something small was calling out...to my surprise as if speaking Canadian English: "Mmmum...Mmm-u-u-m...Mu-u-u-m!"

Watching closely the trees where the cow moose had gone, looking around in all directions and seeing nothing animate...I decided to risk going back to the rockpile! It was fifteen yards distant so I had to be quick. Jogging up to the rockpile, I stepped up onto it with camera ready — but certainly not steady! Well, well...what a lovely sight! Two little auburn-coloured moose calves lay there in the sand and pebbles, basking under the Sun's warm rays! They looked to be less than a day old, probably born overnight or this morning just hours ago!

Looking up and around...seeing no angry mother moose...I clicked the camera as fast as I could. Then one tiny calf wobbled slowly upward...to stand on its long lithe legs! It stood awkwardly...looking at me. Both calves looked my way, with ears out sideways and slightly up. After a few moments the second wee auburn calf stood up on its wobbly legs! I took two more quick shots. Very apprehensive, I kept glancing upstream where their mother had gone! The undulating translucent greygreen snowmelt creek rushed by just two yards beyond them, shishing and gurgling loudly.

Then after several still moments of mutual regard, these sweet wild babies both took three or four slow, unsteady steps following the direction their mother had taken. Again, one called: "Mmum...Mmu-u-u-m!" Then the other little auburn beauty called out the same: "Mmm-u-u-u-m!" The calves again stepped slowly, carefully, straight towards their mother's little sapling pinetree. I took the hint. Their mother would surely be returning soon! In fact, I was surprised that she had even abandoned her twins.

Now it was time for me to vacate — as quickly as possible! Jumping off the little boulderpile, I ran back downstream along the trail, glancing back as I went...excited and elated about this rare meeting. Having noticed a large old alder tree leaning out over the creek from the far bank, I thought: "Why should I leave now? Maybe I should go back up the other side, climb it and wait."

A hundred yards or so downstream was a small low railway trestle which I crossed over, then jogged back upstream along another animal trail through buffalo brush and sapling birch trees. Buzzing with apprehension, I watched the woods closely. The cow moose was not in sight and I was soon safely at the leaning tree! Climbing easily up to four yards above whitewater...high enough to be out of reach...I sat waiting, with legs dangling down. From this point I could see the two calves standing still, just where I had left them a few minutes before. Their mother had not yet returned!

I kept looking upstream for her, then back at her wee ones. Two or three minutes of time passed...so I started to worry for the calves, hoping I had not made her abandon them completely. More minutes passed. Then glancing back downstream over my left shoulder — there she was! She stood at creekside about ten yards from her calves...glaring at me with ears flattened down and hair on her back standing straight up along her full body length! But I was well out of reach... as long as this heavily leaning tree's roots held! Here, she surprised me again by returning from the opposite direction that she had recently left, on-the-run! Lucky for me, I left when I did! She had circled around to come at me from behind!

Her two calves now slowly walked towards her on their long, unsteady young legs. After staring at me a few minutes she seemed to calm down...with ears perking up and hair on her back flattening to normal. Now the threesome were again together, standing on the sandy, pebbly pale grey gravel. But my being perched in a tree seemed to puzzle the cow, since she behaved as if danger were still on that side where she first saw me. When she finally decided to lead her calves away, she stepped into the cold creek rapids about ten yards downstream from my perch...then began crossing to the side that I had just come to! Stopping in rushing water about one foot deep...she looked back at them.

Following her, the wee calves tiptoed out into shallows then stopped and stood still. One yard away the swift whitewater waves undulated past them! She waited...looking back as if coaxing the calves to come. Although seeing me up in the tree, she still maintained that danger was on their side. Now another kind of apprehension raced through my mind and body! This creek's fast-moving water was too deep in the middle and on my side for these very young calves to safely cross! And the vertical cutbank on my side, about two feet, was impossible for these wee calves to climb.

I thought: "Oh no! What have I done? The current will take them down and they might drown!" I mentally tried to tell the cow moose, thinking hard: "Go back! Go back! I'm on this side...the danger's on this side!" Maybe I should have yelled it out loud, though.

She then stepped out into the frothing, wavey deep water to more than halfway across the creek. One calf waded into deeper water, then the other a few steps behind to ankle-deep. The first one kept going. The second calf stopped. Now up to its elbows and knees, the first little moose was swept off its hooves as the icy swirling water pulled it downstream, bobbing along in the white froth out of control! Somehow keeping its head above water for fifteen or so yards, the wee auburn beauty drifted on the current...until finally carried into the calm downstream shallows of a gravelbar, still on the creek's far side. There, its little hooves dug into gravel and it waded out onto the dry bar to safety! Seeing this, tension within me began to ease a bit.

Then the second wee calf stepped forward into deep greygreen whitewater where it too, lost control...but only for a few moments...as its little hooves grabbed onto a shallow foothold, allowing it to wade ashore slightly downstream but onto the same bar it had just left! As the first calf made its way alongshore back upstream towards mother, the cow decided that crossing over here was not safe. She was still standing in deep swift water near my side from where she had watched both calves' attempts to cross. She turned back, walking slowly to dry land. During all of this, I did use up several frames of film although knowing the images would be not very clear.

There she waited calmly on the gravelly sandflat as her wee ones returned to her. Soon together again, back they went, slowly walking past the bushy dark green spruce tree that I had ran to about eight minutes before. She was a good mother, waiting and leading her precious babies very slowly across the sunny gravel flat. Within a few minutes the wild family quietly stepped into thick willow brush, poplar and pine saplings out of sight and safe.

Now I was very happy and much eased: happy to have seen my first moose calves in the wild, for so long and at such close range...and relieved that my presence as something dangerous — in the moose mother's mind — did not lead to tragedy for her wee ones! I remained in my perch up the old alder tree for several more minutes. All appeared clear. I climbed carefully down then jogged away downstream beside the shishing creek, heading back towards my old Ford ranchwagon... leaving the moose family in peace...hidden safely among willow, poplar, spruce and lodgepine forest. And this creek's little hidden canyon would now have to remain unexplored for quite some time.

A Change of Heart and Mind

While working at a small town along North Thompson River I decided one early summer day to go fishing. Having been told by a few local people about dollyvarden trout in the river, I thought this would be a good excuse to go for a Nature walk. They said that corn kernels were good bait, since dollies would eat corn from a sewer drain, an unpleasant thought…but also said that raw stewing beef cubes made a bait irresistible to them. Whether or not such was legal, I did not know. Never much of a fisherman, I had a small casting rod that I rarely used. Not feeling right about killing anything, even so I had been socialized at a young age into fishing for fun and food.

Putting half-a-dozen beef cubes wrapped in wax paper, into the left lower pocket of my green-and-black plaid Pioneer coat, I then slipped on my canvas World War II army shoulder-bag. Picking up the rod, I walked under lodgepine and white birch forest to riverside, then headed downstream. Following a very old inconspicuous trail overgrown with thick hardhack, snowberry bushes, tall leafy cow parsnip, scrub birch and willow, I pushed my way through.

This packed-down trail could be seen at first only by pushing bushes aside and looking underneath. It must have been a packhorse trail in the 1800s before the railway was built, connected with Hudson's Bay Company's trade routes. After a half-mile I came to an old abandoned farm with partly collapsed log barn and log toolshed, but no house. Just an indistinct rectangular outline remained where the house once stood. The large cleared area, about eighty acres, was now a meadow of wild grass and cow parsnip with clumps of maroon and white-barked birch and wild willow dotted about.

This interesting discovery I had to explore! The barn was empty but was no doubt at times a haven from rain, hail or snow for rodents, birds and other small animals. I hoped to see barn owls but there was no sign of them. A couple pair of barn swallows were nesting in it, though. Attached to the barn along its southern wall, the log toolshed with a low gently tapered roof, was still intact.

Looking inside, there were pliers, a hammer, axe, shovel, nails, wire, nuts and bolts on the dusty grey workbench…all dry and hardly rusted after all of those years. The overhanging cedar-shake roof was still doing its job! The workbench of solid four-inch thick planks ran the whole length of about twenty feet along the shed's south wall, which itself was windowed for almost the full length. The long low windows had no glass but served their purpose of lighting up the bench: well designed for a place with no electricity.

Draped over a pole-rafter on the shady north side was a bit of North Thompson history — a treasure to me — composed of leather, wood and metal: an old packhorse saddle! I thanked the oldtimers, whoever they were, for leaving it and leaving it in a protected place. An unusual packsaddle, this one also had stirrups. The saddle had no mould, little rust and had hardly been chewed by rodents. By its condition though, I could see that this old packsaddle had gone through a lot of use probably until the 1920s when by all appearance, the farm was abandoned.

Leaving the saddle, et al, to be taken later on another day, I went back to the riverside trail to continue downstream looking for a pool where a dolly or two may have been waiting silently at riverbottom. Walking for some long distance, I saw nothing likely. Even so, I continued onward since the day was quite pleasant, with a mix of blue sky and high white cumulous clouds drifting slowly about. And…mosquitoes were not too numerous!

At a stretch of semi-open hardhack, snowberry and willow brush that stood from two to five feet tall, the trail became more visible. Here, my eyes detected a little dash of movement just five yards ahead on the trail! I stopped, stood still and waited to see if some small animal would show itself. A few moments later I was rewarded with the appearance of a tiny rustybrown weasel cautiously stepping into view at the trail's right side! It was a short-tailed weasel, I thought probably a juvenile.

Big eyes looking at me, it stood motionless with shiny brown and pink nose twitching…and head lifting slightly as it tested the air. I kept still, enjoying this little animal, visually attentive of it while the wee weasel's olfactory system gathered what it could of me. Its glistening dark brown eyes seemed to be assessing for the possibility of danger. After half-a-minute the wee weasel took a few steps towards me, then stopped. Sniffing the air continually, again it stepped cautiously my way! Closer and closer it came.

By now I realized it could smell the raw stewing beef in my pocket: the reason for its apparent curiosity and persistent approach! I kept still and silent. Only my eyes moved slightly, watching. The little animal came to one yard away then sat up…nose and whiskers twitching and vibrating while holding tiny paws and forelegs straight out. Then it scooted towards my boots where I could no longer see. Slowly tilting my head to look down, the weasel was too close to see, standing now very near my gumboots! For fear of scaring it, I kept my head perfectly still while looking down the best I could.

After a short pause…there came a gentle tug on my left pantleg. I could feel its individual steps pushing and pulling slightly as it climbed slowly in a stop-go fashion, up the bluejean pantleg! My left arm hung straight down with bare hand below and behind the coat's pocket level. The tiny carnivore slowly climbed almost to my hip, past my hand then onto the pocket. Now its head, face and little forelegs came into view.

Still maintaining caution, its yearning for food kept the animal focussed as it climbed a few steps higher. It seemed quite fearless of the human that it had just climbed onto! Now so close I could see clearly it eyelashes, twitching nostrils and the shine of its black vibrating whiskers! Over the pocket's edge it went, nose-first and down, with its short black-tipped tail following bit by bit until the wee carnivore disappeared completely inside! I could feel its gentle movement as it curled around inside the green-and-black tartan pocket while taking cubes of raw beef into its mouth…and could see the tiny weasel's body movement pushing the pocket out here and there in little undulating bumps.

Enjoying immensely this most unusual experience, I was…in a different way and certainly more than the young weasel was! After maybe thirty seconds…up popped its head with cheeks bulging. Next, up came wee fuzzy front paws and legs to hook over the pocket edge as it looked about a few moments, moving head from side to side. Then down headfirst it went, tiny sharp claws grasping my coat and bluejeans but this time steadily to the ground nonstop. At my boots, it hesitated a second or two then quickly bound away along the trail behind me…looking quite happy with life!

I just stood motionless for some time…pleased, energized and thinking how fortunate to have these intimate few moments with this fearless short-tailed weasel. These elusive little animals are seldom seen in the wild — alive and free. Most often, all that is seen are their wee footprints in mud or snow. But if seen bodily, that is usually as dead or dying in a trap! To me though, weasels are worth far more alive than dead. With such feelings and thoughts, I turned around heading back along the old riverside horse trail, walking upstream towards home in the same direction my happy weasel had gone.

Slipping left hand into pocket, two pieces of beef were still there. So I dropped them onto the trail knowing that my tiny friend-of-the-moment would return in the very near future. Now, this was an exciting experience to tell people about although I thought few people would accept it as true. But whatever…I knew.

Later this same summer I again tried my luck as a fisherman but much farther downriver. After trampling through a lot of willow brush and past small trees of alder, birch and spruce, I came to a calm pool that looked good. Fish would probably be here, down deep. Baiting the hook this time with a worm though, and casting a short distance, I let the hook sink to the bottom…then slowly reeled in. Waiting for a tug on the line, I repeated casting several times.

While at this…the wide, silent river flowed peacefully by. Cool fresh air, faint earthy smells and beautifully curving large ancient white birch trees across the water brought a soothing peace, as if paradise were right here. The lightgreen-leaved birch were time-decorated with long pale green lichen, dangling motionless from white time-bent limbs and branches. These trees, the deep greygreen treed mountains beyond, the pale blue and creamy white sky, all reflected from a glowing brown mirror of river surface…while altering slightly to a beautiful shifting, moving abstract that was created by the river's slow current, water-billows and swirls. Oblivious to the absurdity of this beautiful circumstance and my deceptive purpose, I fished on. After a short while a sudden jerk on the rod and a quick succession of tugs redirected my dozey relaxed mind into the action-of-the-moment!

An excited energy in the line telegraphed the frantic action of a fair-sized hooked fish! Keeping the line taught but not too much, I slowly reeled in the desperate confused fish. Now and then it would flash a pale orange in the murky brownish water…but soon tired. Upon leading it into the gravelly shallow, the fish, side-spotted with yellow and orange, was identifiable as a dollyvarden trout. Landing it and removing the hook that pierced its upper lip, I then put the foot-long fish into my old burlap army bag. Not wanting to cause it unnecessary pain I did not club it to death, thinking it would soon go unconscious from being out of water. Then continuing to fish, I cast several more times…with no more bites. It was not long until a sort-of boredom set in…so I packed up and headed for home.

About half-an-hour later I was in the kitchen with my catch. Now ready to clean the trout, I took it from the old canvas bag. At this…the fish flipped hard — almost out of my hands! It was still alive! This was such a great surprise, I marvelled at this dolly's tenacity and will to live. So…I plugged the sink, quickly filling it with cold water. Being so impressed by this fish's unusual will to live I wanted now to see how alive it really was! Quickly putting the big dolly into water, it turned over sideways then belly-up…but its gills continued moving slightly out and in, out and in.

Many years previously I was told that fish have float bladders and if filled with air, the fish loses balance, turns upside down and dies. Now that seemed to be the trouble, so held it underwater in the normal upright position. The dolly began burping out air bubbles! "A good sign," I thought. Keeping it upright...the gills began gradually moving out wider and quicker. The fish was regaining vitality! Within three or four minutes of holding it thus, the dollyvarden could remain upright without my hand assisting. Running more cold water into the sink to provide fresh oxygen, I left it to recuperate from the shock.

I was so affected by this fish's persistence that I could not kill it as a food item for supper; I decided to fill the bathtub and keep it awhile as a pet! At this time I was married with one sweet little daughter about nine months young, not walking alone yet but liking to walk holding onto furniture or the wall or my pantlegs. As the tub filled, I picked Amber up to show her our new pet in the kitchen sink and held her hand out touching the trout, as I said: "Fish...fish...fish." When the tub was half full, I transferred the dolly in a bucket, leaving this special fish in the tub to recover more.

Next day, we fed the dollyvarden little pieces of stewing beef, dogfood, bread and other leftover human-food. Each day I would pull the plug awhile and replenish fresh cold oxygenated water. After three days, this unusual pet surprised me again by rising to the surface to eat from the palm of my hand! My little daughter really enjoyed this fish...such as most children, being so delighted by the presence of other living things! She would crawl over to the bathtub and stand up, holding its edge to watch our new pet trout and to help feed it. I held her up so she could feed the dolly from her little hand in the bathtub water. The big trout slowly rose to the surface, gently taking pieces of bread from the palm of her hand...much to her delight! How did we have a bath? Well simply, our pet would go temporarily into a four-gallon bucket of water.

We enjoyed this aquatic animal for ten days then I took it in a bucket of water back to the same pool where it was caught. As I crouched in the sand at water's edge with our special dollyvarden firmly in my hands, I felt very happy that it was alive...that I had not killed it and that the fish would in a few moments be free and wild again. Holding the big dolly in shallow water, looking into its beautiful golden eyes, I let it go...saying, "Goodbye..." as if it were a friend. Our bright-spotted pisce slowly swam into the pool's murky greybrown deep with tail swaying gently side to side and happy I guess, in a fish's way.

But since I had gotten to know it as a pet and in some way as a friend, as a friendly being that demanded nothing, while bringing us much pleasure and cheer — yet needed my positive human mental attitude for its survival during those ten days — I felt the sadness of this loss, as did Amber, I'm sure. It was only a fish but to me was an unusually special fish. Its will to live, friendliness in capture and its sparkling black pupils encircled with golden iris...all conspired to turn me into a nonfisherman! This lowly dollyvarden trout somehow had the power to act as a catalyst for significant positive change in my perspective about Nature's living beings.

Three months passed and winter had settled in. Now the upper North Thompson valley was quilted with two feet of dry powder snow. The river was partly frozen with thick clear ice along shoreline, projecting ten or more yards out and growing daily. High rounded mountains on each side above were lovely with pastel grey, greygreen, greyblue and deep navy blue shades: the vast unlogged evergreen and tamarack forest. Nearby the river grew hemlock, cedar, spruce, birch and cottonwood too, and all had that special winter appearance...with drooping branches adorned in thick rounded blobs of snow.

One day, now off work, I thought of getting some exercise, fresh air and a change of scenery by going for a walk in the snow. A calm grey-sky day, the temperature was a dozen degrees below freezing. I strapped my Chestnut snowshoes onto felt-lined snowboots then proceeded towards the river at a point where terrain was fairly flat with only minor undulations. Powder snow had drifted on blizzard wind over several days previously, so the depth varied from two to four feet making my first steps uncertain. Shallow windswept parts were hardpacked while the deep drifts were airy-soft, making me sink suddenly to knees even with snowshoes!

So this walk was difficult but good exercise and a direct, experienced education about snow and ice. Once closer to the river, I could see large white ice sheets all along the bank tapering here and there from shoreline downward into the water…making great danger! I kept well back from the river's edge as I snowshoed upstream. Several dead salmon lay at water's edge in gravel and frozen mud and a few live kelt salmon were in calm water near the shore. Kelts had spawned not long ago somewhere upstream, then losing energy, had drifted on the current while slowly dying…but were probably satisfied with life after serving their final purpose.

I thought the salmon's lifecycle to be an excellent example of giving: simply by its very nature and role in life! Here in a calm pool were three live kelts resting near shoreline, their grey bodies scarred and scraped with white and cream streaks and spots, likewise fins and tails in tatters. Looking as if experiencing no pain, they were calmly waiting for their last moment when little sparkles of consciousness would transfer from this earthly physical life to somewhere-and-sometime else: a realm unknown to most earthly beings until they die. Then their bodies would become food for various other material beings, including indirectly their own offspring.

I thought about these fish giving of themselves throughout their complete lifecycle: from egg to smoult to adult. All along in time and place they fed many other animals of water, land and air, besides human beings. And I remembered the enjoyment that salmon gave me when a boy. They were always a lively pleasure just to see as spotted young fry swimming in clearwater creeks or as bluebacks jumping in the green saltwater and in autumn, scarlet and green or mottled greys swimming up rapids to spawn. Such living experiences induced great appreciation in my young mind. And I wished that more of humanity would regard the lowly fish in a more realistic, more appreciative manner.

Thus came and went thoughts with attendant moving visual images…as I plodded along with legs wide-stepping in the powdery snow. Now on more level ground, the snowshoes crunched through the snowcrust and sank to only four or five inches, keeping me up and making it an easier walk. Coming to a slight dip, the steep bankside curved into a gentle slope. Visible in this dip was a long dragmark in the snow, running from a low gravel bar at water's edge and upward away from the river. Kneeling down for a close look…very recently something about four inches wide had been dragged through the snow.

Along one side of this snowstreak was another pattern: little indentations and tiny holes. Here, a small animal had been hard at work! These wee tracks were left by a weasel! They looked to be just minutes old! Footprints, body and tail marks all indicated that it was a longtailed weasel. I thought what an incredibly strong animal this is for such minute size…apparently pulling a salmon through the snow!

Now with my interest piqued I followed these dragmarks which led up the gentle incline onto an open flat bench, then along towards a thick grove of thinly snow-coated branchy grey cottonwood and poplar. After a short walk of about thirty yards, there it was: a salmon kelt, partly chewed but otherwise whole! From this fish, very fresh weasel tracks led away into the woods on a run! Now I knew that my arrival had definitely chased this little carnivore away. I knelt down for a close look.

The salmon was about fifteen inches long and must have weighed three or four pounds! How could such small animal pull this large heavy object? That it did, there was no doubt. This was an amazing feat! Again, I was most impressed. Peering steadily into the shadows of low snowcovered hardhack brush where the tracks led, I hoped to see the tough little carnivore. But no…the wee white animal in white snow was not to be seen, although I felt it was watching me from somewhere among the shrubby bluegrey shadows. Knowing how important the salmon was for this weasel's survival and seeing how hard it had been working to get the big chunk of food home and hidden, I left right away, retracing my steps downstream. Even so, I was much cheered by this rare benign juncture of snowshoe and weasel tracks!

Winter passed, then spring…as Earth spun on its axis and orbitted the Sun…until one hot mid-summer day arrived. Now out for a hike just above another river somewhat farther east and carrying my goldpan, I came to one little tributary that was beginning to dry up. Following the stoney creek downstream I came to a shallow clear pool that was the consequence of rapidly dropping water flow. To my surprise, there in the pool looking up at me through black and golden yellow eyes was a good-sized trout, about thirteen inches long!

With large rounded white and grey rocks between the little pool and creek's main stream, this fish was trapped. The four inches of water was warm and no doubt quickly heating up under the very strong sunrays: the trout would certainly die from heat exhaustion within an hour or so. Then it would become food for a raven, weasel, hornets or flies; such be one of Nature's hard facts. Here was a circumstance that presented me with a choice — a decision — whether to save the fish's life or leave it to suffer a slow death in the baking sunshine…thus transforming into a meal for some hungry animal.

Looking into golden eyes, a nonverbal, nonconceptual communication passed from the mottled green-backed trout's eyes into mine. That same sort of individual consciousness was there looking back at me as had been with our pet dolly of almost one year ago. Slowly reaching down, I picked up the fish with both hands and quickly carried it about fifty yards down to the river. Sinking the big trout at water's edge, I held it upright awhile to make certain that the float bladder was in balance. This fish had pale yellow and bright orange-red spots with circles of pale blue, dotted on its sides…a living abstract beauty! After some half-a-minute, I loosened fingers and quietly watched the speckled trout glide slowly outward…into deep greenish-brown water where with gentle side to side tailwags, it disappeared into the cool shaded, life-giving aquatic environment.

Since I happened to be at this place and time and could intervene for the trout's sake, I did so. By this action I had no doubt denied food to one or more animal. Even so, I was happy to have directly saved a life! Meeting this brightly spotted trout at such crucial juncture in its life reinforced a lesson about life that another of its kind had awakened in me: that kindness and sharing should extend beyond humanity to our nonhuman companions…as much as possible and within reasonable limits. By our present-day social standards this concept seems strange and extreme but if viewed from Nature's standards, too many of humanity's rules are themselves inappropriate and extreme! For some unknown time I sat on the gravelly riverbar…pondering this subject and wondering if Canadian society at least, would ever grow up! Will we ever adjust to the higher values that Nature and the Universe express?

FUR AND FEATHERS

The leafy ground seemed alive! Constantly changing curved and pointed patterns danced in colours of ochre, pale green, rust, greybrown and brown. These lively lights and shadows brightened and dimmed in unison with sunshine filtering from above...through shimmering, rustling aspen, willow and birch leaves. I was following downstream alongside a wide slow-moving creek, searching for a beaverlodge. There was a good chance of finding one in this sort of mixed lowland forest. And this part of the creek had some silty mudbank stretches which beavers would like.

Of course, bears also frequent such brushy woods so I remained alert and moved slowly, especially where the view ahead became restricted. After skirting by a short brown boulder-strewn whitewater rapid, the slope levelled and creek slowed again into deep quiet meandering dark green water. Here, just around the bend and across, a beaverlodge came into view built against the silt and clay bank. Inconspicuous in such thickly treed area this beavers' residence would be found only if one walked right to it, so I was lucky! On its top several freshly chewed pale tan-coloured sticks and small barkless logs indicated an inhabited lodge. I set my camera for the dim shady light, then sat down on the sandy shore under a large poplar. With back against its wide grey trunk...I waited for whatever activity might eventually ensue.

It was a surprisingly short wait. Within just minutes my reward popped up...as two little fuzzy corks suddenly appeared at water surface in front of the lodge about seven yards away! Two tiny beaver kits surfaced...one, then the other quickly behind! Their fine fuzzy fur kept them much afloat, seemingly without effort. It was a wonder that such young beavers would be out alone! Each kit was only about eight inches long from nose to tiny tailtip! Paddling after each other, similar to human children playing tag, they were oblivious of my presence...so focussed on play!

Swimming to each other...nose-to-nose, these cute-faced babies floated motionless with little tails straight out and flat on the surface. Then grabbing one another with front teeth on the right side of their necks at jugular vein area, they tugged and paddled themselves into a slow clockwise circular spin. Around and around they spun! The wee beavers were so enjoying this tug-of-war game, continuing to move in small circles...drifting closer and closer towards the shore on my side. After some moments they drifted into very shallow water...and almost onto the sandy shore! The lively little balls of fuzz were now just two yards from where I sat!

I thought it be a good thing I was not a coyote, mink or some other large carnivore! These young beavers would be easy picking...so close to shore and in only one foot of water. They continued entertaining themselves — and me — directly in front, so close that I could see the blue sky above reflecting from their little brown eyes! As yet they did not know about onshore danger. If they had seen me, danger did not register in their young innocent minds. No doubt I was the first human they'd seen; but since I remained motionless the wee beavers had no fear, probably not recognizing me as something animate.

I began wondering where the parents were. The kits gradually drifted back out into deeper water, still moving in clockwise circles all the while…quietly enjoying their play. But it was not long until the answer came from just upstream — a loud smack and big splash sounding across the water surface! That same instant, in a split-second and without a sound the baby beavers vanished into the deep green water!

In circles where the kits dove, little wavelets rippled outward…soon meeting with larger waves from the adult's tail-smack. Large waves touched shoreline, bouncing back and forth, peaking and kicking up silt and mica that swirled and sparkled at the sandy edge…then soon levelled as energy dissipated. Again, the creek's surface smoothened into multicoloured streaks of straight flowing current with green, grey and brown of trees and pale blue of sky reflecting mirror-like in a spotted, lined, shimmering pattern. I waited and listened for quite some time, hoping for a reappearance. But no one returned. Not a sound came from the lodge.

This cheering experience now dominated my mind. From fifteen yards upstream to my right the adult had noticed me. Slapping its big tail as it dove under: this was the beaver's danger signal! The kits instantly understood the meaning, probably instinctively. Young beavers may have a natural fear of loud sounds in water; whatever…this was a good lesson from a caring parent! I wondered if this was their first time disciplined by a tailsmack!

Not far from this lodge was a small lake, my next destination. Entering the spruce and pine forest…I followed a little animal trail that was depressed into thick moss about one foot wide and a few inches deep. It led to the lake then ran along lakeside just above highwater mark under willow, pine and tamarack trees. This pathway was the sort used by marten, mink, coyote, lynx, bobcat and fisher. I had met a pine marten on this trail one day previously but today was alone on the trail.

The lake was calm: an imperfect mirror reflecting the upside-down image of dark blue rolling treed hills, angular pale greybrown rocky peaks and sparkly white snow jutting into the robin's egg blue of infinity. In the near distance just across a little bay I could hear a faint high-pitched sound carrying along the watersurface. This was a sound unfamiliar to me. Since I was walking that way, I expected to soon meet some other wild pleasantness! Now I proceeded along the brushy willowed lakeshore with more positive anticipation.

Moving silently I followed the trail while listening to the sound which was almost continuous but oscillating up and down in volume. Upon approaching closer, several separate little chattering and squealing voices became discernible. How many, I could not tell. There were from four to six baby animals calling out, no doubt for food…and sounding very demanding!

As I arrived, pinpointing their location was easy with their nonstop piping chatter emanating from the base of a large bluegreen spruce tree! This old tree was right at the deep water's edge. Its bark of big grey and rusty brown scales were much spotted and streaked vertically with milky amber and clear yellow pitch. The large exposed basal roots curled, twisted and crisscrossed up, down and sideways above and into the water.

Out of sight within these tangled roots — although giving their position away with such loud raucous chattering — these baby animals were safe from even a bear which would not easily dig apart the large tough roots. This was the perfect place for a nest: so protected by deep water on the southern side, under thick strong roots…and dry beneath the tree's numerous umbrella-like needly boughs. From the unique, slightly raspy sounds of these young voices, I guessed them to be a type of large weasel. Openings between roots were wide enough for pine marten or mink but not fisher.

Moving to three yards away, I leaned out over the lakeside's clear turquoise water for a better look. Just inside the shadows were dark, quick back and forth movements as the animals took turns looking out at me. This was no doubt their first sight of a human. I remained silent and still…knowing that their natural curiosity would probably bring them into view. And it was not long until one of the little animals poked its brownish-black head out of the shadows! Its sparkly dark eyes gazed steadily at me as whiskers and shiny blackish nose twitched, gaining knowledge of the human shape and odour.

Moments later another little face cautiously appeared beside and just behind the first. Then another shouldered it as their natural, youthful inquisitiveness overcame initial fear of the unknown. Now in sunlight, three little silky faces with low flattish ears assessed the human: they were baby mink! And all the while their calls for food hardly ceased! Little chocolate brown faces appeared and disappeared from between roots in sudden jerky movements that are typical of the smaller weasel species.

During these several minutes, no adult appeared. Both parents were away, out hunting…and most likely at high speed in order to feed this raucous troop! This was my first discovery of a minks' den, so was almost as excited and energized as these little animals were! But I could not stay long, having a lot of ground to cover yet. As I continued away along lakeside…their steady water-borne chatter slowly faded out as would a pleasant piece of music.

After walking some long distance from the mink's lake, I came to a slow-moving little creek with sand and pebble bars coloured white, grey and rusty orange. Cupping my hands, I drank three times the colourless cold water…m-m-m-m, so good! Then walking slowly downstream along the creek's gravelly bars and shallows, I peered into the transparent-clear water looking for fish hiding at the pebbly bottom. Here were the wee minnows of a fish that I did not know, possibly whitefish. In one little pool at a sharp elbow-bend they were too numerous to count! These tiny fish were well protected by thick overhanging leafy brush of willow, alder and red osier.

Now walking the shallows towards a sandbar about ten yards away, I could see on it near water's edge, large tracks sunk into the wet sand. Stepping closer…the imprints became recognizable as cougar! Oh…oh…these large pawprints were as fresh as my boot tracks! They were made just seconds or minutes ago! The cat tracks pointed towards the creek's other side. No tracks showed on shallow sandy bottom next to the sandbar. It must have jumped across!

Another kind of excitement now rushed through my body and mind! Visibility here was almost nil with thick willow and red osier clumps growing along both sides of the creek. Being completely defenceless, I immediately wheeled around and hastily vacated the area! Proceeding towards where I had parked the car — yet a long distance away — I chose the path of best visibility. Walking at a quick pace I kept acutely alert, looking around in every direction, a three hundred sixty degree horizon…and frequently looking back. This was one of those rare times when the forest silence became very uncomfortable! I crossed an open flat of tall grass then slowly, cautiously entered the shade of a spruce and trembling aspen forest.

Once under the trees I could see a good distance. And now far enough away from the big cat's tracks, anxiety subsided somewhat. But after some minutes in these woods I began to sense that an animal was near: that weird feeling of being watched or that danger may be near. Looking all around I saw only treetrunks, dark dead lower branches and brush...and listening...nothing could be heard other than gently rustling aspen leaves. I kept moving, again with caution and avoiding any thick brushclumps. After awhile though, I thought maybe I had been just imagining things!

But as I walked, this sense of being watched persisted...sometimes on...then off. I kept up my pace through a grove of trembling aspen that clicked and rustled with the gusting breeze. Then at one point the uncomfortable sensation became particularly strong. Again I looked back, rotating quickly around one hundred eighty degrees. Well, well! The sixth-sense was not merely imaginary paranoia...there it was!

Standing motionless just ten feet away with its grey and rust-coloured head held low and fuzzy pointed ears up, the animal stared at me through creamy-yellow eyes! Suddenly I was at ease: just a young coyote! Here was a scruffy-looking juvenile adult, probably two years old and on its own for the first time. I smiled at it...very happy that my tag-along was not a cougar or some other large carnivore! Then quickly waving my left arm sideways, the curious follower instantly turned and leapt away! In a firm loud voice I said: "Just keep going! I'm too big for you!" And it did.

About two months passed by. I decided one day to go for another walk up a more distant mountainside to see what rock types were higher up on its slopes. This was a warm, blue-skied early September day...just right for such a hike. After slipping on a little yellow backpack but this time also carrying my 30-30 rifle, I went zigzagging upward under small birch, pine and yellowing tamarack trees. Squirrels were at the sunny treetops busily nipping off cones that would tap and bonk as they fell, bouncing haphazardly from branch to branch to ground.

The forest floor was covered in some places with an unusual combination of thick green moss, wild herbal plants and small berried bushes. After considerable steady climbing I had worked up a sweat so sat down to rest on a mossy rotten old log. Here the spongy emerald green carpet muffled the sound of pine and tamarack cones as they hit the ground. Faint shafts of sunlight slanted through the pale green and yellow canopy of needles and leaves. I had entered another calm, peaceful place...mottled above and below with pleasant greens, soft yellows and encompassed within vertical uprights of white, grey and reddish brown treetrunks all around. From these trees, branches jabbed sideways in a pattern of multiple triangles, some perfect but mostly not, projecting outward and upward in varying sharp angles. A living mosaic of geometric shapes and colour completely enveloped this little space. Here was a three-dimensional natural abstract that felt most comfortable and still...yet unusually alive!

After some relaxing minutes thus, a dark blur of motion appeared suddenly on the right about six feet off the ground! Instantly turning my head, the spotted form of a large owl silently gliding with legs and talons outstretched...then flapping its wide rounded wings and fanning out a big white-spotted tail...came to perch on one sturdy branch! Hitting with a crackly crunch, the large toes and talons grasped onto dry birchbark. Then the big bird's head swivelled left to look at me through big brown eyes. Perched in the tree just five yards distant and only ten feet up, it was close!

This arrival jolted me somewhat out of my dreamy rest! Now adrenalin had my body energized and mind perked. Its head was large, rounded and completely spotted with tiny creamy white dots. Big dark brown eyes sparkled, staring steadily and calmly. The big bird seemed fearless. But I kept still, wanting it to remain with me as long as possible.

We kept staring at each other: the bird being as inquisitive about me as I was immensely enjoying it's presence! This was a rare occasion, being so close to the seldom-seen barred owl!

But shortly, it broke the mutual regard by quickly swivelling its head to peer into the forest horizon and at leafy ground between distant trees. The big bird was on the hunt for a mouse, vole, grouse or snowshoe hare…whichever unlucky one presented itself. Of course, the squirrels nearby were now silent! After a short moment, the owl's head and steady hunting eyes swung back towards me…again becoming eyes of curiosity and interest.

For a few minutes thus, we observed and studied each other. Then the big mottled beauty gave me another surprise! It leaned forward and left its perch. Without the faintest sound, air flowed against fuzzy soft feathers as the owl glide towards the birch tree that stood just an arm's length from where I sat! With a heavy, crisp crunch, yellow toes and long black talons met with dry bark as it came to perch on one dead limb just two yards above me!

I kept motionless…and as silent as the big bird was. The same intense mutual observation continued. This lovely owl looked down at me some moments, then turned its head in seemingly neckbreaking turns of one hundred eighty degrees or more to scan the forest horizon…then back towards me; for about two minutes it repeated this headturning and observing. The beautifully feathered owl was certainly as keenly interested in me as I was in it! Such an invigorating and pleasing experience…a happy smile came to my face: the natural expression of inner positiveness generated by this wild barred owl's presence.

What a beautiful bird: with its creamy white beak, wee white-flecked facial patterns, little rounded spots on its dark brown head, the large rectangular wavey wing and tail patterns and long, slender white and brown vertical chest and belly bars. These all combined into a complex but harmonious display…a visual symphony of white, cream, brown and grey: its feathers and form were as if a silent geometric song!

I could not help feeling inspired by such natural beauty, seeing how Nature's deeper forces manifest in myriad ways on the physical level and how the innermost life expresses in so many ways that are complex, simple and sometimes beautiful. What this owl thought of me…I would never know. What its interest in me was motivated by, I did not know. But an intelligent curiosity within this beautiful bird overcame any natural fear of the unknown it may have had!

Six feet distant was still too far away for this big owl. Again, it leaned over sideways…wings opened out and tail fanned. Then it dropped into a clockwise spiral curve…to land with a heavy clunk on a large smooth lower limb — directly in front of me! How incredible! Here we were, this beautiful wild owl and me, just an arm's length away! If I had reached out with either arm, I would have touched it.

At such close range, looking into the owl's big sparkly brown eyes, its conscious mind became visibly obvious — shining out from within — carefully scrutinizing me by staring into my eyes! Pleasant and still…long moments passed in this mutual regard: face to face, eyes to eyes and in a nonconceptual way, mind to mind. Then as if remembering its primary purpose, head quickly swivelled right with eyes searching the far-off distance between birch and pine treetrunks. Looking…looking…as if far away into space and time…the seconds passed. Then the owl's head swivelled left again towards me for a short moment, a quick look to the right, then back at me; the big bird repeated this urgent headturning five or six times. And each time, eyes met eyes.

Finally though, it did not look back but slowly leaned forward, spread its big fuzzy-soft mottled wings and left the limb without a sound. Gliding away downslope just a foot off the ground, the big barred owl tilted slightly to dodge jagged dead branches and treetrunks while effortlessly, silently floating on air. Shrinking in size and into space and time…becoming one integral part of the pastel yellow, green, white, grey, rust and black geometric mosaic, this special owl approached the distant beyond…where the mountainside's curving slope appeared to rise. There, my owl disappeared within a white and maroon pallisade of birch treetrunks.

"What a fortunate meeting," I thought, still sitting on the mossy green log and charged with a most pleasant cheerful energy. The owl was hunting either for itself or maybe a fledgling family or both…so had to go. Even so, its innate natural intelligence and curiosity allowed the beautiful barred owl to pause awhile from mundane necessity to share a few minutes of its busy life. This was a special juncture of time and place in the lives of two very different beings…a rare experience that for this human certainly increased his appreciation of our western wildlife and no less of Nature as a whole!

Little White Dots

Puffy billows of pale grey clouds edged with bright white and sending out long thin translucent white curls from below, were drifting northeast over the Rockies. Mountaintops were yet covered with large pale blue and white snowpatches and lower down, bluegrey rock scree was warming in the late spring sunshine. Lower still, the greygreen and yellowgreen-patched forest had already livened in a myriad natural ways: such be the way of Nature in a four-season northern country. These wide valleys and high rugged mountains were the all-new residence and experiential setting of a young man working for the first time in a remote part of western Canada.

Since the day was just beginning and I worked nightshift, there was time to venture out on a hunt for something to shoot…with my 35mm camera. Firing up my 1953 ranchwagon I was soon chugging slowly along a vacant new highway, watching the upper slopes and valley-bottom forest. It was not long until wildlife appeared in the distance above. Quite low on the mountain's southern slope, a group of tiny white animate dots was barely visible a half-mile away!

A small herd of mountain goat-antelope was loitering on a steep rise of soft-looking whitish earth…no doubt a mineral lick. There was a challenge! I stopped, got out to have a good look and wondered how close I could get to them without being detected. This venture would be a most interesting and entertaining way to pass the day! So…I planned the best route up to them. To the west there was a long narrow stretch of poplar and aspen trees running upslope; that would be good cover. Those trees were my only chance, bordered on each side by treeless boulder scree and thin buckbrush which was too open.

I checked wind direction by wetting one index finger and holding it up to the gentle breeze. I was in luck! The air current was moving from east to west. Having no telephoto lens, I would have to get very close for a good photo. Remembering what hunters in the past had told me about mountain goats: that they were extremely difficult to stalk and get close enough to for a shot…my never accepting their song-and-dance, thought I would prove otherwise.

Slipping on my western jeanjacket, then with camera in hand, I carefully manoeuvred through the lower part of thick brush patches and boulders…hoping to not bump into a bear or big cat! I had seen fresh cougar tracks on the sandy bar of a nearby creek a few weeks previously, so was apprehensive. My only protection now was a very short, old dull hunting knife that I wore on my belt; it was almost useless as self-defence. Even so, some tall poplar trees were quite climbable! Winding around the rectangular boulder blocks, I moved bit by bit, higher and higher.

Approaching closer, I again checked wind direction. It was still blowing from east to west and the goats were to the northeast. As long as I could remain unseen and unheard, chances were good. Luckily the strip of tall leafy aspen, poplar and cottonwood trees was adequate cover right to the top edge, where began a little flat bench. After a half-hour climb I was up at the same level as the mountain goats and only about one hundred yards away! Now they were visible through little open gaps in the pine and aspen forest.

As yet unaware of me and busily enjoying their mineral lick, I moved higher yet...planning to get above them. At this higher level the mountainside curved over into the semi-open bench which I then followed eastward...slowly and silently closing in on my target. Here, under small whitebark pine and trembling aspen trees grew a large patch of rusty brown-stemmed bushes, some short and others quite tall, with tiny light green leaves just beginning to sprout. As I stealthily approached the mountain goats...at times crawling and avoiding dry branches that lay on the ground...an unsuspected odd beauty appeared.

For quite some distance along this bench, dwarf juniper and soopolallie bushes which varied in height from three to six feet, looked as if they were decorated for Christmas! Except these decorations were all white: dots, streaks and dangling threads of very fine fuzz. On closer look, balls and variously shaped pieces of fluffy cottony material had been caught and held randomly by sturdy branches, making the brush also look a bit like cotton plants. The closer I got to the goats, these Rocky Mountain cotton bushes became thicker and thicker with white fuzz. That mountain goats much frequented this high bench was now obvious!

Acting as natural brushes for the mountain goats' springtime moult, branchtips thinned out their fine winter undercoats each time they walked past. It was a pleasant sight, with tiny pale green leaves sprouting amid many fluffy white bits of wool. Picking a handful...to my surprise, warmth surrounded my fingers almost immediately! This extremely fine wool was a most perfect heat-retainer...and so light and soft, my fingers' touch-sense could barely feel it! I picked more, stuffing it into one jacket pocket as a little keepsake.

Now right above the mineral lick, I observed trees nearby for an escape route in case a protective nanny goat thought it necessary to chase me! Just right for this were two branchy whitebark pine trees close to the bench edge. They were an upright eighteen-inch diameter pine right on the claybank's dropoff edge and a smaller leaning vee-trunked snaggly pine...about twenty feet farther in. Setting the camera for the open light and goats' white wool, I walked on tiptoe avoiding twigs and crouching low. Then closer...crawling to the dropoff and lying on the ground, I peeked around the eighteen-inch truck. There they were...just fifteen yards away!

A cheerful moment this first close sighting was! Excited, my heart pounded hard and hands shook! They had not yet detected my presence. There were six animals: nannies and young. Trying to calm down, I waited...watching, enjoying the antics of two little kids playing follow-the-leader! The smallest two were very young, just born this spring. One yearling and three adults calmly scratched and licked the powdery greyish white soil. The adrenalin that made my hands shake seemed to remain a long time, so how was I going to get a reasonably clear photograph?

And now I was upwind from them! Soon they would smell danger in the breeze. One wee kid walked out to the tip of a little clay-like finger. There...it stood a short while looking triumphant...until the punky-soft earth broke away under it! Down it tumbled, head over heels...for about ten yards! Unscathed even so, the young mountain goat regained its feet and climbed deftly back up with the rest.

After these few entertaining minutes, the largest adult female, the herd's leader, lifted her snout and began sniffing the air somewhat persistently. She had caught wind of my scent. Her sudden alertness indicated that she knew something dangerous was closeby. I decided to try a few snapshots now, before they bolted away! So, slowly standing up, but still hidden behind the eighteen-inch pine tree and using its trunk to steady the camera, I began clicking. They seemed to hear the camera but were not afraid, probably since it was unrecognizable and barely audible at fifteen yards distant. Now all three adults were raising their snouts…testing the air and looking about!

Then the large senior nanny had my position pinpointed as her head turned to steadily face me and my tree. She focussed on what little of me showed along the treetrunk edge…with steady eyes, ears perked my way and shiny black nostrils open! She and now the other adults stared intently, not knowing what I was…more than half-hidden behind the tree. I slowly stepped out into full view, standing motionless at the claybank's edge to indicate to them my benign intent. As the adults eyed me, the younger mountain goats too, one by one looked my way.

They became slightly nervous, walking randomly about their grey knobby mineral-lick while rapidly moving their heads in different directions. After half-a-minute of this, the dominant nanny-goat abruptly walked straight up to just below the bench edge with her two tiny kids following closely behind. Placing my camera onto the ground by the treetrunk, I walked to the vee-pine tree and stood nervously beside it, ready to climb. Jumping up onto the bench, the big she-goat was now just ten yards away! Her two precious ones scrambled up closely behind then stood beside her. All three kept still…eyeing me with shining dark amber eyes and with their long pointed ears out sideways, listening keenly. Within a few seconds the two younger adults and yearling had jumped up onto the flat. Now all six stood silently on the bench and all looking…looking…this unusual setting would have made a beautiful photo with them standing next to the white-and-green-spotted brush! She took three steps angling towards me then stopped…staring hard!

With right hand on my branchy climbing-tree, I stood motionless but ready: observing the big nanny's eyes, ears and body position. We all seemed to be held by the stillness and silence… watching each other but waiting for the other to move first. After maybe half-a-minute the big nanny goat turned her eyes and head to the left, then began stepping slowly along what appeared to be a main pathway. Following this trail brought her closer to me but she was angling more northward. I could see that she just wanted to pass by, showing no aggression! So…I just stood still as she calmly walked past about seven yards away with the twins at her heels and the other three close behind. At about twenty yards distant she stopped to look back a few moments, and so did the others…their necks twisted back almost a hundred eighty degrees. Then she led the little herd at a quick pace eastward towards a faintly audible creek, one by one disappearing into the white-and-green-spotted soapberry brush.

I just stood there for some time loaded with excited energy and enjoying the fresh clear memory! Walking back to my camera at the bench edge, I looked down at their mineral lick. It was well-trodden with hoofprints and little hollows where the animals had nibbled up the tasty earth. Far below, I could barely see my old cream-coloured wagon parked by the highway. It would be a long walk back. But the Sun was still high so I decided to not leave yet and instead, hike farther up.

Following the route taken by the herd I was on a well-used animal trail about two feet wide, winding under pine and tamarack trees. The goats had not continued along this trail but moved off towards the creek, which was running through a deep rocky gorge. They were not to be seen. I walked this main trail which followed a gentle upward slope and paralleling at a distance the unnamed creek. Easy walking for about two hundred yards, the animal trail then began to roll, curve and dip down at a steep forty-five degrees, making visibility poor. Then above, I could see that it bent at ninety degrees to the east onto an open grassy slate ledge.

I never liked walking where I could not see at least twenty yards ahead so stopped before the dip under a twenty-inch spruce tree. Tumbling whitewater hissed and echoed from the creek below, the little canyon being very close at this point. Walking off the trail to the gorge, I saw that it was cut for ten yards or more through grey layered hardrock in an absolutely vertical dropoff! Here the rushing, swirling water's sound was very loud, apparently magnified somehow by the rock walls. I wondered where the mountain goats had gone; certainly they would not be able to cross this deep rockcut. They had not come up the trail that I was following. Now I debated on whether to climb a bit higher to see what newness would be up there.

Walking back to the trail, I procrastinated. Beams of sunlight brightened pine, spruce and tamarack boughs while lighting up the animal trail behind me in a pattern of curving patches, little ovals and circles of shade and light. Back under the big spruce, in its dark shade the air was cool and fresh with a delicious aroma of pitchy bark and evergreen boughs. Everything here was so peaceful. Leaning against the treetrunk, I quietly enjoyed it all for unknown time…then farther up from the northeast began a faint, indistinct animate sound.

The distant repetitious pattern gradually increased in volume…soon changing to an intermittent, low-pitched solid thumping…becoming more and more distinct. Some large animal was definitely approaching and it seemed to be coming along the trail! I visually scanned the nearby trees for an escape route — one that I could climb fast! My twenty-inch spruce seemed appropriate enough. Still not knowing the animal's identity, I set the camera for shade and at about six-foot focus onto a large exposed root that grew across the trail just in front of me.

I crouched onto knees…out of sight behind the spruce trunk, listening and waiting. The sound seemed too loud and too solid for a bear or cougar. Maybe it was a moose or elk? The closer it came, the clearer. Now I knew by the hard solid beat that it was a hoofed animal…so tension lessened while excitement remained up!

The sound quickly became loud and sharp! The large animal was no doubt coming along the trail but did not seem to have the rhythm of elk or moose on-the-run. With camera held tightly against the treetrunk's right edge, I waited, looking up in that direction. Pounding hooves were now very close! Then from behind little pine trees at the open rockface above, the animal appeared just twenty yards away…galloping along the trail, now past a dwarf juniper patch: a handsome lone billygoat!

The billygoat swayed its head from side to side as it galloped, looking most happy and enjoying life to the fullest! It's long fine beard curved back, rippling in the breeze created by its own forward motion. Now slowing for a large branchy log that lay across the trail, the billy's head bowed down, then suddenly up as it glide over! Reaching the ninety degree bend in the trail, it slowed and turned sharply left, then disappeared down into the deep dip…coming directly my way!

Kneeling on my knees and hidden by the tree, the billy was oblivious of my presence. With right eye, I peeked overtop the camera along the scaley grey treetrunk bark. Up came the goat into clear view — bounding straight along the trail towards me!

With head swaying side to side and bobbing up and down, its long black horns glowing and ears angling back…the billygoat pranced along with big sparkling amber eyes and a face that emanated cheerful self-confidence! Solid hooves pound the hardpacked dirt with loud galloping thumps!

Pressing the shutter release, I caught this regal mountain goat in mid-air with front hooves up and long soft beard flowing, curving almost straight back. At the same instant — hearing the camera click — the billy hopped two short braking steps, slowing to a quick halt right beside me! Standing broadside and motionless with head swivelled backwards at about one hundred thirty degrees…the goat silently eyed me! I too, remained completely still, as if frozen to my treetrunk security…my head turned at an angle and looking back at the big billy from the corner of my right eye.

This was too close! If I had reached out my right arm I could have touched its fuzzy white wool! I kept perfectly still…looking at its eyes and face while feeling an elation that was simultaneously tinged with fear. Knowing that if the goat felt threatened, one defensive jab of its long black horns would easily be the end of me, I remained absolutely still! Time seemed to have suddenly expanded…as mere seconds felt like minutes.

Both of us were now apparently frozen in time! The billygoat's beautiful amber eyes and black parallel pupils continued a steady gaze…studying and assessing the human. Long moments passed…as silent mutual observing continued. Then I noticed that this goat was maintaining a nonaggressive expression and stance. It seemed to be far more curious than fearful!

I thought now to try for one more shot. With right thumb and forefinger very slowly advancing film to the next frame, I adjusted the approximate focus, a visual estimate of three feet to its face. At this slight motion the billy remained still…just watching. Now slowly bending my wrists, moving the camera to point back at it, with this slight movement — a blurred white flash and loud thumping of hooves came instantly! Two bounds down the trail then a lightning-quick left through soapberry brush towards the creek gorge — and it was gone!

Once again I was alone with the silent trees, feeling their calm steady peacefulness. I stood up, looking to where the goat had vanished so quickly. With a wish to see it again I cautiously followed its tracks and direction towards the noisy whitewater canyon. Soon standing at the upper edge…this deep rockcut was too wide for even a mountain goat to jump across and no hoof-hold was visible anywhere on the sheer dropoff. I was puzzled. It had been leaping at full speed straight to this gorge so…where did it go? This billy and the little herd, I thought, certainly knew something that I did not!

Pacing back up to the pathway, excitement and energy charged about within me. Turning back down along the mountain goat trail, the billy's cheerful proud face and prancing gait replayed on my mind's visual screen…and I thought of how its expressions were those of a wild being that was fully loving life here on these beautiful Rocky Mountain slopes! And…so was I! This day's experience certainly induced great cheer and a positive lifelong memory, thanks to these peaceful mountain residents.

Two Voices In One

The area was one that I had never been to but looked interesting on the map. Remote and rugged enough, I thought it would be a good place to prospect and explore. Along with a sleeping bag and grub I brought my goldpan, rock sledgehammer, rifle, spotting scope and camera. Following a pothole-ridden logging road that paralleled a boulder-strewn river, I headed upstream in no hurry. Above this wide valley two very rugged mountain chains ran north-south.

Most of the valley had been logged off over the past fifteen or twenty years, so trees of various small sizes and berry bushes in bloom filled each rectangular or square cutblock. The few huge old trees still standing were hemlock, larch and fir...all beautiful with pale yellowgreen lichen hanging from big zigzagging limbs and clumped randomly on the deeply grooved trunk bark. Lower down and alongside the river were large spruce and the less populous cedar. Several giant red cedar remained standing, some with bare broken-off tops. Others had long spike-tops, lumpy with large knots. On their trunks were tree-sized, j-shaped limbs that are known to loggers as schoolmarms or widowmakers!

One advantage to me created by this vast clearcut valley was that I could see unobstructed the mountains on both ranges. Beautiful they were in both form and colour! From the distance these geological giants seemed to grow from valley bottom as smooth deep green and deep blue, flattened parabolic curves, then rising steeper into mottled pale green subalpine meadows and buckbrush that met with fan-shaped grey and rust scree slopes; above them towered sheer cliffs of squared and rhomboid solid-rock peaks, encompassed by snowpack and small shining white and grey glaciers.

The glacial ice was mostly pale grey but where sunshine penetrated...little dots of gem-like turquoise blue. Looking at the mountaintops through my twenty-power spotting scope, there were wide stretches of gently undulating snowpack that was pink! This was the first time I had ever seen pink snow which years ago was told existed but only half-believed. What would colour snow pink at high elevations? I thought it may be caused by either pollen or lichen.

Most rock in these mountains appeared to be granite and granite-like but was difficult to identify from such long distance even with a twenty-power scope. Lichen growing on rock will often mask the rock's colour with its own. But even so, little feeder creeks gave me some idea about local rock constituents. Stopping to pan out gravel in three creeks along the way added to this knowledge: mica, quartz and feldspar were abundant. Every time on the pan's bottom glowed a few pale pink garnets but no blacksand and nothing metallic. This was what I expected, so was not disappointed.

Anyway, my primary reason for being here alone was to experience Nature...to get to know it a bit more and enjoy what it gives, what it expresses. On a calm sunny springtime day at a time of season before flies and mosquitoes arose...the predominant phenomenon of this wild mountain valley was silence! A powerful silence, so pervasive one could not help but absorb it: the effect was a deep but light calmness in both body and mind. More probable though the silence absorbed me, bringing on this peaceful experience! The only chitchat I heard came from my own thoughts, the sounds of ravens, chickadees and siskins.

Driving onward…eventually I stopped at one larger shaded whitewater creek. Sitting on a boulder beside it to cool off, listen and watch…loud whitewater noise filled the air! But now and then within this din, most unusual sounds were coming up from below little waterfalls that tumbled over the large rounded boulders: continual high-pitched squeals, low murmurs and faint whistles! These sounds seemed quite human…but were emanating from under the bubbly white and pale green clear water!

This odd chorus sounded much like little children in a playground giggling, squealing and having fun! Hearing these…I could easily understand how ancient people would have imagined there be some sort of invisible beings living and playing in this singing whitewater. Whatever the cause, I was fascinated by these playful and semi-conversational sounds continually emitting from the fast-moving creekwater! They gave this crystal-pure creek an unusual liveliness that was both comfortable and amusing while likewise arousing curiosity and wonder.

After some long peaceful moments beside this pleasant, happy-sounding creek…time came to venture farther along the gravel road. Now the day was fairly advanced as late afternoon shadows had crept along imperceptibly, lengthening and deepening. I drove on, looking at shadows and colour changes that were becoming more prominent on the mountainsides. By now I was about twenty miles along and with more unknown bumpy road to travel. Crossing over one small wooden bridge then rounding a curve, the day's first large wildlife came into view: at the roadside stood a cow moose with her yearling calf! Stopping immediately, I shut off the motor to watch. The brownish-black cow looked a bit concerned, with large drooping nostrils opening and closing while staring at the truck, ears perked straight up, yet standing still.

They had been loitering along the road, nibbling leaves and buds of roadside poplar saplings and brush. Loud tumbling water from the nearby creek had prevented them from hearing my truck approaching…so this sudden arrival disturbed their placid day. The mother trotted across the road with her light brown young one following closely behind. Their peculiar leg movements were pleasing to watch as they jogged along right past the truck; extra long, slender legs that looked like stilts added to their mirth-inducing appearance. They continued in a high-stepping trot into narrow riparian woods by the creek. There, once under poplar and cedar trees they stopped, glanced back then moved away in a slow walk following the creek downstream towards the distant river. Since daylight was fading and with the valley in shade I never attempted a photo.

Firing up the truck, I drove onward looking for a wide area to park for the night. Another mile along, there was a wide flat gravelpit. In this open flat area a yellow frontend loader was parked for the weekend. Gravel had been taken out for road surfacing, leaving a vertical cutbank about twenty feet high along the northern edge. Above that a gently sloping clearcut was full of blue and black huckleberry bushes just beginning to bloom. This spot seemed a perfect place to camp overnight. I parked, then climbing into the truck box, dug out some grub from a big green plywood storage box. Quite hungry, I wolfed-down supper…all the while likewise feasting on the visual beauty all around!

High above to the north were two huge grey mountain peaks with a beautifully curving solid-rock bowl in between, streaked with many parallel grooves that had been cut by a slow-moving glacier during some long-distant past. Near the top of this bowl was an extensive snowpatch glowing soft creamy white and strong pink in the late afternoon sunlight — more of the enigmatic pink snow! These mountains were perfectly beautiful! I had arrived at the right place, at the right time.

Watching the big sweeping shadows encroaching upward on south slopes, cast by mountains to the south…slowly…slowly they climbed from treeline up the grooved grey mountainside then across the wide snowy bowl. Puffy clouds floating high to the northeast in a deepening blue sky were quickly changing colour from cream to pink and pale orange…then mauve and dark grey as the Sun's rays were blocked by a mountainous southwestern horizon. It was not long until trees nearby and on lower slopes turned from deep olive-green and blueblack to black. Soon the Sun's last lightrays no longer struck the grey solid-rock eastern mountain tops, which then turned deep navy blue. The greyblue eastern sky now darkened quickly…and soon evening's first stars began to shine and twinkle soft white from the dark grey deep of outer infinity directly above.

Ever so slowly the curving eastern horizon rolled over and darkened…bringing the planet Venus and far-distant stars to rise. Gradually the silent sky became a lovely expanse of countless stars, brilliant or softly glowing! Larger stars continually blinked and flickered in changing colours from white to pale orange to red and yellow or pale blue and back to white. Here I was seeing light emitted from stars, suns, galaxies billions of years ago…a phenomenon of Nature difficult to comprehend. Now I was enjoying this natural lightshow from the long, long past but in the present moment! I thought the past, present and future must really be one long, vast continuum.

The sky and forest had now darkened into night, so with nothing else to do I stretched out across the truck cabseat. For safety's sake, I was in the habit of sleeping this way even though a bit awkward. Not quite wide enough to straighten my legs, I adjusted to this by lying on my back or side diagonally. I kept the key in place. And loaded five bullets into my 30-30 rifle which was then laid alongside on the floor. This was a time before the arrival of pepperspray on the market.

One more benefit was that I could watch the sky through the windshield and windows, much like having a glass roof! As I watched the twinkling colours…sleep and the realm of dream-consciousness gradually, surreptitiously overcame the earthly daytime mind. Soon oblivious of the waking-state world…I was gone into the relaxed but little-known realm of physical and conscious sleep.

I had been asleep for maybe two hours when a deep-toned distant sound entered my slumbering consciousness. At first this was just a part of my dreaming mind…off in the background. Then a second sound of the same pattern and tone but a bit louder and closer, drew me back into a semi-awake state. Now I recognized it to be not a part of dreaming but the deep voice of a large bear! Even so, I lay on my back still half-asleep…but listening. My eyes opening, the sky was deep grey and full of a myriad beautiful twinkling stars. Black forms of evergreen trees jutted up along the sky's mountainous lower edge. Moments passed and all was silent.

More moments passed…until in the near distance to the northwest another deep growl broke through the dark silence! This time it was very deep, louder and closer: "Oooooo-rrrrr …Oooooo-rrrrr."

This growl was actually composed of two distinctly different sounds being vocalized simultaneously, not in sequence. By the depth and volume it was recognizable as that of a grizzly…and a large one! The growl's increasing volume indicated that this bear was slowly walking my way through the huckleberry clearcut. Approaching from the west above the gravel cutbank, it continued to vocalize now and then with the same very low-pitched sound. Feeling safe in the truck…I just lay quietly listening but still not quite awake.

When directly behind and above me atop the high gravelcut, the bear vocalized again: "Oooo-rrrrr!" This grizzly's voice was very deep…a most powerful sound!

Now suddenly more awake, I began mentally debating what this bear's intention may be! It was about twenty yards away at the top edge of the gravel cutbank; I knew the bank was too high and steep for it to come directly down, so was not worried. A few moments of silence passed until another: "Ooooo-rrrrr!"…this time more distant as the bear had moved eastward, farther away above the high gravelcut. I remained still, on my back…listening.

At ground-level everything was pitchblack and completely silent. I began feeling a touch uneasy…as the quietness stretched out in time. Then finally, the bear sounded out again from an increased distance; it seemed to be just passing by and was now walking away! I began to relax again but still waiting for another, more distant call. No sound came as more long moments passed…and wanting to hear another more distant message, I fought my doziness by watching stars twinkling in the deep silence directly above.

Again the quietness lasted and lasted. This night was a breezeless calm. The tree boughs were absolutely still and silent. Black treetop silhouettes stood motionless along the jagged mountain horizon. I waited and waited for another confirmation. But with this long, dark, peaceful silence and gently twinkling stars…my eyelids were slowly lulled to a close. And I was so cozily warm under the sleeping bag. The bear must have wandered away.

Drowsily, I thought…"The bear must have just been passing by."

In this calmness I began drifting away into the mind-realm of sleep. But then, one very loud, very deep roar exploded from the blackness right behind the truck: "OOOOOO-RRRRRRR!!!"

That jolted me instantly upright — as a bolt of electricity flashed through my body and mind! The big grizzly was at the truck's tailgate! While I — suddenly sitting at the steering wheel — honked the horn, turned the starter key, pulled the light switch on, all almost simultaneously with near-lightning speed!

I felt a strange electrical sensation on my upper back and the back of my head while imagining — and expecting — a quick swat from one huge paw coming through the glass! But the truck motor started immediately. Pumping the gas pedal to make more noise while glancing back, I saw just dark grey starry sky against the black shapes of low brush and sapling poplar trees…and the reddish glow of taillights reflecting from gravel near the truck's backend. Expecting to see shining eyes or the silhouette of a bear somewhere in the dark, I felt a touch eased with it gone! Apparently the truck's sudden loud sounds, lights and exhaust fumes were a perfect surprise combination — scaring the big bruin away at least some unknown distance!

Turning the truck around with high beams on, the animal was not to be seen. Even so, the bear must have been not far away…probably less than forty yards to the east at the clearcut edge where willow, larch and poplar saplings were tall enough to hide it. Sitting in the idling truck — hands shaking from adrenalin and fear subsiding — I peered into the shadowy darkness and at pale whitish headlight reflections on trees and brush…hoping to see the bear. I was now regretting having not seen the big grizzly!

But feeling safe now and a bit relaxed, I thought about this incident and wondered if the bear was after me or grub that was inside the big plywood box in the back. Then I remembered the toasted cream-cheese sandwiches that I had unwittingly left there! It seemed most likely the strong smell of cream-cheese, butter and toast had been the prime reason for this nighttime visit! And…I thought, it was a good thing I slept in the truck cab — not in a tent! I knew that a hungry grizzly would eat anything edible: cooked or raw, plant or animal. Well, my stay at this gravelpit was now over. The big bear was too close for comfort and it might come back!

So I drove slowly along the rough unfinished road westward…as far from the bear that I could get! Only three miles along, the logging road stopped. Parking there and then, I grabbed the flashlight then climbed up into the back, opened the storage box and got out the tasty sandwiches. In the pitch black I wolfed them down, thinking I should have had them for supper earlier! I did not want to attract another bear! Then lying back in the cab I watched the sky…all aglow and sparkling…while listening to a little nearby creek going, "Sh-sh-sh Shhhhhhh…." A long time passed until adrenalin's nervous energy finally dissipated and this earthly mind once again drifted away into the oblivious but peaceful dream world.

With Earth slowly rotating, stars curved across the wide deep sky to gradually set in the mountainous west…as cosmic time brought the Sun to rise ever so slowly in the evergreen tree-lined east. Warmth and light of the early morning sunshine soon brought me consciously back to Earth. I was happy that no more visitors dropped by overnight! Stepping out onto the rough newly bulldozed road, I stretched my arms upward and breathed in deeply. The morning air was cool and energizing and my mind cleared upon breathing in the resinous, clean forest air. Another quiet calm day was beginning. I looked up at the beautiful high mountains steeply slanting into the sky above…and feeling very appreciative!

Beautifully clothed they were in deep green and bluegreen forest to halfway up. Then higher up, grey and brown solid rock, pink and white snow and turquoise glaciers…huge, silent and still…gave to me their visually and emotionally pleasing expressions of form and colour. Those giant geological formations brought cheer to this little human mind. Likewise a lively but relaxed, smooth energy seemed to flow into this wee human body standing far below. Even so, this little mind could appreciate emotionally that great beauty and power…which too, was something significant and large.

I thought of how beautiful Nature was and how dangerous…thought of the powerful deep roar of the grizzly's double-sounded voice — how big its throat must have been…how unforgettable last night's experience would always be! But now hunger began dominating my senses and therefore my mind. Taking two tincans from the green storage box, I wolfed-down a quick breakfast cold and straight from the cans. This was a manner of eating sufficient to stave-off hunger, albeit not so healthy. Canned food though, was safer in remote regions, having no food smell to bring bears around…that is, until opened.

Soon after this bush-breakfast, with goldpan, little ladies' shovel and 30-30 Winchester in hand I walked twenty yards to the gurgling, shishing creek. This creek's bed was of rounded grey, brown, black and white rocks all less than boulder-size but jammed together like bricks and deposited almost flat across, sloping gently at about two percent. In small undulating waves, the clear cold water hurried past and over them. Cupping hands I scooped up a handful of water, quickly drinking it down, satisfying that metabolic yearning — thirst — with pure, almost tasteless mountain snowmelt water! After two more scoops I was satisfied and no less appreciative, thinking: "Nature certainly is the great giver. Thankyou!"

With the little shovel I pried up a few rocks until enough gravel loosened to fill the pan. Panning it out in my usual rapid manner, soon a small amount of magnetite, garnets and pyrite glistened on the bottom…but no gold! After a few more pans with the same result, I walked upstream some distance to the first bend. I could see that someone had worked the creek for gold a long time ago, probably during the 1930s Depression. The gold-seekers had not stayed long since there were no telltale signs: no log cabin remains, no tent sites and no tincans or glass. After two more pans with the same result as before, it seemed that if gold were here…it was very sparse.

All the while I kept looking up and around — a bit jumpy after the night's experience, especially since all that I could depend on was my eyesight! This creek's many little tumbling rapids were quite noisy. Bears and cougars, I knew made hardly a sound walking on their soft leathery feet; that combined with the creek's lively sound…one could very easily walk up to me, unnoticed! Now I paced back to the truck keeping the path of best visibility while glancing back once in awhile.

Then leaving everything at the truck except the rifle, I picked up my small short-handled sledgehammer and went for a second exploratory walk. Following another little creek, I soon came to a boulder scree slope covered with alternating patches of moss and lichen. I skirted upslope along the scree edge under a semi-open forest of spruce and subalpine fir…a large stretch that was not yet logged. Here I found a different type of rock outcropping under the trees: a pale rock that I did not know the name of. This was the only place I had ever seen such rock. Banging around with the hammer here and there, I looked closely at rock chips through a twenty-power hand magnifier.

That no metal showed in the rock was slightly disappointing but I persisted…looking and banging. Then one piece broke open showing a little hollow, or vug. Inside were tiny sparkly crystals projecting from its rounded walls. First sight of them brought a jolt of excitement and pleasure; maybe this rock would have some dollar value! This was a rare beauty! But what was it?

Sunlight reflected as brilliant wee stars of ruby red on one side and bright shining coal black on the other side! Observing through the magnifier, the red crystals were a most beautiful ruby red…and so clear…as transparent as glass! These crystals were the purest red colour I had ever seen! They looked like minute rubies, dozens of them all in a cluster. My first thought was of silver ore. Could these crystals be what is called ruby silver? Having never seen pyrargyrite or proustite, this was a wishful guess.

The only other possibility entering my mind was corundum, black and red. Red corundum is also known as ruby! Now charged by a mild form of adrenalin compared to the previous night — I climbed and clambered around searching for another piece of the same material hoping to find some larger crystals. But after an hour or so, I had to accept this one little anomaly as my only find. Carrying a few rock samples and the vug back to the truck, I placed them safely inside a box to take home for closer scrutiny later.

In the waning afternoon as I stood beside the truck spying the mountains with my spotting scope, a series of most unusual sounds began from very high up on one of the northeastern mountain slopes. Two beings were communicating in tones and patterns of sound completely unknown to me! At first, I thought of ravens since they are capable of voicing a variety of odd sounds. Yet these did not fit any sound that I knew ravens made. There were yells, yodels, whoops and deep to medium-toned human-like conversational sounds! The yodels and whoops were incredibly ape-like!

"Could they be Sasquatches?" I thought. Those sounds were what one would expect from something half-human and half-ape. But I always thought it extremely improbable that such beings existed; if they did, some definite evidence such as bones would have been found long ago.

My next thought was that it could be a couple of prospectors who had flown in by helicopter some day before I arrived. If so, they would have heard and seen my conspicuous blue pickup truck on the road far below…and maybe decided to have some fun. Well, they were putting on a very convincing performance — whoever or whatever! Yet although possible, that seemed unlikely, too. So I returned to thoughts about ravens, knowing what great scope and expression their vocal communication can have; they could have been ravens with their high-mountain croaks, yodels and whoops being distorted by distance, wind and echoes. But even more probable would be that a couple of bears were in conversation, since they also vocalize in various ways. Here, they would most likely be grizzlies!

By now this blue-sky day had advanced to late afternoon. Happy with my explorations and discoveries I began driving, mostly in first gear back along the ungravelled rough blast-rock road. Soon arriving at the gravel pit where the previous night's big grizzly had been…I stopped to photograph the saddle-shaped mountain above. Then I scoped the whole range to the east.

These were the most rugged mountains I had ever seen. Even at the very tops were huge cubic boulders of various angular shapes! And at one uppermost point was one very large, tall spire that actually glowed a ruby red in the early evening sunshine…looking like a giant ruby crystal! But this could not be. Could it be rubyjack zinc ore? I had no way of knowing since it was impossible to get to, other than by helicopter. Well, that beautiful spire was one more enigma… but even so, one more pleasing discovery in this remote wild part of British Columbia.

Social Animals

Light green trembling aspen leaves were twisting and clicking softly in the cold breeze. Through shimmering canopy boughs could be seen little patches of blue sky…and a brilliant white snowy peak jutting up amid squared and pyramidal solid stone blocks, all coloured in soft hues of rust, orange and grey. Below them stretched long curving fans of bluegreen and deep bluegrey conifer forest, dotted and patched with the pale yellowgreen of poplar and birch groves. The Rocky Mountain valleys were once again warming up…awakening to spring.

I was slowly walking through open woods, enjoying the gentle rustle of aspen leaves above and the shuffling and little snapping sounds of dry leaves and twigs under my boots. Then on my left, from behind grey and black treetrunks, emerged a large dark object moving quickly my way! In the air maybe six feet from the ground a huge bird with large head, big yellow eyes and broad mottled grey wings was swiftly gliding without a sound — straight towards me! Was it attacking?

Coming so fast — all that I could do was stand still, watching a very big owl gliding closer… its wide eyes staring! Its flight seemed effortless, gaining elevation the closer it came…the big bird silently glide directly over, just three feet above! The owl was only passing by, fortunately! Although I had never seen one before, I recognized it to be a great grey owl!

It flew on southward between trees, banking and dipping, deftly avoiding contact with jagged dead aspen branches that reached out like bent black and grey snags. This owl was verily beauty manifested in form and colour, so mottled and spotted with greys, white, greybrown and creamy tan. Excited and alert, I watched the big beauty fade away from sight…gliding past the oval black eyes of aspen and poplar trees to disappear into a maze of vertical treetrunks of white, grey and pale green. For some moments I stood silently fixed on this most pleasing image…then walked on, revelling in the new experience, short as it was! Then moving onward in the opposite direction towards a long wide meadow, I too, had a destination in mind.

Last year's meadow grass lay as pale cream-coloured hay parallel to the ground in a pattern of streaked curves and waves, a living natural carpet. Through this, projecting straight upward were a myriad of short bright green grass sprouts, as if tiny double-edged swordblades pointing to the blue-sky zenith. I was following the edge where meadow met forest and the poplar and pine trees led up onto a gentle north slope. At some distance eastward in the lower meadow stood a dark bluegreen clump of small spruce trees. I continued towards it, enjoying the warm sunshine and soothing silence of a calm, early spring day.

As I came closer to the thicket a dark animate shape appeared...up high among the spruce boughs: the dark brown head of a cow elk looking out at me! Approaching closer still, her tan and rust-coloured chest and legs became visible through the lower boughs and brush. She stood as still as a sentry, staring steadily...unmoved by my approach. Taking the hint, I stopped to watch her! Her shining dark eyes glared back! Her ears were out sideways and angled slightly back in what seemed to be an aggressive gesture.

Wanting to photograph this elk but not having a telephoto lens, began to nervously step closer. When about twenty yards distant...a loud strange sound rang out — as if two large planks of lumber were clapping together! Much surprised, I stopped and looked all around, wondering what was the cause! Simultaneously she slipped back into the tightly-growing spruce trees, out of view. Having never heard this sound before I could only assume the elk had somehow vocalized it...even though elk be usually mute. I guessed it must be a danger call, a warning call!

Then I began slowly circling clockwise around its hiding place. This was an oval-shaped thicket about thirty yards long by twenty yards wide. The cow elk soon reappeared at another point standing at the tree-edge as before, directly inward from me. Again she stared hard! I took one distant photo of her, knowing there was slim chance of getting closer...safely! Then I walked slowly, again clockwise away from her.

She just kept silently steadily watching and holding her position. Then another cow elk stepped out from the thicket into view, standing at the northern edge! She stood as firmly as the other, also intently scrutinizing. Again, that loud strange sound rang out! But now I saw that its source was definitely this elk! And now I understood that these elk were serious...that I was in danger. They were telling me to keep away!

And that I did! Before, I was somewhat apprehensive but now my hands began trembling. Unwittingly I had brought about this dangerous circumstance. Thinking I should increase distance without turning my back to them, I began circling again while slightly angling away. Slowly and carefully I stepped through the tall dry yellowish grass...all the while being watched closely by the two elk. Again, not far from the second sentry another cow elk appeared — standing firmly the same way as the other two!

By their unusual, persistent behaviour, the thought entered my not-so-quick mind: "There must be one or more cow elk calving inside this little spruce grove!" Here, out of sight from predators...cow and calf would be safe and easily guarded if need be.

"There is no other explanation," I thought, while circling gradually away at what I hoped would continue to be a non-threatening distance. When three-quarters around, a fourth cow showed herself, standing on guard where saplings met meadow! Her dark eyes sparkled and her wet nose glistened in the sunshine. She too, silently, keenly watched me angling away...back uphill to my original starting point.

As distance increased I began to relax, knowing that the elk would remain where they were since I was now no threat to their wee ones. This co-ordinated behaviour, an obvious showing of intelligence, had a most impressive effect on me. These elk had been guarding the spruce grove on four sides as if four compass points! This short meeting gave me some insight into behaviour that was socially intelligent; it was something definitely beyond merely blind instinct. That these large deer were co-operating in such manner was clear evidence of communication that was specifically for the benefit of the herd!

As I neared the aspen woods on the slope above, the fourth sentinel remained in position... watching. Now near the shimmering, rustling aspen trees about forty yards away from the elk, I sat on an old branchy grey log to look back awhile. Across and all along the wide grassy valley... everything was still, calm and quiet. To north and west, rising far above rounded bluegreen hills of pine and spruce, were ten or more peaks of pale grey and brown solid rock, each topped with bluegrey and brilliant white snow. They too, stood as still as sentinels...silently projecting into the motionless blue sky. And I felt happy being here a short while as a benign participant in this wild, living natural environment.

The last cow elk stepped back in between the shady spruce trees, out of view. I remained for quite some time sitting on the old log...watching and waiting. But after seeing and hearing no more I left them with a silent, "Goodbye," walking into the pine-forested slope higher up. After some distance upward I could hear a high-pitched, "Eeek-eeek...Eeek-eeek!" This sound was new to me, so wanted to see what little animal was speaking out! I turned in that direction.

Making my way under lodgepine forest towards the sound, in a short while I was nearing the base of an old scree slope. Angular boulders and smaller rock pieces were beautifully patterned with thick grey, white, cream, rusty orange and greygreen lichen...growing in circles, ovals, streaks and oddly shaped patches. Again, that little high-pitched statement penetrated the silence! Some small animal was hiding among these triangular and cubic rocks. Standing still, I visually scanned the slope for animate shape or any hint of movement. Several minutes of silence passed. Then a little rusty brown rabbit-like face emerged from a narrow gap among the boulders. Its ears were short and round. "Must be a pika," I thought..."What a sweet little animal!"

The tiny face watched steadily...keenly scrutinizing me. Keeping still and smiling happily, I waited...hoping to see more of it. Time passed seemingly slow and long, until the little animal cautiously stepped out onto the lichen-decorated boulder where its whole body became visible. It certainly was like a miniature rabbit, except for its very short ears and just a wee bump for a tail! Only about seven inches long, this cute little animal looked more like a child's stuffed toy than a living being.

Enjoying this pika's company for maybe five minutes until it returned under the big boulder, I then paced slowly onward along the scree slope's base where green grasstips and wild herbaceous plants were sprouting in the bordering meadow patch. Here, little pathways ran through dry grass, trampled down last year by pikas. Alongside their wee trails, pale green succulent sprouts were poking through, curling and lifting up from under the old brown, tan and white stems, leaves and grass. Among these were many little round rodent-chewed holes dotting the meadow, a sure sign of voles also resident here. This meadow patch, next to a rocky scree slope, was habitat perfect for the colony of pikas and a population of voles which apparently lived here as good neighbours sharing the same food supply.

Continuing again along my path of discovery...higher up two more pikas called out in the near distance. Communicating in what seemed a more eased manner, a soft but long drawn-out: "E-e-e-e-e-e-e-e-i...E-e-e-e-e-e-e-e-i," they sounded happy and at peace in their little rocky world. And I felt much the same...as I slowly wandered homeward, now through an open forest of old trembling aspen trees. On the ground at one point lay a large brown antler, dropped by a bull elk last winter. Regarding this boney beauty a few minutes, I left it there for the local rodents and porcupines to chew on.

Quite some time passed in this Rocky Mountain paradise...as the local wildlife had parented, fought, played, grown up and moved on...in unison with Earth's rotation and orbital movement around the Sun. Spring moved into summer...which in turn, into autumn. Now early September's cold nights had induced the willow, larch, aspen, poplar and cottonwood trees to turn yellow and golden. Between and beneath the trees, tall grass and herbs were once again a dry pale green and ochre yellow hay.

Now late morning, I was driving twenty-two miles to the nearest town for groceries, chugging along the vacant road at about forty-five miles per hour. This was a time that I felt great about life: having a good-paying job that also happened to be in this almost-untouched wild region! How fortunate I was to work and reside where hardly a human lived for many miles! As I drove along, due to natural interest my eyes were keenly alert for any hint of wildlife in the woods near the road…eyesight keyed for any unusual shape, colour or slight movement.

And surely enough, about three miles along on the hillside above to the south, there began a steady shaking and swaying of lodgepine sapling tops! I braked and pulled over to roadside, shutting off the motor. Moments later along with crackling and swishing of branches, there appeared a most impressive bull elk pushing his way out of the thick lodgepine forest! Seeming to barely notice me, the big bull never hesitated as he jogged onto the open grass and shrubs of the roadside clearing just ten yards away. He appeared to have his mind set on some particular agenda, therefore almost oblivious of my presence! This one was different from locals I had seen at times during summer along the familiar drive. Here was a stranger.

This bull had just arrived for the soon-to-begin elk rutting season. Its head and unusually long mane were all black, unlike the more blond and rust local elk. Its antlers were a good-sized five-point, no longer in velvet, reddish brown and white-tipped. Eyes sparkling and with head held high, it trotted along angling towards the road ahead of me to twenty yards distant. The big bull looked to be unfamiliar with roads and pavement since it slowed…then cautiously tiptoed at roadside…suspecting the flat odd-smelling pavement was something to avoid — before dashing across as if over redhot coals!

No doubt, this powerful-looking elk had just come from the remote area of vast rolling evergreen forest and rugged mountains to the south. With each breath, white mist shot from the shiny black snout as its hot exhalation met with cool autumn air. The big bull's high-energy, head position and leg movements — its powerful demeanour — brought a similar excited, strong energy to me…as I sat with arms on the steering wheel, visually and mentally absorbing every split-second of its presence! Here was a prime specimen of natural masculinity designed by Nature. Extreme self-confidence and power emanated from this big elk's very physical appearance and manner of movement! I thought it was good that this road was yet so little travelled, not too hazardous yet for the wild residents!

Prancing along with big-racked head held high…this energetic bull looked ready to fight! Moments later it stepped into the shady subalpine fir, spruce and aspen forest below. Although charged up myself, I just sat still…closing my eyes and mentally rerunning this short meeting: watching it on my instant three-dimensional, full colour memory screen. This was an experience that made life a bit more worthwhile; here was another life that was interesting beyond the mundane! The big bull was gone…but memory, I knew would extend these mere seconds of time into the far distant future.

After some time unknown my mind switched back to the present moment. Firing up the engine, the old wagon once again chugged along towards town. Just another mile farther along the valley widened out and opened as grassy meadow dotted with a few small islands of aspen, tamarack, subalpine fir, willow and spruce trees. Out there, a herd of fourteen elk were peacefully grazing and lounging. One large blond bull stood among cows, yearlings and this year's calves. He looked to be in his prime of life, displaying huge six-pointed antlers! The younger black-maned bull was certainly heading this way. Now I understood his seemingly singular agenda and destination!

Would the young outsider elk have the audacity to challenge this royal elk? By all appearance, I thought it would…without a doubt! But for now this herd was together and at peace, some animals lying down in the grass chewing their cud and enjoying the warm sunshine. Being in no hurry, I stopped to observe and enjoy them. Taking my twenty-power spotting scope, I sat quietly on the grassy bank above about fifty yards away…watching. In a short while a pattern of silent gestures, non-verbal communication within this herd brought my interest and energy up!

As this big bull slowly stepped and grazed among the herd, the largest, eldest dominant cow always held her grazing position. When he came close to her, she stayed. Whenever he was close-by, she seemed more interested in him than he was in her. But apparently his mind was elsewhere for the timebeing. He kept stepping ever so slowly with head down, grazing as he moved indirectly towards one particular young cow. She was smaller, probably just one year-and-a-half in age. When he reached a distance of about ten yards from her, she made a casual but definite move away several steps.

He stopped to graze a few minutes, changing position slightly. Then from another direction he began again slowly moving closer to her. Although never looking directly at him, she was keenly aware of his presence, more by sound than vision with her ears constantly pointing back or sideways. Yet, typical of female behaviour…she ignored him. This pattern persisted as he continually moved inch by inch in her direction. And likewise she continued with her mild rejection of him! She was the perfect example of female coyness!

A subtle slow-motion chase, it kept on for the half-hour that I was there. This interplay was quite amusing and also surprisingly informative! Here, it was manifest that the social life of a wild herding animal had some basic commonness with the civilized two-legged herding animal. It was so much — too much — like the natural behaviour of normal healthy male and female human beings! After seeing this quiet little social interaction, the realization came that humanity is not so very different, as it thinks, from wild animals.

Once again, days and nights passed…as the relentless motion of Nature's energy and space interacted, manifesting as the flow of life and steady change. The forested slopes had become more and more mottled in deep green, dark blue, grey and bright golden-yellow. About two weeks later, one evening I was looking out the cabin's eastend window watching stars rising and brightening on the black-treed horizon. Slowly, the pale bluegrey eastern sky darkened…while filling with more and more stars…until the whole sky turned dark grey, yet brightly lit with countless aeons of tiny twinkling, shimmering white and pulsating lights in pale shades of blue, yellow, orange and pink.

Then…carrying on freezing night air from the black distant forest was a strange metallic piping sound! A bit puzzling…this sound I had never heard before. Starting very high-pitched, it probably began actually inaudible to human hearing…then steadily tapering down to a deep voiced double-sounded ending: "… eeeeeeeeeeee-OW! OO-oo!"

This could only be the call of a bull elk! Yes, the rut had now officially begun! That distant call was a most fascinating phenomenon bringing the silent black woods to life…also a spontaneous feeling of cheer inside my chest and a smile to my face.

Quiet moments passed. Then a second call farther away resounded through the still, dark forest. "Were these the two bulls I had seen two weeks ago?" I wondered. Back and forth…their metallic piping calls continued…carrying on the cold calm air along the valley, through forest and up the mountainsides! Soon, another bull entered the conversation from a third direction!

Their wonderful wild calls continued communicating for a half-hour...then silence returned for the night.

These Rocky Mountain elk were seriously at play, enjoying life in its present short moments! The setting was perfect: with a touch of frost and fresh cold air to activate the bulls' breeding impulse; with wide grassy meadows to clash antlers in; with open forest of poplar and pine, birch and tamarack, willow and spruce...to run in. Above this elks' playground there spread from mountain to mountain a skyful of silent, countless-billion-year-old lights flickering and softly glowing white, blue, green, yellow, orange, red and pink. And this cold dark valley was very awake, very alive...much as the sky...sparkling with subtle animate life-light, as it had for countless aeons and would for countless more!

Yukon
and
Northern British Columbia

RUSTLES, SHUFFLES AND WHIMPERS

The drive from southern British Columbia to my destination in Yukon would be about two thousand miles and I knew not whether by such venture, I would make or lose money. Springtime had arrived in the far North, the time for morel mushrooms to grow in the boreal forest. I decided to take a chance. Pickup truck loaded with grub, camping supplies, two spare tires on rims and various spare parts, I was on the highway from morning until late at night. By end of the second day I was somewhere along gravelly Highway 37 where arose the lovely wild Cassiar Mountains.

That long stretch of road was a most pleasant one since almost no human lived there: no powerlines and no fences marred the naturalness which came right to highwayside! Logging had only began in the area, so forests, valleys and meadows were much like a thousand years ago! At one point a huge blond grizzly bear was grazing grass in the right-of-way, but in a humorous manner…with front legs down onto elbows while its back legs stood straight up! As I approached, braking and slowing down…a wide massive head turned my way. With a long snout and narrow eyes, it looked a bit funny-faced but was simultaneously very serious and…somewhat scarey. I stopped to watch and it watched back for about half-a-minute. Then the powerful, long-clawed beauty very slowly rose and stepped casually into tall willows, out of sight. This was the largest grizzly I had ever seen!

Some time later a great grey owl was standing perfectly still on the gravel shoulder with its back towards me and just looking away, staring down the long straight road. Slowing down, I thought it would fly but no…it kept motionless on the spot as I passed. Later on I thought it may have been sick…maybe poisoned by wolf-kill bait? I hoped not! But kept driving…driving…into Yukon…driving…driving…until finally, late on the fifth day under a big orange sky, I arrived at the morel mushroom area. Quickly finding a good place to camp beside a grove of trembling aspen trees, I parked, then fell asleep almost immediately!

Late next morning I went on an anxious scout up onto hills a half-mile above camp. With one four-imperial-gallon bucket in hand I entered the mixed forest of spruce, pine and poplar… slowly zigzagging up a steep semi-open clay slope, working towards the bench above. Here a handful of mushrooms presented themselves, widely spaced on this forty-five degree slope… discouraging but likewise raising hope that something better was ahead. Finally, I reached the top edge then stepped onto flat ground, happy for that! Now I could see that this was an extensive forested bench of mostly lodgepine and trembling aspen. Here too, was a patch of numerous young morels but too small to pick.

Little openings in treetops lit up the leafy canopy with spots of bright blue and white sky. This beautiful forest ceiling was spangled with emerald green fine-pointed starlets and dotted with pale green leafy ovals and hearts. Shafts of sunshine lit up the shadows with bright stripes and wide transparent bars of light. And the moss-and-lichen-covered ground was a variegation of green, white, ochre and rusty-red…dark or glowing. This was a very silent place and almost breezeless. Walking farther northward…I was crossing over a quiet thick patch of moss when in the near distance, faint indistinct shuffling sounds brought me to a halt! Directly ahead came the rustling of swishing brush…along with barely audible high-pitched whimpers and squeals. Then, filtering past the treetrunks and bushes came a few short low-pitched doglike sounds, but also quite indiscernible.

I wondered, did I have the company of other pickers out with their pet dog? So, avoiding that direction I began working away southward along the wide bench. Mushrooms were growing sporadically and although sparse, this area had not been previously picked. I could see over extensive ground more tiny morels here and there, also too young to pick so planned on returning some other day. Once at the southern end where the bench pinched off, I moved down a steep western slope onto the lower flat of swampy dips and little rolling mossy mounds.

Here were some old moose tracks in the dried mud and another sparse pick of morels. This walking up and down, over and under, was physically hard work…but the day was most pleasing with its soothing silence and almost no mosquitoes! My total pick was one four-gallon bucket in about three hours. Back at camp by early afternoon, I spread them out onto a plastic tarp for drying in the sunshine and slight breeze. The sky looked benign…mostly blue and with a few distant white cumulous clouds on the southern horizon, so it was again safe to leave camp at least an hour or so.

I thought now to scout for awhile the easy way, by driving the highway. Less than half-a-mile along two adult moose came into view! Standing under tall old trees in the open poplar forest about forty yards off, they looked as if planning to cross the highway. One was a cow and one a bull with short velvet antlers just starting to sprout several knobs. I slowed…then stopped to watch. But on seeing my truck come to a stop, they panicked and bolted back into the woods running at full speed! That was most unusual! I had seen moose near roads farther south many times, remaining either unconcerned or only mildly afraid.

This fearful response I thought could be explained in just one way: moose must be heavily hunted here from the highway. Having driven several thousand miles of Yukon's highways and roads over the years, I saw very few of these stilt-legged animals although most of the ground be prime moose habitat. For such vast areas of perfect habitat, moose numbers were strangely sparse! I thought that was not due to a harsh winter climate — as Yukon's government song-and-dance says — but was and is…mostly due to excessive uncontrolled hunting. With such thoughts, I continued along the highway some distance so not to interfere with the two moose.

Coming to a forest of aspen and poplar, I stopped and went exploring on foot. Among these trees some lovely wildflowers were beginning to bloom, looking very similar to the deep pink wild bleedinghearts of Vancouver Island, except these Yukoners were two-coloured: pink and yellow. This area was quite flat with patches of large old spruce, trembling aspen and lodgepine growing as separate groups. Few morels appeared but the presence of one snowshoe hare, a spruce grouse and three-toed woodpecker…all cheered me up. And near the top of one very tall, thick-boughed old spruce tree…were the sandpapery voices of hungry fledgling redtailed hawks, safe in a big nest of sticks and twigs. The parent birds were also quite vociferous but only about my presence nearby on the ground below. I did not linger. After walking a lot of dud ground, I did manage to eke another half-bucket from this flat, though.

With varying success in other parts of this boreal forest over the next three days, I was becoming more and more skeptical about the possibility of making reasonable profit. Then on the fifth day I climbed back up to the bench that I had first scouted: where the enigmatic sounds had been. This time I went in that same direction following the same route, picking mushrooms here and there along the way. Again the woods were very silent in the almost-still air…other than a few squirrels chitchatting to each other and at me! A lovely forest this was with the ground patched in alternating green moss and grey or tan lichen under the pine and spruce, while sturdy-stemmed bushes of a type unknown to me grew under the more open poplar-treed parts. Walking over one thick moss patch I came to a packed down animal trail about one-and-a-half feet wide and six inches deep, running through it.

An old trail, it ran approximately north-south by compass. Stepping over the trail, I wandered eastward scouting and getting familiar with various natural markers in the forest, which I would use as directional bearings now and possibly in the near future. About half-an-hour later, curling back to north and west then pushing through thick buckbrush, I entered a little opening with a yellowish-tan coloured dirt-mound at its edge. Large footprints of three to five-inch diameter were moulded all around into this dry hard dirt! This was a most pleasing sight to me! These tracks had been left several weeks previously when the ground was yet muddy from spring snowmelt and rain.

Now I took a cautious, closer look at the rounded mound. Nearer to it were some very recent, indistinct scuffmarks in the dirt. On its northeast side was the entranceway of a den…where small prints predominated the pattern of four-toed footprints. The entrance gently sloped down at about thirty degrees some indiscernible distance past a network of tiny rootlets and into the silent darkness. Now I was excited! This was a wolf den!

The old tracks and fresh scuffmarks of pups at and near the entrance indicated it to be very recently abandoned. So…this was my answer to the uncertain sounds of four days before! My presence then must have brought the wolf family fear or caution enough to move farther away. Well, I was happy at least that the pups were grown sufficiently enough to travel on their own legs!

Certain that they would not return, I kept scouting for and picking morels. Nearby were numerous large wolf tracks in dry clay where the ground was open and devoid of moss. As I worked some distance west of the den the bench began sloping downward. A short way down, lay an unusually large old ground-snag with its big roots twisting and winding up towards the sky. Rusty brown and grey, this barkless long-dead giant spruce tree was about three-and-a-half feet in diameter at the butt…unusual for the boreal forest! I went down for a closer look. Right beside it was a sight both pleasing and amusing!

Growing from inside of five very large wolf pawtracks were several good-sized yellow and bronze coloured morels! Never before had I seen anything like this. Wolf tracks of various sizes were stamped into the half-dry mud everywhere, all around the ancient snag…and mushrooms were growing among them. From this trampled ground and almost countless pawprints I could see that the wolves had, for their own reason, much favoured this old rooted snag as the place to be! It must have been their lounging area and sentry post, I thought. Wishing I had brought my camera, I was hesitant to pick the mushrooms…but too far from the truck to go back. So…I just sat on the wolves' big rooted log awhile to look at and enjoy this rare sight! From this point, the wide open view to west and southwest was a panorama of the broad flat valley and distant dark bluegreen rounded mountains. This big old snag was an excellent lookout for the wolves!

But then reluctantly…I picked them, fifty-some-odd morels, and moved on higher up then to the northwest. A couple of hours later with two full buckets, I proceeded back down…eventually coming to an old half grown-in, windfall-laden mining company's road which I followed. It led in a long curve back down towards the truck. This day was cloudless and hot! Now out in the open…sweat beaded and dripped from my face and ears. Sections of this roadway were of very fine pale grey and tan dust, varying from two to five inches deep: a mix of ancient volcanic ash, fire ash and clay particles. With each step the dust would kick up into small expanding clouds that drifted all around, making breathing difficult.

As I paced downward to a switchback, one set of animal tracks appeared…sunk into the dust in the distance ahead. Coming closer, I could see that they were wolf tracks and very recent — as fresh as my bootprints! One adult wolf had passed by only minutes or at most a couple of hours ago. So…I was not as alone as I had thought! The forepaw was another five-inch long track which I measured with fingers and palm of my right hand. And these tracks led along the road directly towards the back of my truck!

Two hours previously when I parked, no tracks were there on the dust-laden old road. The wolf had momentarily stopped, apparently inspecting my truck. Then it passed by the left side and trotted away down the road in the direction of my camp. This happened probably while I was above on the bench at the wolves' wintering den. The big adult wolf had been inspecting my mobile den at about the same time!

Several days later, carrying two four-gallon buckets I went upslope onto the same bench not far from the wolf den but a bit north, through a narrow hardrock ravine. Near the upper end of this big-treed ravine, on the ground as if materializing from a greybrown void…a half-dozen very large morels suddenly appeared three yards ahead. So perfectly camouflaged by twigs, needles, sunshine and shadows, they were invisible from the near distance and almost invisible from just one yard away! I was both amused and wondered by the way that Nature could hide them!

These morels were in a variety of muted natural colours which changed chameleon-like as sunlight intensity and shadows changed: grey, brown, yellow, rust, pink, green and black. Their ribbed and mottled pattern would imitate twigs and combined with shape, at times looked like spruce or pine cones lying on the ground. Even so, with experience I had acquired a fairly good but imperfect eye for them.

Snipping off their tops with a pair of plastic-handled scissors then moving up onto the flat bench, I checked ground a bit southward…then retraced my route northwest, carrying an almost empty bucket. Now that inexplicable feeling sometimes known as the sixth-sense…forced its way into my consciousness and physical body as an indefinite sensation of danger nearby. I was familiar with this experience from other times when alone in the woods. Not merely fear or phantasy, it had been real several times, more often than not — so I knew to take heed! I stood still and quiet…listening and looking carefully around in all directions. I heard nothing and saw nothing unusual.

Not to worry though…since I wore a holstered pepperspray on my right hip as self-defence. It also acted as an inducer of courage; I could walk the woods without fear. Entering a stand of tightly growing small lodgepine trees, I plodded slowly along as quietly as possible…keeping the two buckets, handles held in left hand, away from treetrunks and ground-snags…while still looking and listening keenly in all directions. Another thirty paces or so…then I decided on turning to the right at a point where one bushy green pinetree was lying on the ground. I thought to climb over the fallen tree and check that way.

As I turned, stepping towards it, one bucket banged against an eight-inch pinetree — sounding out a loud drum-like, hollow clunk! A split-second later — a rustling and solid thumping on the ground began from just behind the bushy green tree! And a large, almost invisible translucent tan and rust cloud billowed up into view. My eyes strained to identify this amorphous, pale moving object. Then recognition struck — a large cinnamon bear!

Standing broadside yet half-invisible in the cloud of rusty-tan coloured dust, with its big fuzzy head cocked sideways, the bear eyed me! Distance between us was a mere five yards! Slowly…I reached to my right hip, lifting the pepper spraygun to my side, then to chest while flipping out the orange safety-wedge with right thumb. The bear stood motionless…watching. I too, stood still…staring back.

Its sleepy-eyed, yet otherwise expressionless face and ear position indicated that — although as surprised as me — the big bear had neither fear-of nor ill-will towards me. By the big cinnamon's droopy eyelids and relaxed body expression, it looked to be still half-asleep! Maybe it was not sure if it were still in the dream-state or awake in the matter-realm? Our silent mutual observing continued for ten seconds or so. But since this bear seemed so docile, I decided to make the first move — away. Under this circumstance…that seemed both prudent and appropriate!

In slow-motion I stepped back behind the eight-inch pine, then rotated slowly ninety degrees and began casually longstepping away. The bear just stood still, silently watching…and I kept glancing back at it. Since the trees here were growing quite close together, I could quickly disappear from the bear's visual perception. I stepped around trees keeping as straight a line as possible towards the ravine, while listening keenly and continuing to look back over my shoulder to the left in the bear's direction. The big cinnamon bear remained motionless, with head swivelling only slightly while watching me quietly step away…as more and more little pine trees filled in the visual space between us. Within seconds I had vanished from the bruin's sight and it from mine! Back at the rocky ravine's edge I stopped to look back and listen…nothing in sight and no sound. The cinnamon beauty seemed to have no interest in following. Even so, I made haste straight down the shady gully!

By remaining silent, nonaggressive and slow-moving, I never gave this rust-coloured blackbear an excuse to become aggressive. And once out of its sight and maybe its hearing, below the bench edge I moved as quickly and silently as possible directly down the hillside towards the truck. I thought of how lucky I was to have accidentally hit a tree with one bucket! Thumping out that dull drum-like sound, so unique to an empty four-gallon plastic bucket — the cinnamon bear was awakened from its cozy daytime snooze! Comfortably shaded from the hot mid-day sunshine, it was hidden, lying under pine boughs and almost directly in line with my planned route over the fallen green pinetree. This time, I could thank my noisy carelessness! Otherwise…I would have walked almost to the bear and while hopping over the bushy pine boughs — would have stepped right beside, or worse — onto it!

SIX ARE COMPANY SEVEN ARE NOT

It was late spring when I drove to a small town in northern British Columbia to hire a floatplane. After a few days there I met a good bushpilot whose flight rate was more affordable than others in town, so arranged to fly over several high mountains about twenty-five miles to a small lake. I had three weeks' supply of canned grub, 30-30 rifle, two pepper sprayguns, tent, tarps, barrel-stove and various other necessities for camping out alone…and was ready to go.

Two days later under a big all-blue sky the pilot arrived in his silvery grey floatplane. Fuelling and loading up took about half-an-hour, then with a full load we taxied out onto the smooth deep blue lake for takeoff. This was my first flight by floats and my first time going out alone so far from human amenities. I was quite excited and a bit apprehensive. While idling at the bay's north end the pilot briefed me about safety and emergency, then pulled the throttle back. The engine roared…and in a few moments pontoons left water! Now floating on air…we were looking at the sky!

As the plane rose higher we curved to the right over town then flew straight, following along a wide valley. I watched the ground below for wildlife, hoping to see moose or caribou. We flew above rounded dark-treed humps…over open pale green subalpine…then near some high treeless rocky peaks. There, I was hoping to see white dots which would have been Dall sheep or mountain goats. The rugged rusty mountains were lovely but devoid of both white animal species!

Animal trails were conspicuous on mountainsides and in open valleys, but the higher trails seldom-used now because mountain goats were shot out long ago and Dall sheep shot out not-so-long ago. The pilot pointed out mountains where he would in the past see Dall sheep as he flew by, mentioning that they were now almost extinct in these mountains — killed off by hunting guides! In the open valleys below were tiny pale bluegreen lakes, brown ponds, shiny meandering streams and distinct moose trails…but I saw no moose and no caribou. Obviously their numbers too, were low. Silently, I wondered how many hunters this pilot had flown out over the years.

Time also flew. Soon my lake became visible, glowing silver-white in the near distance. Now gradually decreasing elevation we approached the lake, circled over twice…then set down in a southerly direction onto the glass-flat surface…a very smooth touch-down! Near the lake's south end we taxied slowly to a safe docking point where shoreline was devoid of large rocks. I stood on the right pontoon with the rope and watching for large rocks just below surface in the crystal-clear water. When in maybe a foot of water, I stepped off and tied up to a sturdy-looking lakeside willow bush. Taking one pepper spraygun from a pontoon, I looped it to my belt, quickly paced up onto a small flat bench then into the sloping pine woods to check for morel mushrooms. Yes…I could see some here and there as singles and little groups! I was in luck!

Picking a few, I ran back to the plane to start unloading. We had docked at the perfect spot. Except — mosquitoes were immediately on the attack, telling me that this earthly paradise could also be hell!

We unloaded…and to start I carried my tent, rifle and second pepper spraygun up to the little semi-open flat under lodgepine trees just above lakeshore. This little flat was a very old campsite, a good place to set up the tent. Old axe-chopped stumps, scarred treetrunks, rusty nails and a crudely-made table told a mute tale of visitors who were here long ago. The table and stumps were well-decorated with thick limegreen lichen growth which I estimated to be sixty or more years old! No one had camped here since then.

The pilot mentioned that he would be flying over this way at times and if I wanted him to stop, to put out a signal. I had a bright red teeshirt which we agreed to use; as a signal I would tie it on top of a particular willow buckbrush at lake's edge where the floatplane was now docked. I gave him the handful of morels to take home then he taxied slowly northward some distance, turned around and pulled the throttle. Standing at lakeshore I watched as the shining silver plane roared southward, lifted and flew past! I waved as he passed by. He circled back homeward, then gave a wave of the wings. The floatplane slowly shrank in the sky and then vanished around one beautiful brown rocky mountain peak. Suddenly its engine drone too, became nonexistent.

All that I heard now were mosquitoes buzzing and tiny wavelets trickling softly at lakeshore. During these few minutes I squashed a lot of mosquitoes…which were unrelenting! They were certainly starved for blood! The time was about eleven a.m. so I had a full day ahead yet. Pacing quickly back up to the pretty little moss and lichen-covered flat, the first object I looked for in my bags was a bottle of canola oil which I opened immediately to smear onto hands, face, ears, head and neck. This was my nontoxic mosquito repellent. It did an adequate job, preventing about ninety percent from biting. Then I made haste to set up the puptent and organize camp; it seemed that my only complete escape from mosquito harassment would be inside the tent!

Anxious to scout the ground for morels…as soon as I set up the tent, I looped the compass string through a buttonhole in my left shirt pocketflap, then picked up a four-gallon bucket, scissors and was away up onto the gently undulating slope just above camp. Fairly recent moose tracks were on the ground so I had to watch for that big animal. And I was happy to not see any bear tracks! But there were also two old sets of wolf tracks in the mud. Even so, I had some confidence in the pepper spraygun. After a short walk through spruce and pine forest, something else brought a smile to my face: the good crop of mushrooms! Morels at various stages of growth were consistent on this ground so the four-gallon bucket was full in about an hour!

Returning to camp, I laid out two large plastic tarps on the ground where sunlight would shine most then carefully dumped the fragile fresh morels onto one tarp for drying. The day was beautifully sunny with only a few small nonthreatening white clouds and a slight breeze blowing from the lake: just right for solar drying. By now I had worked up a hunger and it was also time to rest a bit, so walked over to the bench edge for lunch. There, one large root that curved and curled at the base of a good-sized spruce tree, made a perfect seat and scenic viewpoint. The lake was a lovely ripply calm and completely clear close to shore. A loon called from across the lake…as if it be a welcome to this peaceful wild place! I loved the sound. Of course, it was not meant for me but most pleasing anyway.

Opening two cans, one of peas, the other of herring, I wolfed them down cold and while at it noticed how this spot would be best for placing the barrel-stove…for safety sake and for enjoying the wide-open view up, down and across the lake. Next, I levelled gravel and dirt near my big curving root-chair then placed the stove there, assembled and attached the chimney parts: three straight lengths and one adjustable elbow. The long chimney tapered upward past the big spruce, fastened with wire and hung from a sturdy lower branch. The last step was to plug the pipe-stove connection with little pieces of aluminum foil which I pushed into the joint cracks with a knife blade. That done, I went back into the woods carrying two buckets but this time following a mossy animal trail.

This trail, I noticed went right through the middle of camp but was not recently nor frequently used. I hoped it was not due to be! Following through a low bushy area there appeared a small short-tailed, rusty coloured rodent…so busy in the moss looking for food that it was oblivious of my presence three feet away. It was a cute little redbacked vole, the not-so-fortunate creature whose existence is crucial as a major food source for several carnivores: weasels, marten, fisher, fox, owls and hawks. They are probably a secondary food item for wolverines, wolves, lynx and bears too.

After this pleasant meeting, I left the trail and climbed higher to a semi-open area that was beautifully coloured with little random patches of wildflowers. Here were tall fragile plants with multiple stems drooping over in little clusters of two-coloured flowers of brilliant yellow and deep pink. This plant I had seen for the first time in Yukon and not knowing its name, seeing its similarity to southern British Columbia's wild bleedingheart, called it the Yukon bleedingheart. Other flower patches separate from these were blooming a solid deep yellow and on closer inspection, their yellow daisy-like petals and circular domed brown centre showed them to be brown-eyed susans. These were the visual pleasures all around to momentarily enjoy as I hiked in search of morels.

Just above this bright flowery area was a good mushroom patch then another to the north of it…so by late afternoon I had filled two more buckets. Following the same way back to camp I could hear in the distance to the south another of my favourite little woodland friends — the northern threetoed woodpecker. I felt good about this, knowing I would one day soon meet it at close range! And I was happy with the crop of morels, sensing that it would pay for the flight cost and bring in some profit beyond that…as long as the good weather continued for adequate drying.

Once back down at camp, I spread out the mushrooms onto a second tarp to start them drying in the late afternoon sunshine. By now I was too tired for another pick so rounded up some wood and fired up the stove. Dumping two cans of food into the frying pan, my only cooking utensil…I relaxed somewhat, while not swatting the odd mosquito. Heat from the stove along with some leaking smoke kept insects away; I sat as close as possible to the stove! Now I could enjoy the bright peach-and-orange sunset sky!

A short time later, sounds of swirling water began in the near distance to the north along lakeshore. I could see through overhanging willow and upcurved leaning spruce trees, the large dark form of a cow moose slowly walking in the shallows towards camp. Sitting still, I watched and waited. As she approached closer, she came into full view and beside her nearer to shore, tiptoed one tiny calf! It was a sweet little thing, with dark auburn-coloured coat and looking to be one week young or less. Seemingly fearless of me, the cow walked past just twenty yards below with her wee one at her feet! Their appearance so close to camp was another most pleasant welcome. It felt good knowing that I was not alone…having some animate neighbours other than mosquitoes.

Cow and calf just kept walking calmly southward along the shallow gravelly shoreline, soon disappearing behind willow and dwarf birch bushes. I sat happily on my root-chair listening to them step away in large and little swirls of water. The brightly coloured western sky gradually faded then began to darken as evening was setting in. Mosquitoes became more numerous and I was tiring of their irritating buzz, so went to the tent for relief. Once inside, I lay on my back looking up and listening to the steady humming of countless thousands outside!

Through the pale blue tent top, black shapes of mosquitoes were visible in the hundreds either perched, flying or landing on it. Now I could actually enjoy their hum from a relaxing distance of two feet or so! A maddening buzz outside, it now became an almost musical hum! And the geometric pattern of their countless legs and bodies too, perched everywhere on top made a quite pleasing ceiling decoration of black and blue. So many of them landed there and on the tent sides that soon most light previously filtering through the thin cotton fabric was blocked out by their almost solid-black mass. I was certain that in this area a person would either go insane or be actually drained dry of blood or both, without a mosquito-proof tent as an escape. But on this night…they literally hummed me to sleep!

Early next morning I awakened to a deeply calm silence. The air was cold and still. Unzipping the tent entrance, I crept slowly out…holding a pepperspray in front. Then lifting the tent-fly, first visually scanning the shady camp, I saw no large unwanted visitor. Now the brightly lit far side of the lake and sunny westward mountains attracted my eyes. Standing up, I pivotted around in a circle to make sure I was alone. Even mosquitoes were not yet up, with the air so cold. The dark blue eastward mountain too, was in shade and pale yellow beams of sunlight streaked through its uppermost canyons. The Sun was yet behind the mountain…still low in a light blue cloudless sky. What a beautiful morning this was!

Walking to the stove and scenic-view lounging spot, I stood soaking in this visual beauty… while breathing in some slow deep breaths of cold fresh air. The air was both invigorating and subtly pleasant, so filled with the aroma of spruce and pine trees. And far off in sunshine at the lake's shallow south end were my two friends: the cow moose and her wee calf! Mother was out feeding, standing in water to her chest and surrounded by yellow-flowered pond lilies while baby stood in the shallows, also chest-deep. I went back to the tent and dug out my twenty-power spotting scope, returning to the big-rooted scenic kitchen to watch them awhile.

Not yet ready for breakfast, I took a bucket and scissors then walked towards a little creek that I had seen from the air before landing. It was a two hundred yard walk south of camp. There, I was happy to see the fast-moving water — and crystal clear — running in a deep but narrow gravelly channel. Kneeling onto fours, I sniffed the water and dipped fingers into it. This water was almost ice-cold…and certainly potable! Cupping my hands and scooping water up, I tasted, then drank it. Water could not be better!

Beside this creek and in the lower dips nearby grew thick willow buckbrush and dwarf birchbrush. Here visibility was too limited for comfort. Although I had not seen bear tracks yet, I was afraid of meeting a bear at close range. I had hoped any bears would have vacated the area to go fishing for salmon which were spawning in a river about fifty miles away. But now I was curious about what lay beyond the little creekside jungle. Jumping across the creek, I pushed and fought my way through this thick tangle until breaking out to a semi-open forest of spruce, lodgepine, poplar and birch. On the flat ground between these trees were extensive patches of yellow and pink…more of the same beautiful wildflowers of yesterday! And nearby in reindeer lichen and ash were mushrooms, not numerous but mostly good-sized.

I managed to half-fill the bucket and while so-doing noticed a fairly recent wolf track among several older sets of adult moose tracks. With my curiosity satisfied, I turned back towards camp with a plan to return on another day. Heading back, I took a different route following the cold creek upstream some distance along its south side, then pushed slowly through more tough thick willow bushes…stepping onto precarious, wobbly rounded pillows of thick floating muskeg, crossing to the creek's north side. Although these spongy moss-pillows wobbled with each step, they held my weight!

Just upstream lay a wide, long stretch of clear calm water with many such muskeg pillows blotched with maroon, green, tan and yellow colours…little islands, separate or in small clusters, all afloat. I was not certain what to call this water body: pond or lake? But since its water was absolutely clear, clean, freezing cold and good to drink I preferred calling it a lake. I thought this very unusual water body must be formed by melting permafrost underneath and across at the shady eastern side.

Skirting along this unique little lake a short way then angling downward through a predominantly spruce stretch, when nearing camp a different cow moose with her large yearling calf were foraging in shallows at the south end near the main lake's outlet! There, a small swift-moving river began dropping quickly into noisy rapids. The two moose were only about fifty yards away, close enough for a good look; I peeked at them through the lower boughs of a thick spruce tree. They had not heard me…no doubt due to the loud river rapids between us. She was submerging her head completely, pulling up lakeweeds and lilies then with big floppy ears pointing down and back, peacefully gazing about as she munched them down. Her yearling was also foraging underwater but closer to shore. Sparkling clear water ran off and dripped all around.

These moose were a cheering sight but I had work to do so continued onward out of their sight, heading back to camp. By now sunlight was shining strong into camp so I set out the morels to dry, got the stove going and fried up some breakfast. Next, with two buckets and rubberboots stuffed with plastic grocery bags I went uphill to the benches, ridges and slopes. This day was a good one. In two trips up, I was rewarded with five full buckets. On returning to camp in early evening, for supper I opened a few cans of grub and heated it in the frying pan on top of the smokey barrel-stove.

Sitting on my big spruce root overlooking the lake, to southwest I could see the same cow moose and yearling still grazing at the lily shallows. Near them a pair of goldeneye ducks were paddling, dipping and diving. By now the Sun had dropped below the deep blue and maroon-brown western mountains which with Earth's rotation, seemed to rise into the sky. Above them, sunset clouds hovered…changing very slowing as shades of cream, orange, peach, pink and mauve. So calm and peaceful…this was a dreamlike evening.

As shadows deepend imperceptibly all around, once more from the north came sounds of shallow water splashing! There they were, yesterday's cow moose with her tiny auburn calf… again wading along lakeshore towards camp. She stepped into deeper water and her wee calf, following closely behind, began swimming. Continuing thus closer and closer until almost below camp, now spying me, she turned back and slowly waded away but deep enough for her calf to keep swimming. She was a bit shy this time; I knew not why. The two silhouettes gradually blend within the dark greenblack leaning spruce trees at lake's edge, disappearing behind them.

Such natural beauty and the silence attendant with it induced a deep calmness within my body and mind. This relaxed calmness was a phenomenon that I had not experienced back out there…in the realm of civilized humanity. And my sitting very close to the stove kept a hundred or so mosquitoes far enough away, as they shunned its radiant heat and the little wafts of escaping smoke: that, along with a newly acquired ability to mildly ignore their obnoxious buzz…allowed a degree of calm enjoyment of the living beauties all around!

As evening sky darkened to the east and zenith from pale bluegrey to grey, stars began faintly showing. I walked calmly back to the quasi-safety of my little tent. Again out of their reach, I listened to the pleasing distant hum of thousands just outside while nodding off slowly into the realm of dreams. I slept on my side with one ear to the ground. Some unknown time later, a distant but heavy solid pounding…coming through the ground…brought my consciousness back to a semi-awakened state. Mixed with a dreamy mind and although apparently coming from some distance away, I recognized the thumping as not part of dream! Opening my eyes… the night was in its fullest darkness. It was also very cold. Even the mosquitoes had retired in silence…too cold for them to move.

I lay on my side, left ear to the ground…listening. There were now two distinct drum-like sounds approaching from the south towards the tent: one set was slow, deep, heavy and solid while the other quick, faint, light and delicate. Closer and closer…the animals were very near, now just east of the tent. I smiled with pleasure: knowing what, who, they were. They kept on northward…I was in no fear. Actually a real enjoyment this was to hear…the hoofbeats of my friendly cow moose with her wee baby following closely behind! As their hoofbeats gradually faded away, midnight's gentle silence returned and a happy mind soon drifted back into the realm of dreams.

Next morning, I listened intently for unwanted sounds in camp…before cautiously crawling out of the tent doorway! The air was still and cold. Silence pervaded the forest…I was alone and mosquitoes were not yet up. Walking over to the stove, I could see the second moose cow with her yearling calf breakfasting at the lake's south end, near a little island about two hundred yards distant. Above them the sky was perfectly clear blue and beyond, dark early morning shadows accentuated the greygreen treed hills and rocky brown bluffs across a blue-black lake. Pleasant plunking and trickling sounds of splashing and dripping water moved unhindered along lakesurface to my camp…while cold fresh air with a subtle scent of sprucetree pitch acted quickly to clear my sleepy mind.

I slipped two pepperspray holsters onto my leather belt and started the fire. After wolfing-down breakfast I went down the bushy bankside to lake's edge to wash out a couple of tincans. Cleaning out cans right after eating had always been my way of keeping the camp food-smell-free…so that bears would have less reason to approach! As I walked over thick spongy muskeg approaching the shallow lakeside, a sudden swish-and-plunk sound brought to me to alert! What was this? Looking hard and long at the water and reeds I expected to see a little mudcloud somewhere beneath the crystal-clear water, with a frog or toad under it. But there was nothing. It seemed to have disappeared; whatever the cause, now had me wondering.

Thoroughly cleaning the cans, I took off their paper labels then squashed them flat. Next, they and other cans of the previous day went into a plastic grocery bag with a short rope tied to it. Then submerging it under three large rocks, I tied the rope to one sturdy willow bush in case a storm brought heavy waves. Following my steps back to camp, still on the low lakeside flat I passed the short, moose-trimmed willows and another specie of bush that varied from two to seven feet tall. This was a patch of dark green-leaved shrubs, aglow with little deep yellow buds and five-petalled starlike bright yellow flowers.

Then climbing the steep dirtbank to camp and eager to start working, into one bucket went the scissors, a small bottle of canola oil and a bottle of drinking water from the little deep creek; I headed uphill carrying two buckets. It was not long until a few good-sized morels were visible in fire ash, moss and needles, along with more that were too tiny yet to pick. Seeing these was encouraging and likewise energizing...so I worked hard and fast! As I wandered up slopes, along ridges and gullies, the warm morning sunshine felt so good on my face. But mosquitoes too, activated by it, were becoming more and more numerous. I stopped at one little flowery bench to smear on a layer of canola oil. It went on especially thick over hands, ears and face!

Here were little clumps and loose patches of the brown-centred yellow daisies and one set of large but very old long-clawed bear tracks. Nearby was an old pile of bear dung consisting completely of plant matter, dropped by a grizzly. By all appearance this evidence was left the previous year...which was comforting! Also running through this flowery flat were adult wolf tracks but more recent...of two or three weeks before I arrived. I was hoping to see a wolf but thought it unlikely since a year or two previously there had been a British Columbia government wolf-kill in this region!

Now from the pine-treed slope above came pleasing sounds of a little docile bird, one that I had become well acquainted with at other times in the northern forested wilds. Always cheering to hear, it was a high-pitched: "Gkee...gkee...gkee," then a medium-pitched, rolling, throaty: "K-k-k-k-k-k-k-k."

This chattery bird was probably the same one I'd heard two days ago. Wanting to see this little feathered friend, I headed uphill towards its calls. In a short while the bird became visible...at its nesthole ten feet up a small pine snag. It was a male with conspicuously brilliant yellow forehead patch. I had always felt befriended and accepted by these gentle black-and-white woodpeckers since they allowed me to come so close to them.

A female though, would be far more cautious, less approachable and would take longer to accept me near her nest. Even so, they had rarely been upset by my presence. Having only three toes on each foot they are called the northern three-toed woodpecker. The sound of these birds and their young chattering almost incessantly from the safety of their snag nest-hollow, is always the most pleasant and entertaining music! But here the chicks were either too young to chirp or the eggs had not yet hatched. The nesthole was silent. Probably, the female was sitting inside.

I continued on...busy in my way as the birds were in theirs. In a few hours both buckets were full plus one plastic grocery bag, so I returned to camp. More blue and orange plastic tarps were laid onto the ground, leaving a narrow walkway between in the shape of an L about eighteen inches wide. Carefully, I dumped the morels...spreading them onto tarps for drying in the warm sunshine and breeze. Others from the first day's pick were now almost dry enough for bagging up. After a short rest of legs while enjoying the lovely lake and bird sounds in the trees around camp, I went out again for another pick...returning several hours later with another load.

By now my legs needed another rest and I had worked up a hunger, so got the barrel-stove going and heated supper up. While relaxing at my big root-chair, at least to a degree allowed by buzzing and biting mosquitoes...a more pleasant sound, a coarse vocalizing from the lake began filtering through spruce boughs and just beyond thick lakeside dwarf-birch bushes. Walking closer I could see a rust and grey-coloured mother goldeneye duck with eight fluffy grey ducklings, all paddling slowly past a rounded boulder and very near to lakeshore. I had my camera ready but they were too distant for a photograph. The ducklings looked to be just a day or two old...more little wild neighbours!

Again while sitting by the warm smokey stove as afternoon slowly transformed into a multi-coloured twilight...the air cooled and lakesurface shimmered, reflecting a myriad of bright spots in everchanging pink, mauve, blue, black and white. Now and then from the lake's far side, sounds...of ducks dabbling and a loon with its throaty yodel...drifted on the breeze. Just north of my vantage point the first cow moose once again appeared just on time, slowly wading knee-deep in the shallows with her tiny calf following. She came towards camp, out deep enough for her calf to swim...casually wading by just below about thirty yards away as her wee one swam closely behind. I sat silent and still thus to be nonthreatening, benign; this was the way to be accepted into a wild, nonhuman neighbourhood. Now I could see the behaviour pattern of this mother moose: every day she took her baby into the lake where it would learn about water and how to swim — crucial for safety from wolves, wolverines, coyotes and bears!

A short time after they had passed I went down to lakeside to wash the frying pan and wash-and-squash tincans. Once again on my approach there was that sudden little swish-and-bloop of water! I knelt down...looking and looking. The little perpetrator could not be seen...although the water was clear to bottom! What was this shy, invisible animal? Still puzzled, I returned to camp brushing by the beautiful yellow-flowered bushes which were now even more in bloom.

Now with sky darkening and air cooling, it was time to cover the mushrooms for the night. Extra tarps were laid over then weighted down along edges with rocks and wooden poles; this procedure was to protect the morels from nighttime dew and possible rainfall. Then I retired to the tent. I lay beside my loaded rifle and pepperspray — which were my security, my teeth, self-defence. Very tired...I was soon asleep.

Early next morning from dreams I snapped into a semi-awakened state, drawn back by an unusual sound above my head just outside the tent! Half-awake, I listened intently! Some animal was a mere foot or so away and about half-a-foot above ground level uttering a soft but raspy, medium toned: "Ih-ih-ih-ih...Ih-ih-ih-ih." I thought this may be a pine marten, porcupine, fisher, fox or wolverine.

As quietly as possible, I left the tent with pepperspray and flashlight in hand...but saw nothing in the early morning twilight. It could not have been a porcupine since it was gone within seconds. This animal was so very fleet-footed, I thought it must be either a marten, fisher or fox. If a wolverine, it would likely not have ran away! The air was very cold. Sunrise was about an hour away. Mosquitoes were yet semi-frozen to their overnight perches among the leafy brush. The cold air was so fresh, most comfortable without the mosquitoes! And this enigmatic twilight visitor was not far away just out of sight! Maybe I had not been cleaning out the frying pan enough?

I crawled back into the tent and nodded off to sleep. A couple of hours later, bright sunlight brought me back...another day was beginning. I got up, chopped wood and fired up the stove. Having noticed the first day here an old tincan dump overgrown with moss just below the bankside, I now went to see what good junk may be there. Kicking cans to the side with my high gumboots, I found two Hudson's Bay Company rum bottles embossed with the company's name, year 1670, shield and logo: "Pro Pelle Cutem." They were of the 1920s and 30s vintage, confirming the old camp's age. One bottle was a twenty-sixer, the other a half-pint: two nice keepsakes of the Depression years or before.

Happy with these I returned to my open-air kitchen and Nature viewpoint. Now I was surprised to see in the far distance at the southend shallows, this time three adult cow moose: one with wee auburn calf, one with its yearling and the other alone. So now I had five moose neighbours! Placidly grazing the aquatic plants, all three adults and yearling stood belly-deep in green and yellow-dotted skyblue water...completely submerging their heads then lifting up to chew and gaze about. Water ran and dripped off...creating brilliant white sparkling ripples on lakesurface. Each time, a few moments later the soft splashing sounds arrived at my side of the lake.

After breakfast, going down to the tincan washing spot as slowly and quietly as possible I looked hard at the shoreline muskeg and reeds. Peering into colourless still water, I tried to identify some small animate life-form but saw only the natural abstract patterns of aquatic plants, shadows, reflections, mud and twigs. Kneeling down very slowly onto the muskeg, I moved a can towards water's edge.

Once again, a quick swish-and-plunk of water just two feet out! Little silent ripples moved through the reeds imparting a slight totter to them. Reeds and grass waved gently back and forth, gradually slowing to a stop. Again...no mud disturbance showed on the bottom.

This was like looking at an abstract picture trying to see half-hidden objects which appear only bit by bit among the lines, colours and shapes. Bright sunlight reflected starlike from surface and shone to the muddy bottom, as deep green reeds cast vertical, crisscrossing and curving shadows onto the greybrown mud and onto each other. But I remained crouched and still, undaunted. Where was it? After several minutes of steady scrutinizing...from amid this complex abstract there finally appeared a little golden circle with black disc at its centre. It was an eye, quietly looking up at me from underwater among the reeds! Then slowly, bit by bit...this wee being's head and body form appeared...as if materializing from nothing! Almost motionless, now a very slight movement of gillcovers, translucent fins and tail became evident.

Well, well! A grin spontaneously developed on my face...such a pleasure meeting this life-form which was new to me. I could not help chuckling at this funny little being...with its duck-beak and tiger-stripes! It was about three inches long with grey, brown and whitish vertical stripes along its sides and back: perfect camouflage! The relatively large watchful eye glowed from below a flat forehead that tapered forward into a long flat duckbilled mouth. This was my first meeting with a northern pike: one as yet a long way from adulthood! A most pleasing way to start the day, this was!

By now sunshine was beaming down into camp so I uncovered the mushroom drying tarps, exposing morels to the Sun's heat and the breeze. This day, I decided to try panning for gold in the little ice-cold creek and to scout across it again, but as far as possible southward. With pan, shovel and one extra bucket, I went to the creek. I filled the bucket two-thirds for drinking water. Then rolling over some large rounded rocks and scooping gravel up with my small shorthandled shovel, three pans produced a touch of fine blacksand but nothing else of interest.

Slightly disappointed, I jumped across the creek, fought through the buckbrush jungle and continued to the low flowery flat area where I had picked before. Soon though, a cheerful sight came into view just ahead under pine trees and willow brush: little patches of closely grouped mushrooms were growing in profusion over a full acre of ground! This was one of those rare finds where one could pick on hands-and-knees and fill a four-gallon bucket in half an hour or less. I got down and crawled along, snipping morels as fast as I could.

As I neared one large snaggly old lodgepine tree there appeared to be some rusty metal lying at its base. Curious, I walked over for a closer look. To my surprise, here was a large old leghold trap with a short broken piece of heavy wire attached! Picking it up, I read on the bottom, "Longridge." This was a very old trap that looked handmade. By the size, it must have been used on wolves.

This ancient pine tree showed no scars, had no wire or nails in it, therefore was not where the trap had been set. I imagined how the trap would have got here. The broken wire hinted that a wolf...trapped so long ago...may have broken loose but died later at this tree. Or possibly the trap just fell off a trapper's dogsled into the snow? Whatever happened, this was another nice antique keepsake from the wilds of northern British Columbia.

With this rare find and the loaded mushroom patch, another happy day was beginning! The cloudless blue sky above and distant shish-sh-sh-sh-sh of a steeply dropping whitewater river brought even more cheer to this unique place and time. It was not long filling two buckets and two bags which, with the trap, I carried back across the little deep creek. Picking up the bucket of drinking water and goldpan, I very slowly headed back to camp…all that I could carry!

Later, on the second trip back to the wolf trap area, I took a slightly different route closer to the lake through a lumpy muskeg flat. I passed through a boar's nest of tangled spruce blowdowns, snags on the ground and hung-up at various angles…walking became very difficult and slow. Then a loud crash and snapping dry branches just twenty yards directly ahead stopped me! From within a little spruce thicket, a dark blackish brown cow moose jumped up and jogged towards the little river — crashing through brush with her large pale brown calf right behind! Crossing the rapids in a gangly trot, they kept pace up on the other side…through willow and dwarf birch until out of sight. I had come too close to their daytime bedding spot, so was glad that she ran away — not towards me as a protective mother might do! Well, now I knew one place to avoid.

Next day I went to the north and east of camp, up onto one blue and pink flowery slope. Some distance up, the soft sweet high-pitched voices of baby three-toed woodpeckers…gentle music to my ears…were steadily calling from their hollow snag about fifty yards farther uphill. I zigzagged gradually upward towards them, picking morels along the way. Once there, I sat on a small log about ten yards south of the nest-snag to listen…while also watching the parents come and go. As they approached the nest, usually one at a time, the parent before landing would often call out a slow: "Kee, kee…k-k-k-k-k." At that moment or upon hearing wingbeats approaching, there would be a great increase in volume of the babies' very rapid high-toned: "Kee-kee-kee-kee-kee-kee-kee…."

Here I noticed again that the yellow-topped male showed little caution when approaching, usually flying directly to the nesthole to feed the young. But the black-topped female due to my proximity exercised great caution, taking more time and a less direct approach, most often landing on other trees and snags to watch the human some moments first; that seemed like a natural response by the protective-minded mother. But after some time scrutinizing, she accepted me as no threat and began flying directly with a beakful of bugs and grubs to her hungry little gems.

Hardly a day passed without at least one such pleasing, or even unexpected, meeting. This remote place was so alive with wild things that boredom was not possible; they were so interesting, entertaining or exciting! In the same area next day just north of my three-toed friends' nest-snag, where some large bronze and blond morels grew in thick patches…I was hard at it. After picking them, leaving a full bucket there I slowly wandered upward into a forest of small pine trees and scattered trembling aspen.

As I approached one thick clump of lodgepine ten yards above, a sudden loud low-toned thumping of hooves and swishing of branches brought me to an instant halt! Simultaneously glancing that way, I glimpsed through a branchy maze of grey and green, a large dark brown vagueness and wee auburn moose trotting away downslope to the north! Happy I was to see the friendly cow moose and calf! That close, she could have easily trampled me but was kind enough to move away instead! Fortunately, she knew me — knew that I was no threat to her calf since they had waded and swam past camp every evening at sunset. Here, they had been bedded down for the day hidden safely within this shady treeclump. But I spoiled their rest by coming too close.

Continuing upward onto a long glacial clay hill, more mushrooms awaited me. Once I had filled another bucket, placing it in a cool shady spot under thick pine trees, I went scouting to the east...crossing over a wide pillowy yellowgreen muskeg swamp which was actually a long bay, part of the ice-cold lake of floating moss-pillows. Hopping from mossy islet to islet, each bouncing and sinking slightly...I crossed this precarious floating bridge! At the same time, a high-pitched excited piping call began from one distant spruce treetop: "Kee-kee-kee-kee-kee-u!" Perched there was a bird with long yellow legs. It flew closer, circled, then perched atop another sapling spruce as it continued almost nonstop with the sharp warning call: "Kee-kee-kee-kee-u! Kee-kee-kee-kee-kee-u!"

This bird, a lesser yellowlegs, continued scolding for quite some time after I had disappeared from its sight under the trees. It had such a broad sense of space, of privacy or safety...that it was actually telling me of a nest nearby; it would have been better to remain silent, I thought.

Now I stepped up onto another clay and gravel area of rolling humps and dips in mixed pine and aspen forest. Covering a lot of dud ground, I stopped at times to look at rocks. Although seeing nothing of special interest I did enjoy the fresh forest air with its evergreen and aspen leaf aromas...and the billowing white clouds drifting above, almost motionless in the robin's egg blue sky. Few mushrooms were growing but on one claybank I picked up an oddly shaped, large white bone that I had never seen before. It had a hole in the centre, no doubt a vertebra from some very large animal which I wishfully imagined may have been a woolly mammoth or something of that era!

Persisting, I walked the open poplar, aspen and pine forest for some long time before giving up. Returning with the bone and one bag of morels I jumped back across the long muskeg bay from islet to islet, while again being followed and scolded loudly by the yellowlegs. Proceeding along the clay mound under tightly growing lodgepine trees then down, I picked up one by one the two full buckets, heading for camp. Going down, I passed by the three-toed woodpeckers' nest-snag since I was in the mood for hearing their gentle musical speech. There, I paused to rest my legs and listen awhile, sitting on my same log...such sweet little birds, these.

Once back at camp I carefully dumped the fresh morels onto tarps and bagged up those that were dry. Evening arrived in its imperceptible but steady way. Again, the auburn calf swam slowly by...just behind mother. Then night's darkness crept in all around and stars twinkled far above. I lay in the tent with security alongside — rifle and peppersprays — while relaxing away from mosquitoes and slowly dozing off. I fell asleep...stars arose and moved westward in their curving pathway across the dark greyness of outer space. Some time along, a very rapid shaking sensation from side to side pulled my mind somewhat back. I just lay still, awake enough to observe. The side to side shaking continued at a very quick rate. Could this be an earthquake?

As I awoke more, became more oriented and observant, the fast but slight tremor continued for maybe a minute, then stopped. I waited for another...but all remained still. Yes...it was definitely a quake albeit a small one! By sleeping on the ground such tiny tremor was quite noticeable, more so than otherwise. I drifted back into a pleasant relaxed sleep.

Above, the stars continued their aeons-long circular movements and space gradually lightened from east to west. The new morning arrived and tiny warblers began to chip and sing around camp. A squirrel sounded out its all-is-well rattle. And I was soon up...then onto the rolls and dips hard at work, as I am sure my little neighbours were in their own ways.

After another hard leg-workout this day passed into evening. I sat by the stove keeping out of mosquitoes' reach…and watching deep blue shadows advancing slowly across the lake. Hardly a breeze now, the lake was mirror-calm and quiet except for a few peeping shorebirds barely audible, far away. It was not long until the cow moose with wee auburn calf came out of the forest at their favoured spot just north of camp. As I stood up, watching them approach, I accidentally dropped the axe. It clanged loudly against the stove! The mother spooked and — in a panic — started swimming out to deeper water! Her calf naturally followed in her wake. She kept going nonstop farther and farther…straight out!

Her tiny calf tried its best to keep up but lagged behind. I became fearful for the calf…not knowing how far it could swim. It was so young! The little island was near their swimming route so I hoped that be the cow's destination. But no — she just swam by it! She slowed a bit, waiting for her calf to catch up some, but never stopped!

Smaller and smaller, they slowly shrank into the distance…heading straight for the lake's shady far side. This lake was about one-third mile wide, seemingly a long distance for this two-weeks-young moose! I got out my twenty-power spotting scope to watch them. Mentally urging on the calf…slowly…ever so slowly…the pair swam. The cow reached shore where she stood looking back at her calf, waiting. Within the huge darkening mountain shadow I could see a tiny black dot…still at the surface. Another minute passed. Then another…until the little animal finally walked up onto the far shore!

I was immensely eased to see that! Slowly, cow and calf walked northward into the blueblack forest shadows. After this incident, I missed their company for three full days! Happily though, on the fourth day they were back near camp.

The tenth day arrived and as I worked the hills and hollows far above camp I could hear in the far distance the sound of a winged plane. I stood listening to ascertain its direction of flight. It was getting closer and seemed familiar. As the plane came closer its particular sound was recognizable as that of my bushpilot's floatplane. It was definitely coming my way! I wondered if he was just flying by on another mission. I had not put out the red teeshirt flag for him to stop.

Standing by the bucket with scissors in hand, I watched the silvery plane glittering in the sunshine as it circled the lake and lowered in altitude. He was going to stop by, anyway. Grabbing the bucket which was almost full I hurried back downhill towards camp, picking up a second full bucket on the way. Walking back as fast as possible, I was trying to get there before he tied up! The floatplane roared as it touched down onto water out of sight behind pine and spruce trees. Then shortly I could hear the chugging sound of the plane taxiing in. I had a long way yet to go…so alternately jogged and walked.

But as I entered camp, panting and with sweat trickling and dripping from my head, nose and ears…he too, just stepped up onto the camp's lichen-covered ground. I was happy to see him and to have some human communication after ten days. He stopped by just to check on me: to see how I was and how I was doing with the mushrooms. He said that he wanted to see the morels I had picked so far. The ones I just brought off the hillside I dumped onto plastic tarps, carefully spread them out and explained as he watched the hows and whys of drying morels.

I explained that both heat and wind were crucial for drying and solar was the best, least expensive and least work-intensive heat source. But for that, one needed good weather. If it be cloudy and rainy one would need to build a drying shed with a wood-burning stove; a method that was least desirable but would be the last resort and for this, one would need large sturdy wire mesh trays with some way of mounting them above the stove; the work involved would then be three or four times that of solar drying.

After this sort of explanation he seemed even more interested. Then I showed him the large white vertebra that I found on a hill above, asking if he recognized it and saying I wondered if it could be from some Ice-age animal. He did not recognize the bone. Then after a long hard look, suggested it may be from a moose: the first vertebra that connects with the skull. It seemed too big for that but I had to accept this plausible answer.

A half-hour passed in conversation then he had to go. I gave him a small bag of morels to take home. He taxied out...then with a powerful roar that echoed back and forth across the valley...took flight and after a wing-wave, turned away. The silvery floatplane shrank into the distance...dwarfed by billowing cream-coloured summer clouds above. Its sound gradually quietened and within minutes was a silvergrey dot disappearing into the blue of infinity.

Hours passed and I was again beside the stove watching lovely sunset colours slowly changing within drifting clouds. A pale turquoise green horizon-sky glowed just above the deep blueblack rocky-peaked mountains. Broken clouds of mauve, pink and orange constantly reshaped into animated and cartoon-like forms. Now was the time for my friendly moose to take her wee one-and-only for a lakeside walk and swimming lesson. I waited...listening expectantly. Soon, as certain as ever, they appeared on the gravelly shore forty yards north of camp. Mother waded out to chest-deep while baby swam beside, passing below camp and heading towards her favourite feeding shallows.

They moved away in the blackening water amid tiny wave-sparkles of pink and orange...soon to disappear around the curving lakeshore behind greenblack willow brush. After this evening pleasantness I covered the mushrooms then retired for night inside the tent...safely away from the countless buzzing little tykes of hell-on-wings. Lying beside rifle and pepper sprayguns, I stretched out very tired legs then quickly floated away into the realm of sleep and dreams.

Next morning, I was up and out of the tent just as sunshine began filtering into camp. Another day of steady work ensued. Late in the day though, I was fortunate to photograph the male three-toed woodpecker. It paid me a visit, coming into the trees next to camp and let me approach within three yards. Other than this, not much eventful happened except the ground produced four buckets of nice morels. Then one more peaceful sunset, little moose swimming lesson...and I was back home in the tent for another night. In a quiet place such as this — and having worked my legs to the limit — sleep came within minutes of lying down!

I had been asleep for three or four hours when suddenly shaken back by one shattering loud, very deep roar! In a split-second consciousness flashed back into the physical realm of reality — startled but groggy!

"A grizzly!" I thought. Yet half-awake, I tried to orient myself. The roar came from about five yards to southeast of the tent — and my head! A few moments of silence...then another extremely loud deep roar violently shook the air, me and...it seemed the forest and whole valley! An ear-breaking sound — it dragged out for about three seconds: "RRRRRRRRRRRRRRRRRRRRR!"

All was pitchblack in the tent. Quietly...carefully...I reached for a pepperspray and the rifle, listening for any motion on the ground outside...not a sound! Very slowly, I rolled sideways and sat up...then crept forward to the tent's entranceway.

Now crouching on knees at the tent's entrance, listening...I kept silent and motionless. Long moments passed...not another sound. Ever so slowly, I unzipped the tent's front mosquito flap. Moving it slightly aside, I peered out along the ground. There, all was black while black forms of pine and spruce trees jutted into the dark grey sky beyond. Silent stars twinkled brilliant white, pale blue and pink through the cold night air.

Seemingly endless moments of quiet passed. Now I noticed my hands were shaking... adrenalin...in suspense from the long silence, unable to see the ground outside and wondering if the big animal knew where I was! The tent was certainly no protection now! Fear crept into my body and mind. I mentally debated on what the best strategy would be.

Thinking this animal was a grizzly and not certain where it now was — if it had moved or not — I decided to stay put, looking out and holding the pepper spraygun ready to shoot. The rifle was at my side but too awkward and also too noisy if I cocked it. The pepperspray was my best defence: quiet, versatile and accurate. I thought it be best to remain still, silent and alert! I waited, waited...and waited.

The dark silence seemed to last such a long, long time! Moments, seconds, minutes went by with no sound of any sort. I was beginning to relax a wee touch. My hands no longer shook. Maybe it had no interest in me?

I thought about the two roars, focussing on their volume, depth and tone. The volume, depth and vibratory pattern was almost exactly that of a Boeing 737 jet on takeoff! This animal's roars must have travelled audibly at least two miles each way, up and down the valley! Remembering a grizzly's growl of fifteen years ago: just as deep, but not so loud...although it was only three yards from me. There was also a tonal difference: this sound was a single-toned roar but the grizzly's actually two distinctly different sounds that erupted simultaneously. Now I thought this animal may not be a bear!

After maybe ten minutes of waiting in this dark silence and hearing nothing else, I cautiously crawled out a few yards along the ground into the cold. Looking around...all that I could see were the black forms of brush, stumps, treetrunks and trees against the pale grey lake and dark grey sparkling sky. The big beast had tiptoed away, it seemed. And the little beasts too, were not around: their joints yet seized-up by the cold night air. Now in comfort, I listened and watched silently...for maybe another ten minutes before crawling back into the tent. Still highly energized though, quite some time ensued until I was finally overcome by sleep!

When morning light brought me back to the earthly waking state, I crawled out cautiously, pepperspray-first. All was well in camp. I was alone except for a few early-rising little irritators... mosquitoes. Immediately I turned left and walked to the southeast looking at the ground for tracks. Yes...the ground and lichen had stamped into it the large hoofprints of a moose!

It had walked to edge of camp from the slope above, stopping here. Tracks pointed southwest towards the lake and...my drying tarps. Looking around camp, I could easily understand why this moose would stop and become upset: with plastic tarps lying over the ground everywhere, clothes hanging from trees and all of the various attendant smells, so strange to a wild animal far from human doings!

I followed the tracks. To my surprise they led into the narrow eighteen-inch pathway between the drying tarps! This pathway was bordered by tarps on both sides, forming an L-shape. At the ninety degree corner, the path turned left. So did the moose tracks! At the pathway's end into open ground the tracks made another ninety degree turn, to the right...then alongside the tarp's edge and pointing directly towards the lake!

I could not help myself but laugh at this most unusual, even odd, behaviour! In the black of night a moose had tiptoed between the tarps, intentionally avoiding stepping onto them! I chuckled for quite some time, while also remaining excited about this unexpected visit.

Now curious to see if the animal were still in the neighbourhood, I walked over to the camp stove and its open-view vantage point. At the lake's south end one large bull moose with short antlers-in-velvet was knee-deep and grazing alone. The cows, whose favourite grazing spot it was and would always be there at this time of morning…were not there! Apparently, last night the two cows and yearling calf had vacated the area upon his vociferous arrival!

The bull stayed for this and two more days but was alone during the whole time. Likewise, I never saw my other friendly neighbours…the cow and wee auburn one…for those three days. All had departed or were in hiding! That, I found to be most interesting while also humorous enough to smile about. But on the fourth morning the big bull was gone; not coincidentally, this same day all three cows and the two calves were back by the lake. They had accepted my company…but not the bull moose! He would have to wait for rutting season.

On Steep Mountain Slopes

Demanding to be seen, the valley's poplar groves were glowing golden yellow…bright little patches among deep green spruce and hemlock forest. Rugged rocky peaks in shades of grey and tan projected steeply skyward topped with brilliant white new snow. Autumn had arrived in the Skeena Mountains! Now early morning, the air was cool…perfect for the steep mountainside climb that I was just beginning. Following a little noisy creek upward on the forty-five degree slope, I was looking for a large quartz vein that could possibly carry gold or other metal, since this region was known for copper, silver, gold and molybdenum. The day previously I had seen several small white quartz stringers running through the grey slatey parent rock nearby.

Not far up, this nameless creek tumbled through a little narrow canyon of dark grey hardrock. Here the slope steepened even more and the creek became much louder…a slight roar echoing up nearly vertical rock walls. Water flowed and tumbled quickly down in a series of little white waterfalls. Above and alongside the gorge I climbed, wending upward under lodgepine, hemlock and yellowing poplar and birch trees. Warm sunshine beamed through here and there in straight angling bright shafts.

Now and then soft gusts of wind would bring a rustle to birch leaves which shimmered and twisted…jagged-edged, pointed ovals glowing yellow, brown and pale emerald green. Beneath the trees on the moss and lichen-covered ground, sunlight and shadows painted patterns in everchanging shapes and shades of green, white, cream, black and grey: the forest floor was alive with dancing curves, lines, circles and triangles!

Just upslope I came to a little wet dip where a thick clump of tall green and yellow bushes stood in the way. The top ends of their long thin stems were clustered with orange-red berries: round, smooth and shining…hanging down and partly hidden among yellow and pale green slender maple-like leaves. This was a most welcome sight since I had worked up a sweat and a thirst! Reaching out I picked one little cluster, throwing the berries all together into my mouth. Mmm…were they ever good! A perfect coincidence, the tart juice of these highbush cranberries was just what I needed. Pausing, I savoured a few more but left most…knowing that bears, grouse, bluejays and voles also eat them for both juice and the single large seed inside of each berry. Such wild berries are often crucial for their survival but not mine.

Continuing the upward climb, now under pine and birch trees I stopped to watch two squirrels about ten yards away, chasing each other from tree to tree. Jumping from branch to branch while squealing back and forth, they raced at lightning-fast speed: down a trunk headfirst then up another just inches apart from branch to branch in the treetops then back to the ground! Then up another treetrunk spiralling upward one behind the other by mere inches, then again lightning-fast turning back down and spiralling around the trunk headfirst to the mossy ground! Scooting across moss and lichen to a lodgepine tree that stood at the gorge's edge, up they went — one to the top while the chaser stopped halfway up.

Both squirrels suddenly calmed and began nibbling off pinecones. They continued to chatter and squeal softly, not concerned about the human who stood watching. Quite enjoying these sweet little animals, I stood still, looking up and listening. This was a lovely living scene: two red squirrels at and near the pine treetop, nestled amid green starlike radiating needles and rusty brown new cones, with the mountain-rimmed deep blue sky behind and above. Each one sat upright on its branch right at the treetrunk with rusty-red tail held up and curving in an S-shape...each holding a cone with little sharp-clawed forepaws and chewing off bracts one by one to release the nutritious seeds.

They were now content in their little treetop world that appeared to touch the sky...as if an inseparable part of it. Up the canyon's grey rock walls, shishing sounds echoed and mingled with the squirrels' gentle squealing. This place and time was a touch of paradise...so calm and peaceful. Just watching them, a mild pleasure came into my body and mind. By their body positions these squirrels looked very relaxed...expressing a sort of inner happiness that glowed from within their sunlight-sparkling eyes.

Then the lower squirrel stopped chattering, twisted sideways and down, then suddenly froze still...looking straight down at the tree's base. Now its head was cocked in a strange, awkward tilt while its body stretched and flattened even more along the branch! Silent and motionless, the squirrel remained thus with one eye looking down, the other looking up! This extreme sideways body and head position was most odd! At first I wondered if it had lost its sanity.

Next the other squirrel froze to its branch, completely motionless...also staring down at the ground. Strange behaviour, I thought. Following the lower squirrel's line of vision to the tree's base, I could not distinguish any animal shape that would indicate danger. A branchy greybrown clump of brush was growing in direct line making visibility poor at ground level, though. Again looking up at the squirrels, their positions were the same. I looked down again.

Now a dark brown medium-sized animal profile was vaguely visible through the thick yellow and brown-leaved brush. It was perfectly still at the pine tree's base...looking up at the squirrels! I too, remained motionless hoping this unwanted visitor would move into the open or up the tree. My first thought was...a pine marten? Long moments passed as all four of us were frozen in space, but not in time.

The animal seemed unaware of my presence, being mostly hidden from view with my scent blowing away on the upslope breeze and with loud tumbling water just below nullifying any slight sound I might make. It must have come up from the creek, otherwise would have seen me and never approached so closely. Now I noticed that this animal was at least twice the size of a pine marten. I kept still...waiting for the unknown carnivore to go up after the squirrels. If it did, they would have little chance of escape...since no other trees were within jumping distance for them!

But the fearsome animal did not move up the tree. Instead its head turned sideways, now steadily peering at me through the yellow, grey and brown maze of brushy stems and twigs... attempting to ascertain what I was! With that, my only chance for a clear view necessitated that I move. I stepped sideways to look through an opening.

That instant in a dark blur — the animal leapt, angling down the steep cliff towards the creek! A deep chocolate brown, it was long and low to the ground with a long tail. I ran to the edge to look down! But the beautiful big weasel was gone! Here the creek was twenty yards down a steep slope of about seventy-five degrees. Certainly this was a very agile, quick animal that could be no other than a fisher — one of British Columbia's rarest weasels!

Happy I was to at least have a clear one-second glimpse as the big weasel dashed away. Well… now my squirrels would be safe for at least one more day! Of that too, I was happy…although well aware of the carnivorous necessity in Nature's way and that the fisher would not go hungry for long. With such an exciting rare occurrence beside this unnamed creek…of course, I had to call it Fisher Creek. But that was just for my own mental map and memory, no one else.

A few days later still in the same area, I crossed another small no-name creek under large hemlock, red cedar and subapline fir trees, then went up a scree slope that was covered with beautiful thick cream-coloured and greygreen lichen. At the top a jolt of excited energy zipped through me! Here ran a large white quartz outcropping, about two feet thick! After some close scrutiny though, my excitement waned since it was devoid of any visible mineralization other than a touch of rust.

Undeterred, I kept moving upward and along little mossy benches where narrow quartz stringers showed here and there…another half-hour of walking and climbing. Mid-day was lovely…warm and blue-skied. Beautiful wedge-shaped mountains across the valley stretched east, west and south for many miles. Now I was under a mix of subalpine fir and very large mountain hemlock of two-feet to five-feet in diameter and between them grew blue and black huckleberry bushes, white rhododendron, birch and a few sapling pine trees. Traversing a forty-five degree slope of green-spattered mossy ground, I stopped at one small hardrock knob.

I knelt down for a close look at this rock and to rest awhile in the cool shade. Here was a quiet green world under big trees where no human had ever walked…halfway up the mountainside. Through little openings in the boughs above, sunshine entered as transparent bars and thin stripes brightening the moss to emerald and jade where it touched. Between huge treetrunks, visible across the broad valley were grey jagged tooth-like solid-rock giants projecting into the blue! White, grey and turquoise filled their uppermost grooves…snow and ice in the mountains' cavities. Another of Nature's expressions almost overwhelmed one's senses: a touch of paradise had appeared in a way not-so-subtle.

As I silently enjoyed this calm beautiful place, a gentle distant sound…an odd medium-toned vibration…began from some distance directly behind. Very quickly its volume increased while the tone changed to a sort-of ripping — it approached so fast I had no time to react and look back! Now at my right ear was a loud vibrating, "Brrrrrrrrrrr" and a simultaneous puff of cool wind — as its creator zipped past and ahead! A large dark grey wing just missed my ear by a wee fraction of an inch as feathers shook rapidly in the air!

A split-second later I was looking at the dappled grey back and tailfeathers of a goshawk gliding away in front of me! It landed ungracefully in a little white-barked birch tree just ten yards ahead, turned around completely and looked back through its big yellowish eyes. This bird was a fledgling recently out of the nest. Moments later, high-pitched peeping and sandpapery screeching sounds began from behind but this time to my left. Quickly looking back, I saw a second goshawk approaching! It too, landed awkwardly about ten yards away in another birch just downslope; this one perched almost level with my eyes. Both fledgling hawks continued on speaking with their high-pitched screeches…unique sounds that I had not heard before.

Now I was expecting, and hoping, to soon see an adult arrive. Looking around, waiting and observing the young birds for several minutes…no parent came. Where the parents were I did not know, having heard no other sounds. These two birds were big…adult size but awkward-moving. After another minute or so of mutual observing with both goshawks constantly head-turning and screeching, the two beautiful mottled grey-buff birds flew westward together, low to the ground under a steeply sloping shady forest.

Flying slowly between treetrunks, tilting sideways to dodge projecting dead branches or pulling one wing in close to the body to pass by another branch, they disappeared into a distant maze of greybrown and green lines, curves and black-and-white blotches. What incredibly acrobatic flight…even at this young age! Maybe a parent had called them with sound inaudible to human ears? Or they may have been on their own for the first time? But just meeting these young goshawks made the long hard climb worthwhile! Seeing and hearing them was such a treat…a bright few minutes in an otherwise uneventful day.

Not far from these goshawks' mountainside, in the early morning several days later, I was driving very slowly up an unused logging road. In first gear, it was stop-and-go…manoeuvring through useless ditches that had been cut across the deactivated road. A real bother and irritation these, I was attempting to protect the truck's front end. Soon though I could drive no farther. With two pepper sprayguns and prospecting tools I went into the woods taking the easiest route along a gentle slope.

Still perturbed, thinking about some of our governments' ridiculous ideas and dollar waste, I persevered…slowly climbing higher into a thin drifting white mist. This dampness had been generated by night-time rain and was now in broken translucent clouds moving upward through the forest of huge old snaggly hemlock trees. Higher yet, the cold mist thickened into semi-translucent and opaque grey fog. Along the way I watched rock bluffs for any colour change that would indicate copper or cobalt: blues and pinks. Previously I had discovered a wee showing of copper and silver ore in this area so there was a slight chance of more nearby.

As I rounded one bluff, a young bull moose was standing broadside twenty yards ahead quietly looking at me! Its small flat antlers were losing velvet, with bits and pieces hanging loosely down while rubbed-off parts showed red and pink solid antler. I had my camera in the backpack; reaching for it…I adjusted lens, shutter speed and focus while the moose stood still in a pose, watching. This young bull was certainly unfamiliar with humanity since now hunting season was on; it let me shoot away with the three hundred millimeter zoom lens. A fortunate meeting this was for us both! The young moose would live to another day and hopefully years longer, having this time met a nonhunter: one who understands how unnecessary hunting has become in most parts of the supposedly civilized world and…how necessary all wildlife are to each other and to humanity, no less.

The camera's clicking though, brought a certain apprehension to the moose. Turning quickly away it went at a jog along the gentle slope. After a hundred yards it turned downward, now just walking. There the terrain dropped suddenly into a steep moss and lichen-covered slope where small lodgepine, birch and hemlock grew; the bull moose calmly went its way into the silent forest below.

I continued upward through drifting fog until about two hundred yards along where — to my surprise — another animal was standing, quietly staring! A large round-looking blackbear stood calmly…as if just waiting for me to arrive! This was a beautiful bear, probably a four hundred pounder. It looked well-fed and healthy. Thick glistening fur would help to keep its metabolism functioning well during the fast-approaching winter. It too, waited for me to click the camera, then…typical of a dominant self-assured bear…casually walked away about fifty yards, turning at a leisurely pace to zigzag upslope under giant four-foot diameter hemlock trees.

With camera in hand I walked cautiously towards it. Watching the bear…as it slowly moved higher brushing past blue huckleberry bushes…several times it looked over a shoulder back at me while keeping to its easy pace. Then it stopped for a long look back. And I stopped, of course. Now the space between us was about forty yards. The bear's demeanour was nonthreatening so I had no fear. After a few minutes of mutual observation and two clicks of the camera, it moved up and over a little black and white lichen-covered granite ridge. I gave the benign bear a mental: "Thankyou and goodbye."

Here rock was the wrong type anyway, so I turned, heading back down the mountainside. Drifting fog kept moving between trees, at times making visibility poor as treetrunks and the ground would vanish behind a silent white wall. Sound too, was muffled by the fog…this mountainside was very quiet. But soon the fog opened again somewhat, exposing bits of distant greygreen forest and ground-level contours.

I was crossing an open gravelly bluff when a blackish object appeared, moving under small hemlock and pine trees twenty yards down. The dark silhouette was heading upward along a mossy ridge and away from me. The animal was porcupine-sized and had much the same shape. But it seemed to be moving quicker than the quilled tree-climber normally would. The rapid loping motion was definitely unlike a porcupine's! Now…I was excited! Here, I was seeing my first wolverine! It stopped in the dark shadows under small lodgepine trees, turned slightly to its right and gave me a ten-second look…then loped westward over the curving steep slope and out of sight.

This short mountainside hike was difficult to believe: my good luck seeing three different animals within minutes and along a three hundred yard stretch…most unusual. Now very excited, I wanted to see the wolverine again, closer, so walked back a bit higher up to the clifftop edge where it might have still been. Then stepping downslope into shadows under the pine and poplar canopy, slowly…carefully…I paced the moss and lichen-covered ground while eyeing the treetrunk horizon and peering up into the tree boughs. It was futile. The wolverine was not to be seen. Although this animal is fearless, due to shyness — or maybe more astuteness — it did not linger but moved on down the same very steep slope and in the same direction as the bull moose. Even so…I was elated, having seen a wolverine in the wild!

One Wee Lake

Countless bright yellow waterlilies and emerald green floating pads dotted the little oval lake's shallows. Random patches of pink and maroon, the floating blossoms of water buckwheat, brought their mute beauty and faint perfume to this pure northern lake. In the open water farther out an everchanging rippling pattern reflected grey, brown, deep bluegreen and pale greygreen of the distant gently curving treed hills, the blackness of lake bottom and turquoise blue of the late afternoon sky. Here was a beautiful multifacetted gem…but as temporary and changing as the gentle swirling breeze.

The slight wind was not enough to deter mosquitoes that bobbed up and down at various odd angles all around me; they seemed to be quite enjoying themselves much like a raven or crow does on a windy updraft! They were not too much bother though, since I was heavily clothed in bluejeans and western jeanjacket along with a thick coating of canola oil on hands, face and head. Sometimes a little sting came even through this oil, but the only real irritation was when one flew between my eyeglasses and an eye. Even so, I stood my ground holding the camera and appreciating some of the more positive aspects of this boreal forest reality.

Heading into the semi-open woods of spruce, pine and trembling aspen…with each step the soft leafy ground crunched and crackled unobtrusively under my boots. Low to the ground were pale green shrubs and around them years of grey and rust-coloured twigs, cones, catkins and leaves…all very dry. At just twenty yards in I was cheered to meet a wee fuzzy animal crouched motionless at the base of a bushy spruce sapling! So camouflaged, I could have easily stepped on it! But luckily I recognized the particular body shape, long ears and sparkling eyes of a very young snowshoe hare — just one step away from my boots!

Hidden within the leaf and twig maze, this little leveret's still form had appeared as if by magic from invisibility. Now I too remained still, enjoying its presence and hoping it would not dart away in fright. This one was too small, too young to not have its mother nearby…so I wished it not move. And all that did move on its six-inch long body was a slight infrequent nose-twitch!

Its shining brown eyes were no doubt keenly observing the human. Too shaded here for a clear handheld photo, I stepped ever so slowly backwards towards the nearest treetrunk. Leaning the camera against a narrow but firm aspen trunk, I set for dim light and focussed the three hundred millimeter zoom. Through it, I gained a most intimate view of this sweet little animal. From the curved mirror-surface of the wee hare's big left eye could be seen bits of pale blue sky, black aspen silhouettes arching above and even my own human form leaning against the aspen trunk! The little leveret held its quiet position through four camera clicks.

Then I stepped slowly back, not wanting to disturb it, and continued on my way through the woods. Within a few minutes of wandering, some odd hissing, squealing and clucking sounds began issuing from behind thick brown-leaved buckbrush. Although well-hidden, the bird gave away its position by these unwelcoming expressions. Then, as it scooted away in a low crouch, barely visible were the shape and spotted grey, black and brown colours of a spruce grouse hen! It probably had a nest nearby, I thought. Closely checking the ground, watching carefully before stepping, I hoped to see a nest of eggs or chicks behind the buckbrush. But seeing neither, I continued away towards a flat opening of widely spaced trembling aspen and birch. Between these trees a lovely creamy-coloured lichen covered the ground in little rounded mounds, shoulder to shoulder and up to three or four inches thick. Growing in branchy masses, individual stems looked quite like caribou antlers.

Walking for another hundred yards or so through this open flat, I flushed a smaller bird from the ground! Its unique, slowly pumping wingflap and large white wing-dot I recognized as that of a nighthawk. Flying only twenty yards, it landed on a leaning sapling spruce snag. I kept a mental picture of its takeoff spot…walking slowly, carefully that way. Nearing the spot, pebbles, sand and lichen rendered the nest almost invisible. But sure enough, two odd egg-shapes mottled dark brown and grey emerged from the camouflage. The eggs were lain in a shallow depression but on a raised lichen mound where everything was flecked with white, cream and black. Their unusual shape, being very fat on one end while tapering to a quick point at the other: these eggs were specially designed by Nature's versatile genetics — to roll in a tiny circle!

I took one quick close-up photo then walked away, not wanting them to be left by the mother for too long. After some time wandering while seeing nothing more of consequence, I turned back towards the lake and my original point of entry. Trembling aspen leaves periodically shook and rustled as little gusts of warm wind filtered through them. This was a lovely bit of Yukon's boreal forest…so alive and peaceful! And here, away from the lake, mosquitoes were not so bad.

Shortly though, from behind low brush more animate life came out of hiding as rapid flashes of bright white! White spots moved rapidly in short vertical curves as the pale brownish animal darted away between white and greygreen treetrunks. Coming to a stop under dwarf birchbrush, these were the white bottoms of an adult snowshoe hare's big hind feet! Another well-disguised animal, if it keeps still…but when the hare moves, its white footbottoms flash like bright flags giving its position away! The hare stopped under a clump of greybrown brush to pretend it was not there. I thought this adult was probably the wee leveret's mother, being so near to it. I watched it awhile from the distance then circled away.

By now the everpresent Sun, a deep orange-red, was low on the western horizon. Sky and thin distant clouds had transformed into limegreen and shades of orange and soft copper. As I neared the lake, the forest edge and wee hare's hiding place I slowed my pace, watching closely to avoid stepping on it. But the little animal had moved away. Soon back at lakeside, I chose a level gravelly spot right next to the water where I could spend night-time under a soon-to-be glowing and glittering sky.

Sitting just above lakeshore, I ate a supper of tasty dry-roasted Manitoba wild rice and not-so-tasty canned vegetables. A beautiful scene this was with evergreen hills and sky reflecting from the mirror-surfaced little lake. All the while, I was feeling as placid as the silence of this peaceful wild place. The calm weather and open clear sky straight above brought a stillness that felt powerful beyond all concepts…inexpressible in words, which can only approximate the actual experience.

Coming steadily along the calm lakesurface were very faint irregular splashings and the quacking of dabbling ducks at the far southern end. Directly across, the olive and deep bluegreen rounded hills of spruce forest were now developing highlights of copper hue…coloured by the orange-red setting Sun. And where sky met water, insects in the thousands silently hovered, bobbed and darted at high speed in their aeons-old dance-of-life-and-death.

Mosquitoes were abuzz, quickly moving about in their seemingly haphazard way. Dragonflies in four colours of blue, green, yellow and red were hardly fooled as they hovered…then darted in a flash after their prey! Flies, caddisflies and a few butterflies of blue and mottled orange were all in this dance. Just beneath them, hundreds of deep yellow pondlilies pointed their curving petals outward and upward from among large shiny green, notched oval leaves: such be the insects' dancehall floor, their seats and dining tables where they would at times perch to rest wings and to chew.

Slowly…ever so slowly the sunset sky changed. Late afternoon and evening were indistinguishable as the Sun seemed to never set. Here, manmade measurement of time had no relevance. For many miles the only human presence was myself. Seemingly timeless and boundlessly beautiful…this was as close to paradise as the realm of matter-and-energy could be!

Surrounded by and absorbed into this calm environment, I naturally drifted to a philosophical mode: thinking about and wondering why human beings put so much importance on themselves. Here…I was reminded of how puny humanity is. Human being — so creative in so many ways and so intelligent with reasoning power — is simultaneously the opposite. Yet the human animal is also a member of Nature's multifarious family of beings. The human is one of the top predators and more importantly — has developed the highest degree of intellect and creative ability, with the most versatile encompassing mind. Even so, humanity is quite confused about its role in Nature! It seems to me that our duty and role must be to live with Nature in the least selfish way possible, to appreciate fully what the life and forces of Nature do for us…and therefore give back to them…appropriately!

As I settled in for the night, my thoughts, impressions, ideas…concepts and nonconcepts… drifted, came and went much like the insects but slower…as they lively danced in a gentle wind near lakeshore. The sky at zenith and eastward had darkened to bluegrey, allowing the white light of Venus and pale blue and white of a few large stars to shine through.

I crawled into the sleeping bag under a brown canvas tarp, listening to and watching a nighthawk as it continually called out in a raspy, "Kiiii…..kiiii." Infrequently, it dove straight down with feathers-and-air generating an unusual zooming sound that is so unique to this bird! As I lay on my side watching stars brighten to twinkling, eyelids began to surreptitiously close. Listening to the gentle evening sounds, a wee peeping sandpiper far off…sleep's stealthy process overcame the waking mind. Another facet of mind floated into the little understood realm of dreams: where space, time, matter and energy would manifest so differently.

I had been asleep for some short while until a nearby crunching sound brought me back. This was the sound of teeth quickly nipping on wood! Peeking out from under the canvas tarp…just three yards away, floating among yellow lilies, a beaver was happily munching on a leafy aspen branch, eating the bark and green leaves. The animal was mostly submerged bodily but with its head of rusty brown, chocolate and blond-tipped fur clearly visible. Little longtoed forepaws grasped and manipulated the branch. Tiny wavelets moved out from the beaver's rapidly moving lower jaw as four orange front teeth worked seriously. Its wide flat, black tail lifted at times to become clearly visible just below the surface. Sparkling in the evening light, the beaver's happy brown eyes seemed to look at the sky!

Here I was watching the living embodiment of our earliest Canadian symbol…at the moment enjoying its little aquatic world and unaware of this special symbolic status. I thought of how unfortunate our beloved beaver has for hundreds of years been shot, trapped, skinned and eaten

— and still is! Such be the absurdity of Canada: the beaver-as-symbol adorns postage stamps, coins, etcetera yet the real animal remains unappreciated, disrespected and just used for various human consumption. All of that is in consequence of the selfish human ego…that domineering facet of the nonappreciative human predator.

To me, this beaver was worth far more! It was alive and enjoying life; that was its special value. And besides, just by its natural lifestyle of dam building and small-scale logging the beaver was actually creating habitat — new living space — for many other animal species of land, air and water! For several minutes I watched this special animal dining in peace. Then raising its shiny black nose up, testing the air and slowly lowering back down the beaver quietly paddled away…abandoning its partly eaten leafy green branch. Smelling but not seeing me, it prudently vacated. And soon so did I as sleep again became the dominating force-of-the-moment, pushing consciousness into a subtle realm of mind…where dreams become a personal reality.

Morning came early, as it always does when one sleeps under the sky. Sunshine low on the horizon half-awoke me…then distant splashing and dripping water brought on a yawning, almost fully-awake state. Rolling back the tarp covering, I looked across the lake to see three bull moose! Knee-and-belly-deep, they were having their early morning feed of lilies and water milfoil. Two were young, just into their second or third years with short velvet button antlers on their foreheads. But one was very large and carrying a huge set of velvet antlers — destined to grow for another two months yet! Between each animal was a conspicuous wide distance, greater between the youngest and the older bull; its obvious superiority commanded respect… especially at feeding time!

For about an hour I watched them as they remained grazing knee-to-belly-deep while moving leisurely about in the muddy shallows. The two young bulls eventually wandered closer together and when they had their fill, waded ashore one behind the other. High-stepping on stilt-like legs they disappeared into the shady spruce and willow woods. Soon after, the big bull also moved into the dark forest. Some time passed but none returned so I assumed they had bedded down in the cool shade for the day.

Now it was my turn for a walk into the woods. But on my side of the lake the forest was different, with smaller trees, more open and sunny. I went the same general way as yesterday. My tiny leveret was not there this time. I had wanted to explore the lake's far side but after seeing the three bull moose there, thought it wise to avoid! Again I carried the camera…ready for whatever local inhabitant may appear.

I passed by the area of the nighthawk's nest but at a good distance so not to disturb the sitting mother. Shortly afterward when about ten paces from a sapling snag, I noticed the dark still form of a bird perched on top. It had a hawk-like shape. Oddly, it had not flown away! Leaning against an aspen tree and looking through the camera's telephoto lens, I could see that it was a nighthawk…sound asleep!

Taking one photo, I stepped carefully closer avoiding twigs on the ground. After two more clicks, the bird's eyes opened…no doubt hearing the camera's shutter. Now only five paces away, off it flew but shortly landing in a spruce tree just thirty yards distant. It was probably the mate of the one nesting on the ground nearby. Happy with this meeting, I continued on my way leaving the nighthawk alone to have its daytime nap!

Turning back towards the lake I walked slowly, listening to rustling and clicking leaves above…the pleasant music of trembling aspen. These leafy sounds rose and fell in an even flow of volume and cadence in tune with the everchanging breeze. This was real music! Then a low-toned drumming began in the near distance as one male grouse joined the melody while proclaiming territory or calling for a mate. Drumming from a safe hiding place probably at a sunny warm opening on the ground, it was somewhere beyond the visible confine of brush and treetrunks. Here was a lovely little song of the animate and inanimate flow of life. Such peaceful music playing under the clear blue Yukon sky induced an inner appreciation that was quite beyond conceptual definition or expression. And on this day, the listeners were wild animals of the boreal forest and just one human.

But not being lulled by pleasure into a false sense of safety, since in Nature danger and death are always moving or waiting silently, unseen…I remained mindful! Moving cautiously and where visibility was the best, I was also alert for sounds of danger. If such occurred this easy song would no doubt abruptly change into a serious classical! But this day, it continued on peacefully. By the time I returned to lakeshore, late afternoon had arrived. And to my surprise six moose were out among the bright yellow lilies at the far side!

This time though, none were bulls! There were now three cows and three young! The largest cow had two good-sized yearling calves with her, the second-largest had one tiny auburn calf, while the lone cow looked to be probably a two-year-old. Taking my twenty-power spotting scope, I sat on the gravelly shore to watch them more intimately.

Along the same stretch of shallows as the three bulls had been in the morning, all fed on aquatic plants except the little auburn calf. It stood neck-deep as closely to its mother as possible without having to swim! Too far away for the telephoto lens, I never attempted a photograph. Instead, the uncommon pleasure of seeing six moose together developed a more permanent and colourful three-dimensional mental motion picture: memory. This beautiful living scene of deep bluegreen and olivegreen spruce forest behind…with bright yellow lilies floating amid emerald green leaf-pads and pink water buckwheat…dotting the water all around them…how could I forget?

Most active the two yearlings were! They were chasing one another back and forth — just like human children playing tag! With forelegs pumping high and much loud splashing they pranced about and kicked up water, splashing each other! After awhile the two trotted to their mother, jumping…and again with forelegs kicked water at her! Surprisingly, she responded likewise! Chasing the calves…all three quickly dodging from side to side and jogging around in circles — she kicked water back at them! These moose were certainly playing and obviously enjoying it as much as any human would! This unexpected child-like behaviour was really quite amusing!

Here, the often-solitary moose were enjoying themselves and each other's company as a small family group. Certainly, even moose have sociability as an important element of their behaviour! Interesting it was to see also that cows and their young would enter the lake together, while bulls were with bulls only and that the two groups even took turns feeding at this little yellowlily lake. Such coordinated social behaviour patterns told me that other factors were at play in the lives of moose — and other wild animals — besides and beyond merely survival-of-the-fittest. Now after maybe two hours, with Sun dipping low…the cows and young one by one waded ashore, shook themselves just like a wet dog does, then stepping past wild willowbrush moved out of sight into the blueblack forest shadows.

With the brilliant orange Sun very low in the northwestern sky, silently hovering there as if it would never set…another pleasant sound began transmitting along lakesurface from a little bay on the far side. The yodel of a loon brought to me, as it always does…a happy energetic feeling. Never has this bird's call sounded haunting or lonely. To me, the loon's call was a sound of togetherness and life: strong, lively, uniquely musical and fearlessly individual…while simultaneously welcoming. Much like the beaver and moose, this loon was definitely one more wild living expression of qualities that are more Canadian than just symbolic.

Life and Death Beside a Clear Creek

The morning was late and sunshine hot as the pilot and I carefully loaded two weeks of grub, camping gear, prospecting tools and mushroom drying equipment into the Jetranger helicopter. Once loaded almost no room remained other than space for the pilot and me. Cautiously stepping in, I buckled up as he briefed me on safety and emergency procedures. This was not my first time flying out into the northern Canadian wilds but was the first by helicopter, so would no doubt be interesting and exciting! After the short briefing he fired up the helicopter, warmed it awhile…then we lifted straight up, quickly changing to a slight forward tilt and rising. Inside the cockpit, the nearly complete silence was such a pleasant contrast from hearing a helicopter outside!

I silently watched buildings and trees rapidly diminish in size as we flew in a rising clockwise curve over town. Everything below…houses, cars, streets…shrank quickly and also flattened to almost map-like as we gained elevation. High steep hills too, appeared to flatten and look much less rugged than they actually were. And so quiet it was. With only a very faint high-pitched musical ringing of the engine, this flight seemed a bit magical! Now almost everything was a complete visual experience of geometric shapes, colours and patterns. Within minutes we were flying a straight line over mottled green rolling forested hills, small silvery lakes, ponds and creeks.

But ahead, above and all around, the sky and billowing cumulous clouds expanded into a giant three-dimensional reality of silent blue, white and grey. The distant horizon became a vast panorama of low rolling bluegreen hills, accentuated beyond here and there with little thin rows of angular grey and white pyramidal peaks. Somewhere out there about thirty-five miles away flowed a little noisy whitewater creek. That was my destination! Now we were flying over a vast roadless forest of lovely spruce, pine and poplar woods. Dotted below were little turquoise or dark blue lakes and brownish-tan muskeg ponds encircled and interconnected with pale green grass, dark green sedge and bordered with aspen trees.

From this comfortable eagle's view I kept watching for wildlife below. Moose trails were clearly visible running from pond to pond. At one little lake a moose was standing still in the sparkling clear water, placid in its quiet world. After some minutes the terrain became more rolling with many rounded green humps protruding upward…while the pilot maintained the same steady elevation. Details below were very clear. Growing upon these foothills were lodgepine with dark green dwarf birchbrush and whitish lichen in the openings between.

Flying over the top of one such hump only about forty yards above it, I spotted two large blackbears standing straight up on hindlegs, face-to-face! They were wrestling and playfully batting each other with forepaws! As we came nearer they separated…one running, the other chasing closely behind in a series of curves, circles and S-patterns around trees and through the low birch bushes. They even ran a figure-eight around two pine trees! So focussed they were on each other or so accustomed to aircraft noise, or both, the bears remained apparently oblivious of the noisy helicopter, never looking up! A boar and a sow, I assumed, were fully centred on each other and much enjoying rare moments together in their mating play! My last glimpse of them: they were running full-speed in a circle, one just inches behind the other!

Now I wondered how close these bears were to my destination point, where I had planned to stay for up to two weeks. I knew we were getting close. Within minutes, upon reaching the area my guess was that they were about five miles away, at a reasonably comfortable distance. We circled over to assess landforms, forest and creeks below and to look for the presence of any large animals. All looked clear below…no bear and no moose visible. I had to make a quick decision about where to land. The creek that I chose was open enough — but barely! We came down slowly, squeezing between spruce, poplar and pine trees that lined the creek on each side…landing on a brightly coloured gravelly boulder-bar of the whitewater creek.

The pilot shut off the Jetranger and we unloaded supplies as quickly as possible while also planning a method of communicating on another day when he would fly over, so would not have to necessarily land. He gave me two rolls of red surveyors' tape for marking out a date on the ground: when he should come back to fly me out. In about ten minutes he was back in the air and I waved a thumbs-up: "Have a good flight!"

Belting two pepper sprayguns onto my right hip, I stood on the gravel bar listening to the harsh sound of technology fading away…as the gentle sounds of Nature replaced it. The creek trickled, gurgled and shished as its crystal-clear water flowed quickly by and over smooth rounded granite rocks. Kneeling beside clumps of beautiful rose-coloured wildflowers and putting fingers into the water, it felt very cold! I was happy about that…cupped my hands and took a refreshing drink of the deliciously tasteless icy water! This was certainly a permafrost-fed creek. Then standing up I looked hard at the woods and terrain in all directions…turning slowly three hundred sixty degrees while looking for any large animal shape. Fortunately, I was alone. I could relax!

Hastily I moved all supplies off the gravel bar, up onto the flat above highwater line. Under a clump of spruce trees I put up the puptent, a five-minute job…then built a tarp fence allowing for a small yardspace around the tent. Here too, the sky was summer blue with a few billowing white clouds above the rolling bluegreen hilly horizon. Mosquitoes were so few as to be hardly noticeable! This was a perfect day. Next, I walked along the bar and creek a short distance noting the various rock types: they were mostly pale grey granite but with some others coloured tan, pale pink, rusty and greyblack. There was no quartz.

Later, back at camp I stuffed a few plastic grocery bags into my high rubberboots, now anxious to scout the ground for morel mushrooms. Carrying blue plastic-handled scissors I walked eastward out onto a sandy flat. Over a large area…after walking and walking among large spruce…I found not one mushroom! Nor did I see any animal tracks. Then heading upstream alongside the clear cold creek to a gentle rise, morels began to show in singles and little groups. This was an encouraging sign! An inconspicuous animal trail ran through these spruce and pine woods parallel to the creek. Following it, soon a good patch of morels appeared: some were just the right size, others too young to pick. After filling two half-bags I returned to camp feeling good about this area's potential.

Setting out a drying tarp over some open flat ground where it was most sunny, I carefully dumped the morels onto it. Then back to that same area I went, this time carrying two plastic buckets of four-gallon size. These could be filled without the fragile fresh mushrooms breaking. As I hurried along the creekside trail, a familiar pleasing sound greeted me from high up among large spruce trees. The high-pitched squeaking chirp I recognized as a voice of the friendly little northern three-toed woodpecker. A spontaneous smile came to my face and positive energy suddenly flowed through my body. This welcome was much enjoyed and appreciated!

Continuing to the shaded end of the bench where I had previously seen several small groups of morels, I went to work snipping and filling the first bucket. Here the ground alternated as patches of soft tan-coloured dirt or spongy brown and yellowgreen muskeg. The morels were mostly of similar colours. But tiny young ones were dark grey to black or dark greenish black. In the ashy dirt here too, were indistinct tracks of a lone adult moose that had walked towards the creek quite some time ago. After filling the first bucket I carried it to a large spruce tree, placed it at the shady side of its trunk then continued working.

After awhile as I zigzagged around treetrunks looking at the ground, a bit of something white in the distance caught my attention. It was about twenty yards away, up on an open roll of thick muskeg. Looking harder, something pale brownish was also there in a curl next to the white object. With curiosity aroused I stepped towards it. Approaching closer…a pleasing, excited energy charged through me! Half sunk into the moss was the large curving horn of a wild sheep ram, still attached to a small piece of its skull! And ten yards away lay the other curled brown horn showing its hollow, having been separated from the bony skull-knob. This was a very exciting find! Circling the area wider out I searched for other parts but found none. Nothing else remained of this animal: no vertebrae, no teeth or jaw, no bones, no hooves, no hair. Since Dall sheep were known in this area, I suspected it be that specie, although it could also be a Stone sheep or maybe a saddle-back sheep.

Whatever killed and ate this animal had been very efficient. I pondered what carnivore specie had ended the big ram's life: grizzly, blackbear, cougar or wolf? This evidence suggested that most probable were wolves. Since everything was gone…carried away or eaten on the spot…a wolf pack seemed likely. Wolves eat bones but so do cougars. I did not know if a cougar would be that efficient, eating every piece; also, the information I had on this region was that no cougar had ever been seen this far north. While both grizzly and blackbear species could kill an old ram, their eating style would usually leave some bones at the spot.

Leaving the beautiful big horns, I got busy with mushrooms until too tired to continue. Later back at camp I had a good drink of the purest pure icy creek water, then wolfed-down a cold supper straight out of three cans! After that I washed them out in what I now called Clear Creek, and flattened them with a few bootstomps. Put inside a plastic bag, they were weighted down under the fast-flowing water with a few large rocks in order to keep any-and-all smells of food absent from camp! Now it was time for a rest on the warm sunny gravel bar since the Sun was quite low on the rolling dark blue-treed western horizon, too late to go for another pick.

I just sat on the rocks and relaxed, while enjoying the bright, slowly changing colours of the southern and western sky…and the lively bubbling gurgles and shishing of tumbling creekwater. Little clumps of maroon, rose pink and white wildflowers livened up the stoney gravel bar, growing among rocks and sand. This bushy-looking herb, people up here called caribou weed. And few mosquitoes were out and about…allowing a higher than usual degree of enjoyment in this lovely remote Yukon forest. As time passed, twinkling light of stars began appearing in the grey and bluegrey of infinity above. Soon though, needing a rest and with nothing to do in the dark I retired to the security — of a sort — within my little tent. Now I was hidden from view by the tarp fence: far more a psychological fence than physical…but better than none at all!

Next day, I again worked the ram's horns area where the lower bench ended. Here was a forty-five degree rise curving over thirty yards up into another flat bench populated by small lodgepine trees. Zigzagging up I went on a scouting walk, carrying just one bucket this time. Pine trees here were growing in little separate groves. This second bench ran westward until it abruptly stopped at a solid-rock canyon that rose thirty yards above the creek. Near this cliff-edge was a continuation of the indistinct animal trail that I had been using lower down. Here it was more conspicuous…with several sets of small hoofprints impressed into the dry yellowish clay-like soil. The tracks pointed in both directions along the trail but on their last pass the animals had been moving upstream to the northwest. Several wild sheep had walked the trail about one month ago when this yellowish clay was wet and soft!

Here also were three sets of wolf tracks superimposed over the sheeps' and pointing in the same direction! Apparently, they had been following the sheep. Who would have known that in this remote wild place, eventually a human would be following them both? Their tracks never left the trail…winding around rocky knobs and bends just above the cliff-face. Here, I took time out to check the rock for any hint of metal or other mineralization.

This solid rock was granite-like, of a creamy and light brown colour, fairly cracked and weathered. But as usual it was nothing to be excited about, showing no hint of mineralization. Besides…this area had no morels at all. I was carrying an empty plastic bucket that randomly bumped against treetrunks or groundsnags as I walked — resounding with a loud low-pitched clunk! I thought that would decrease my chance of seeing any wildlife and also of meeting a bear too closely…which was okay with me!

At one point on the trail another large four-toed footprint appeared. This track looked too round for a wolf. It was about five inches across, a front paw, looking more like a cat track! It showed no clawmarks as a wolf track usually would. I doubted that lynx had paws this big. And it was definitely not a bear track. Cougars were not known to inhabit this northern region.

But I had seen cougar tracks several times before and these were identical! I had not expected to have one more large carnivore to watch out for! Here though, I was surprised at such clear evidence sunk into the solid clay. The only alternative it seemed, would be a lynx if that big cat ever has forepaws five inches wide…something I did not know for sure. Even so, I thought it must have been a cougar and would be feeding on sheep, young moose and beavers. One last possibility though, which seemed unlikely…would be a wolf track that somehow became distorted in the mud before it dried into this big round cat-like print. Yet I could not help feeling a cougar was alive and well here, so had to be watchful of it!

After this most interesting observation and uncertain conclusion, I followed the animal trail about fifty yards until the site of another kill was at my boots! Again, as yesterday, very little evidence remained. Four little pale brown horns lay on the ground beside the trail, those of what I assumed to be probably an adult ewe Dall sheep and a juvenile ewe or young ram. They had been killed right on the trail. Again, everything had been eaten except the horns…nothing else remained. This deadly wilderness event and the other looked to have occurred two winters before…probably at the same time. Now I was certain that wolves had killed them.

It would be a matter of time until the horns too, would be consumed by smaller animals such as porcupines, squirrels, voles and mice. So these wild sheep gave their lives and bodies to several animals — as is the way of Nature where everything is used, re-used and of mutual benefit — even though their death seemed so cruel. Once again I was reminded of how temporary life is: no matter how beautiful animals such as Dall sheep were, no matter how beautiful was their mountainous home, eventually they would all die. Such sights and such thoughts made me sad.

I stood for a long time wondering, thinking…as the hot northern sunshine burned my face. Gazing into the deep blue sky…puffy summer clouds drifted and slowly changed shape from odd animal beings to quasi-animal or semi-human beings. At times, one would gradually appear even from the space of open blue…while another would slowly vanish into it. Constantly moving, these cloud-beings seemed both magical and alive; the blueness of outer and inner space was their realm!

While consciously drawn into this cloud performance above, I moved off the animal trail to sit on a rough weathered granite knob at clifftop, high above the creek. To the south and southwest stood rounded undulating green hills. Beyond them were squared blue and grey rocky mountains touching clouds and sky. I wondered about the purpose of the Universe, existence, life and death. It was all too complex and too mathematically logical to be merely blind chance! Questions ran through. Why does such living beauty as the Dall sheep…such complexity of life-form — evolve to live such a short lifespan? Why does this lovely animal have to die in order for another beautiful animal — the wolf, bear or raven — to maintain its life? Why is all life so temporary?

Thus be the natural way, the way that Nature functions: of that, there was no doubt in my mind. And the quasi-elevated human animal is not exempt from the same inexorable forces. Of the various world Religions, past and present…none seem to adequately explain the meaning of Nature, life and death. While the various scientific disciples have explained much about how Nature functions, they have not explained the why. The meaning, the purpose, the why… remains just out of reach of both Religion and Science. Even so…it seems to me that the sum-total of Science is closer to the truth of it all…and getting closer each year. But there is one religion or philosophy based on understanding the human mind, that seems to have answers. It is also the only one giving Nature a high priority!

Quite some time elapsed while I sat focussed on this questioning and reasoning state of mind. But my own purpose of this place and time jerked me back. There was work to do if I were to make a dollar profit! Now I proceeded farther along the trail to an area of little rolls and dips. The creek's whitewater sounds echoed up, bouncing along the almost vertical rocky cliffsides, concealing any other sound. As I entered a group of closely spaced trees and stepped over a fallen snag the empty bucket banged against it, ringing out in a loud low-toned clunk! Instantly from the dip ahead, just below the hill's curve began a crackling of branches, heavy thumping and swishing!

That moment I took a pepper spraygun into hand! Was it coming this way or moving away? I stood still — ready and listening! Nothing appeared at the crest in front of me! The random crackling sounds were now diminishing towards the creek…a great relief! But curious to know what it was I hurried ahead to look down into the dip! No animal was in sight. On the gentle slope its large tracks were clearly visible, moving away from the trail at an angle towards the creek. I was too late.

The animal had gone down into the dark green shady spruce thicket by the creek below! For some minutes I stood watching the creek and hill across, hoping to see it crossing or climbing. The animal never appeared…it was either hiding in the trees or moving away upstream, up the creek's canyon. From this distance, track pattern looked to be that of a moose. We had come to twenty yards from meeting face to face! Walking to the tracks where the animal had stopped on the trail and turned away, I saw that it was indeed a moose — and a huge one!

Its hoofprints were the largest I had ever seen! I never realized their hooves grew to such a size…about six inches wide. This was no doubt a very big bull! Now, a negative emotion began creeping into my body, that one called disappointment…because I never got to see the big beauty. Its tracks left the trail at about a hundred thirty-five degrees to the right as it bolted, turned sharply back and trotted away from the strange drum-like sound of my plastic bucket! Why this moose had lived long enough to grow so big, I understood — so alert and shy as it was!

If I had continued upstream I may yet have seen it but to give the big bull some space, I turned back in the opposite direction. From one point along the trail above the canyon I could see my tiny camp far below but very visible…being constructed mostly of bright orange, blue and green tarps with blue tent in the centre. It looked a bit like a carnival and no doubt could be seen for many miles from the air! Along the way back I scouted somewhat east of the trail, finding another good mushroom slope where the bucket was filled in half an hour. All the while, opposing emotions took turns running through my excited, energetic body and mind: happiness and disappointment. From this patch I returned downslope past the big ram's horns and onward to camp.

Back in camp I gathered a dozen large rocks, putting them in a circle next to a larger rock at the bench edge, just above the creek and where the view to west and south was wide open. Then I rummaged up dry twigs, branches and some bits of tree pitch for starting a little fire, which would be a comfort when evening arrives. Next, I took an empty bucket back to the ram's horns. It was a two hundred yard walk along the cool creekside then another fifty away from it. But once there, I remembered that I forgot my camera. Oh well…I was too worn out to go back again so just sat in the deep moss awhile admiring the two spiralling beauties. Lifting the one horn that was attached to a small piece of skull…it was surprisingly heavy; I estimated it to be at least ten pounds!

I thought that wild sheep rams must have very powerful necks and shoulders to carry such weight day and night for years on end! These horns were very thick, like a bighorn's and about two-thirds curl that had been broomed and chewed off to a thick frontal tip. Otherwise they would have been at least one full curl! They were somewhat battle-scarred and definitely had the look of power! These big heavy horns no doubt belonged to a very old ram…one with self-confidence to match.

I placed this first horn into the bucket then picked up the second, holding it in the crook of an arm and against my right side. Thus my last chore of the day, I carried this rare find back to camp. Quite a treasure, I hoped there would be room for these in the helicopter on the flight out.

After this day I had a good idea of how long I could keep busy with the mushroom crop. So, after another voracious downing of a tincan supper, I constructed a red-ribbon pickup date on the boulder-strewn flowery gravel bar next to camp. My pilot could be flying over any time now for the message. Weighting down the ribbon here and there with stones, the number was a ten-foot long twenty-nine. Then back up the bank to my circle of rocks, I lit a little campfire. Sitting there, I rested while enjoying the sunset…then stars awhile…before retiring to the tent.

The next day began as another lovely sunny one. I crossed the creek in my high gumboots heading westward from camp then along a low bench of little rolls and hollows where grew small pine, spruce and willow. Two areas of good morel ground soon appeared which I immediately got busy at. Two tarps were spread out on level sunny ground for drying mushrooms on-the-spot while I picked. This strategy was for saving energy and time; I could pick more while walking less. About an hour later I had these patches picked and drying then walked farther westward scouting the ashy ground.

As I neared a gentle slope of lodgepine and small spruce clumps, in the distance a set of large animal tracks came into view. I went straight towards them. Closer, I could see that they were pointing directly eastward towards camp — bear tracks! Now standing at the tracks, their freshness and long claws were blatantly visible in the soft ash and clay! Suddenly alert and excited — adrenalin ran through my arteries — I looked up and all around, listening...as I took a pepper spraygun from its holster! These grizzly tracks were as fresh as my boot tracks!

Here, the bear had made an abrupt stop then turned ninety degrees to left and curled back walking away to northwest. Kneeling down, I measured the forepaw's width with my right hand and fingers. This was a fairly large grizzly with forepaws about eight inches across, toe to toe! It had been here probably less than an hour ago, possibly only minutes away or less. Apprehension increased, my body tensed and instantly filled with energy! I was now very alert visually and audibly!

The bear's tracks having led away though, was a consolation. It had either smelled or heard me, or both. It could have also seen me from this point where its tracks stopped and turned. But my seeing and hearing nothing, I assumed it was not nearby now. So...being too curious I followed its tracks a short way where visibility was good...until they went over a low hill that I could not see beyond. Not wanting to push my luck, I quickly paced back towards camp distancing myself from this scene, just in case! Now besides threetoed woodpeckers, squirrels, one bull moose, possibly a cougar and wolves, I had an adult grizzly as one more neighbour!

On the way back, passing by the two drying tarps I gathered up my earlier pick of partly dried morels and carried them across the fast-flowing transparent-clear creek back to camp. After setting the mushrooms out again, I went scouting to south of camp wandering for some time and much distance until the faint steady hum of a helicopter could be heard. Immediately heading back as fast as possible, jogging much of the way...the hum quickly became louder and louder as it was coming in a straight line towards camp. The Jetranger flew directly over me and arrived at camp just before I did.

But instead of reading the red-ribboned date from the air and leaving, the pilot decided to land right there on top of it, again squeezing between creekside trees...to perch on the same gravel bar. He was just checking on me to see how I was and how many mushrooms I was finding. We chatted for fifteen minutes or so but I never mentioned the grizzly to him. Then he left, lifting off with a windy whirl that had creekside brush and trees bending and bobbing...within that loud highspeed chopper noise. I gave him a two-thumbs-up, "Goodbye! Have a good flight!" The helicopter sped away easterly as I watched and listened to it vanish.

I was hoping the big grizzly would not come to camp at night! If it did, I knew it would be after me...since I had no food smells in camp and bears do not eat morels, fresh or dry! This day when evening arrived I sat up a long time by the campfire at the creekbank's edge...watching for the bear. Sunset was long and beautifully coloured with clouds of orange, pink and mauve shades floating slowly above the deeper mauve and darkening navy blue mountains. As the mountains blackened, the sky turned dark grey...and white stars began to sparkle above. The big bear never came...fortunately. I retired to my tent hidden from view inside of the flimsily fenced yardspace. Now safe from mosquitoes at least, I lay comfortably stretched out on the air mattress beside my loaded 30-30 rifle and two pepper sprayguns.

Next day, wanting to avoid the grizzly track area, I went eastward from camp onto a flat bench forested with pine and large old spruce trees. There, a few sets of old moose tracks passed through but very few morels were growing. Eventually my wanderings led to a larger, slower moving second creek edged with aspen and willow. Faint remains of a very old campsite lay in the sandy loam at one point beside this creek: a few rusty tincans dating from the 1890s era! The men of yore — probably prospectors — left two rare coffee cans, both embossed with an old man in a long nightrobe walking and holding a saucer-shaped lamp with lighted candle. The embossed lettering read: "Hills Brothers Coffee."

Placing these nice antiques into the bucket along with a handful of morels, I followed along the creekbank walking upstream. A few minutes later I came to three white beaver skulls, each with two long bright orange upper front teeth! These were lying in sand but with bottom jaws missing. One skull was punctured with round tooth-holes and also partly chewed away. My guess from the hole sizes was that this beaver had been killed by a wolverine, fisher or lynx. A young wolf would be another lesser possibility. I picked up the best two skulls, also as keepsakes.

Soon afterward, still near the creekbank I noticed two sets of bear tracks stamped into the dry yellowish clay. These were old tracks from early spring, I was pleased to see. One set was of a small blackbear. The other prints were probably made by my big grizzly of yesterday: the forepaws were exactly the same size and shape! I was certainly camped in the big bear's territory, so hoped it would remain disinterested.

By the time I returned to camp, my little friend the yellowtopped three-toed woodpecker was there busily pecking at treebark…a cheering visitor! But a few minutes later it flew away northward next to the creek. Since evening was fast-approaching, I lit up the campfire to keep warm and…to keep mosquitoes somewhat at bay. Again sitting on the big rock beside the fire and facing mostly westward where the big grizzly had left tracks the previous day, I passed another peaceful evening resting by the little popping fire, albeit slightly tinged with apprehension.

One more night passed slowly as I slept very lightly — all too aware of the grizzly and the possibility of a night-time visit. When morning light arrived I was happy to be alone! I could relax and enjoy the trickling, shishing sounds of the crystal-clear creek, the warm morning sunshine on my face and hands and the soothing silence of forest and sky. The silence was almost tangible…it would dominate everything during calm days and nights. Now and then animate or inanimate sounds, leafy or earthy smells and other sense stimulae would mildly accentuate within this wide open calmness.

On this day to fulfill a secondary reason for being here, I walked up the whitewater creek with goldpan, testing the gravel. At one bend several large rocks had been moved manually at some indiscernible time past. Probably as far back as the 1890s men were here prospecting. Could be, the old coffee cans were left by them. The 1930s Depression years could have also brought men into the area but there was no evidence of that time. Panning yielded a small amount of blacksand but not a speck of shiny yellow colour that I wanted to see.

Following the creekbed upstream and into the canyon, I could see the granite-like rock wall spotted and stained with turquoise blue and bluegreen of copper carbonate! This showing of nonferrous metal certainly aroused my interest! But upon looking closely at this rock, no actual ore was visible and the carbonate merely a thin surface film. The hardrock cliff was partly shattered with hair-thin cracks through which turquoise bloom of copper had penetrated from somewhere below, surfacing here. An ore body was no doubt in the area but hidden very well by Nature. Of unknown size and unknown distance from where I stood, I had no way of finding it…short of a miracle! Continuing for some distance upstream until the gorge pinched and where huge boulders made further exploration impossible, I saw no more indication of metallic ore…fortunately for the wildlife and ecosystem!

After a morning of prospecting, I resumed my primary objective by early afternoon, hiking in a northerly direction from camp. The Sun was still shining as a few medium-elevation clouds, puffy white and grey, slowly drifted about. The weather appeared much as usual and good for drying mushrooms. Focussed on the task, I was a half-mile from camp where large spruce trees stood blocking the view south. After maybe an hour of work, the slight breeze became interspersed now and then with little hard gusts. Shortly after, a large dark grey cloud arrived from the south — too low for comfort! A few scattered raindrops began falling around me… trouble was in the air!

Quickly covering the buckets and leaving them, I ran back towards camp trying to beat the rain, since some of the morels were not roofed over. Most of the way a light sprinkle was coming down. But the huge, now blackish cloud was racing northward very low over the southern hilltop! Wind suddenly blew steady, cold and hard! The rain was still a light sprinkle as I arrived at camp — puffing and panting for oxygen, on rubbery legs and ready to collapse! But now very large raindrops began hitting the tarps in loud splats! Scrambling around, I covered the mushrooms in a hurry, weighting down the tarp edges with whatever rocks and wooden chunks were handy! Big raindrops quickly increased to a heavy pour! And with this very heavy rain came a strong wind — blowing very much sideways!

Even the roofed-over morels now needed to be covered! This storm really made a lot of extra work. So exasperated, the foulest words possible poured from my mouth as I looked up and shook a fist at the immense black cloud! Of course, that did not help other than release excess emotional energy. Finally…the morels were protected! Soaking wet, I slipped into the tent to rest and wait out the storm. The heavy rain and gusting wind continued unabated for more than an hour. Well, it did give me a much needed rest at least! The end result of this storm was a loss of about three dry pounds of morels but if I were three minutes later, the loss would have been much worse.

In the evening another storm arrived. For most of the night, heavy pouring rain angled down in the strong wind. But sunshine returned next morning, fortunately! I waited until afternoon for the muddy ground to dry off a bit before venturing northward on another scout, following back up the animal trail where the huge bull moose and I had almost met face to face. This day was a cloudless calm and soon became hot. I passed beyond its big tracks. While walking over a lot of dud ground, sweat trickled down my forehead and dripped from hair and ears as I climbed up, up and up…through a large open southwest slope. At last, near the hilltop a good patch of morels showed within and near a lodgepine grove. After a short sit-down in the cool shade of small pine trees, two buckets were filled in less than an hour.

Visible to the north from this point was a high steep rocky peak not far away, jutting almost vertically above the green-treed hilly horizon. For a better view, I hiked to top of the next rolling hump. Standing under another clump of little lodgepine, I observed the broad treed valley dropping gently for several miles to the northeast. Here, the cool shade was again just what I needed! Taking off the backpack, I sat down with back leaning against one treetrunk. Then a few mouthfuls of liquid pleasure from my little waterbottle…Clear Creek water…brought the present moment to almost perfect!

Directly ahead was a lovely expanse of natural beauty completely untouched by human doings, thanks to its remoteness and the long harsh winters. At this wide valley's western edge the creamy white and pale grey peak rose abruptly skyward to dominate the whole scene. This unusual mountain was about a half-mile distant with a series of lovely green-treed rolling hills between it and where I sat. Partly open-faced, I could see on the pale southwestern cliffside, five tiny white dots among little green patches of meadow about halfway up. I thought these must be either mountain goats or Dall sheep!

Reaching into my backpack, I took out the twenty-power spotting scope. Through it the animals were clearly visible: they were Dall sheep! Two rams and three ewes were grazing along the narrow grassy ledges. They looked very placid and quite enjoying the warm sunshine. A good-sized ram with more than three-quarter curl lay near one cliff edge looking out across the wide valley to west of its lofty home. So...I was right about the horns: they were from Dall, not Stone or saddleback sheep.

Up there, the sheep were certainly safe from carnivores! But the lower treed hilly area was a danger zone...where I had seen three sets of horns on and beside the trail several days ago. I was bothered by this herd's apparently sparse population and with no lambs, which would have been a month or more old by now. I hoped there were more ewes with lambs just out of sight over the bluff at the mountain's eastern and northern sides. If not, this was a very endangered herd! But there were still herds of Dall sheep in other parts of Yukon, so...not to worry. Or should I? Supposed management of wildlife from far-off places has proven — over and over — a sad failure all across Canada. With most wildlife it is just a matter of time until they will all become endangered...then extinct. The foremost reason: Ottawa's policy of excessive immigration, no management of human numbers! Second to that, there's a variety of long-standing economic-ecological mismanagement.

Two days later, another balmy one, I decided to return west of camp where the big grizzly left its tracks. On previous days from across the canyon I kept a good eye on that area, never seeing a hint of the bear...so now thought it should be safe to return. Crossing the creek, I followed a small rocky ridge picking mushrooms as I went. In about an hour I was up to the grizzly tracks, so followed them a short distance over a little open hill and to some thick muskeg moss where they became untraceable. The only wildlife around now were three or four squirrels...squealing and chattering in their all-is-well conversation as they gathered and nibbled cones up in the spruce and pine boughs.

Following this pine-treed ridge farther westward, I stepped atop one little rocky knoll. Looking down, an unexpected but most pleasing sight was stretched out on the slope about fifteen yards below! Like a forest in miniature but instead of green, this one was coloured yellow, brown and grey! This unusually thick extensive patch of treelike morels was a rare beauty to behold! Once again, I did not have my camera and being too far from camp could only tuck this visual experience into memory.

But I did have a pocketwatch. With it I could time the filling of one four-imperial gallon bucket; maybe I could set a new record here! Stepping down then onto knees, with bluehandled scissors I began quickly clearcutting this miniforest...only eight minutes ticked by until the bucket's top edge was level with mushrooms! Before this, my fastest bucket was twelve minutes. Such thick patches though, have always been few and far between!

After finishing this fast-dollar patch I walked the ridge more westward, high above the pure whitewater creek. Far to the north, the Dall sheeps' beautiful mountain home again came into view. Too far away and not having my scope, I could not see them but was sure they would see me. Looking their way...I gave the sheep a mental, "Goodbye," since tomorrow the helicopter would come for the flight back out.

As late afternoon arrived I began packing and organizing as much as possible for loadup. The pilot would be arriving at an unknown time, probably morning. I hoped to wake up early enough to break camp and be ready. The tent, fence and some drying tarps would have to be dealt with in the morning. By now though, I was quite exhausted...so on this night slept deeply.

Well...when morning arrived I was rudely awoken by the loud rapid sound of heli-propellers already almost above camp! I rolled over, quickly pulled on my bluejeans and boots, then scrambled out! I was far from ready. He arrived earlier than expected. While hastily untying knots and folding tarps...I noticed to the southwest one gigantic black cloud that completely enveloped the horizon. Its bottom extended right to the ground as a black and dark grey sheet that was definitely a downpour of very heavy rain. And within it were frequent flashes of bright pink or pale blue lightning. There — was the pilot's reason for coming so early!

The Jetranger landed on the flowery gravel bar. My pilot got out and waited there while I broke camp as fast as possible! He helped with loading up. Meanwhile the stormcloud slowly, stealthily approached. As I jogged back and forth across the swift little creek to the bar, the flashing black cloud billowed larger and larger. In less than thirty minutes we were ready for takeoff. By then the storm looked to be about five miles away and would likely arrive in fifteen minutes. The pilot fired up the helicopter, lifted straight up above the creekside trees, rotated... and we made our escape! I was lucky this time.

Flying quickly away towards a beautiful cloudless blue sky...behind us, the flashing electrical cloud now appeared to cease its advance. Such a pleasure it was being once again back in the air looking at forest and mountains from this magical perspective! But all-too-soon this special enjoyment was over. Only a half-hour flight back, we landed and unloaded. After paying the pilot, I immediately drove away in search of a secluded sunny place to finish drying morels of the previous three days' pick, which were at a risky stage yet.

Along one dusty dirt road a grassy little meadow soon appeared...perfect! In about ten minutes, tarps and morels were spread out in the sunshine. Now I could lay back and relax in the field of grass and wildflowers that were blooming all around in yellow, pink, white and blue. But then a chorus of delicate high-pitched, steadily rolling chirps of young birds began sounding out...from a black circular hollow in one old trembling aspen tree just a few yards away! Four or more hungry young woodpeckers were all gently yodelling a quick: "Krreee-krreee-krreee-krreee-krreee-krreee-krreee...!" And it wasn't long until a rapid swishing of feathers and brightly yellow-flashing wings brought one parent to land with a slight crunch at the black oval. Simultaneously the wee chirping voices raised up: loud, urgent and demanding! Here, another wild treat for me had arrived...the beautiful yellowshafted northern flicker.

And far away on the southwestern horizon the black thunderstorm, barely visible...was imperceptibly creeping northward. It would not be coming this way. Now the morels would dry safely. Likewise, I could watch and enjoy flashes of pink and pale blue randomly lighting up the distant black clouds...as they bit by bit enveloped a pale bluegrey chain of pyramidal hardrock Yukon mountains.

Chirping Squirrels

With blue sky in every direction touching the mountains I shouldn't worry about the flight now…I had been afraid of getting that nauseous motion-sickness. The pilot and I loaded two weeks of supplies and equipment into his floatplane then taxied slowly to the bay's north end and turned to face south. He gave me a quick but clear briefing on safety, then we put on headphones for easy communication during flight. The powerful engine roared…the yellow plane's pontoons skimmed lakesurface…then lifted into the air! After gaining some elevation the pilot banked his plane and we curved in an easterly direction over pine, spruce and aspen forest. We continued gaining elevation but now at an easy rise. This sixty mile flight in northern British Columbia would certainly be a beautiful visual experience.

We flew above rounded evergreen rolling hills…over pale green and tan-brown moose ponds, then little lakes in various blues that dotted the dips and plateaus far below. Ahead and to the south stretched a vast expanse of deep blue forest with hundreds of bright silvery lakes reflecting the sunshine. Ahead, rugged rocky mountains in shades of grey, tan and rusty brown appeared to expand and grow upward as we approached. Soon we were dwarfed to very minute by a huge peak as we flew past…over a cleft in the mountain range. For a short while it seemed as if a wingtip would touch this gigantic vertical slice of mountainside as we skirted by the peak!

As if in slow-motion, we passed over the mountain range. Crossing to its eastern side, we were now flying high above a vast broad valley that ran north-south as far as one could see. To the east stretched an extensive forested plateau with countless tiny lakes, some sparkling, some dark. The longest lake in that valley was my destination, still far off but visible as glowing pale grey. The floatplane lowered gradually…approaching straight towards it. The lower we descended the more rugged-looking became the dark-treed rock bluffs along its western shore, while the lake's eastside terrain remained rounded and docile. We were soon to touch down at an eastshore bay but first had to circle above the partly burnt forest next to it.

Still fairly high…too high, I thought…we circled over as I visually scrutinized as best I could the semi-open forest and open ground below for any presence of large carnivorous animals. I could see nothing obvious — thankful for that! Even so, it was not possible to be certain. A bear or wolves may be down there under a tree or brush lying down and out of sight.

After two passes over, the pilot turned northward then banked to southerly now dropping quickly lower and lower to the deep blue wind-protected bay. We touched down very smoothly onto lakesurface then taxied slowly to a finely gravelled grey shore. I got out first, taking the rope from the rightside pontoon, stepping into shallow transparent-clear water and tying up to a firmly rooted shoreline willow bush. My pilot helped unload supplies onto the pebbly beach.

Within maybe fifteen minutes he was back out…yellow pontoons gliding over sparkling water, then into the air and after a slight wave of wings, was angling back towards town.

I stood a few moments watching the plane recede in a big blue sky…then carried rifle, pepper sprayguns and tent over the loose pebbly beach to the flat moss-and-lichen-carpetted woods just above the lake's highwater line. Standing under a large spruce tree, I watched and listened to the floatplane's engine drone steadily decreasing as its form shrank then disappeared into a greyblue mountain-filled horizon. Silence and soft sounds of Nature now enveloped me. Wavelets trickled and plunked at shoreline as they pushed and pulled the smooth rounded gravel, rolling it up and down…generating a multitude of harmonious clicking sounds. These were a gentle, most pleasant music that was naturally easing away the tension I had carried here from the human realm. Distant chirrs and chitchat of a few red squirrels accenting the musical piece were my first animate welcome to this wild place! Humanity had almost never stepped onto this shore or into this forest.

Arming myself with two pepper sprayguns in holsters belted onto one hip, I felt confident of having adequate self-defence. Anxious to get scouting, I picked a good spot for the puptent on level mossy ground under a clump of small pine and spruce trees. Hurriedly I set it up then constructed a blue and orange tarp fence around the tent, thus creating a little yardspace. This flimsy structure also acted as animal blind and psychological barrier. A biffy was dug next, beside and under a little mossy log back in the woods. Within twenty minutes I was longstepping into the semi-open woods over flat deep-muskeg ground…towards a rounded poplar-treed hill.

My 30-30 rifle was left in the tent. It was not worth much anyway as defence against a grizzly or moose except at very close range: less accurate and probably less effective than pepperspray. And besides, I did not want to kill anything! I was in wild animals' territory now…of my own will. This was my risk, not theirs. I did not belong here and was merely a temporary visitor so had no right by Nature's law to kill anything.

After five minutes of difficult bouncy walking over thick spongy muskeg, I crossed a little boggy leafy-green creek at the poplar hill's bottom edge then went up onto more solid grey-and-yellow-clay ground. Following the slope southward just above the little green creek until reaching a boar's nest of tangled fallen spruce and poplar trees, I stopped there…somewhat puzzled and disappointed. I had expected to see at least a few morel mushrooms but saw none! As a consolation though…in the dry pale dirt were stamped several old moose tracks while in low dips among the moss were low shrubs loaded with clusters of edible crowberries, shining a mirror-like black. Turning uphill, gradually zigzagging higher, I soon became aware of how difficult this area would be to work — with so many fallen trees tangled and crisscrossing in all directions!

Walking was hard and slow…having to clamber over and under several of these boar's nests. But eventually, higher up mushrooms appeared in singles and small groups. Encouraged slightly, I was spurred onward. After about an hour though, the general pattern of these hills was becoming apparent. Very sparse it was. In disappointment I wandered for another two-plus hours checking different ground hoping there would be some thick morel growth somewhere.

But no…they were just not there. To catch my breath I would sit on a log or stump now and then while gazing at patches of deep blue sky…openings to infinity between the puffy white and pale grey clouds: my solace in an otherwise unhappy circumstance. Just a few hours after arriving I knew that it would be impossible to pay for the six hundred dollar flight cost. And worse, the pilot would not be back until morning of the fourth day! I would be stuck here for three nights and two more days. I had gambled before this way and won…but this time, lost.

By now afternoon was late and I was really tired. Slowly manoeuvring around, under and over groundsnags and stumps…I proceeded back towards the lake and camp. Along the way, one cheering sight came fluttering by as a spot-backed northern threetoed woodpecker and it landed on a nearby pine treetrunk! Flipping its long pointed black beak rapidly from side to side, the little bird was inspecting bark for insects and larvae hiding inside. Between pecks, it spoke softly in woodpecker talk: "Gra-a-a-k…Gra-k-k-k." Then another bird replied in like manner from the near distance southward. Always pleasing, these sweet birds were often my only close animate company.

Soon after this, I came to the very fresh tracks of a yearling moose. I followed them a short distance to where they junctured with the larger tracks of its mother. The two moose were going south while I headed westward, so didn't expect to see them. Then a lot of medium-toned whistling chirps above, musical chatter from a flight of crossbills, was my next enjoyment as they passed overhead flying northward. And from within nearby spruce trees came another cheerful sound: high-pitched peeps of tiny unseen birds that were either kinglets or chickadees…I was not sure which. A short while later I was almost back to my original point of entrance on the bench above the little green creek. Here, in the soft dirt was a set of small animal tracks about three inches long and very fresh…only minutes or at most a few hours old and pointing southward.

Kneeling down, I could clearly see the front paws: distinctly squared in a bear-like shape and with tiny but long sharp claws. At first glance I thought a little grizzly cub had left these impressions, probably at the same time I was higher up the slope! These tracks were not here when I had first come up from the creek about three hours previously. Now apprehension overcame my physical tiredness and emotional down! Looking up and around…listening… there was no animal in sight, large or small…and no sound other than rustling poplar and aspen leaves. The ground showed no other tracks nearby, neither the mother's nor a sibling cub. But since these tracks angled southward towards the little boggy creek, I assumed the sow grizzly was going the same way through leafy greens or muskeg at creekside. I was glad of that since my camp was to the west and north!

Biological electricity and adrenalin now had me on alert and energized! Closely watching the brush, I kept to the most open way back. Stepping as quickly as possible through the green creek and almost bouncing over the muskeg, I headed back towards camp! Then, as I was passing by a pinetree clump — one very loud boom! A sudden inner jolt and an instant stop, I stood as if frozen! Two spruce grouse exploded from among crowberry shrubs — up into the air ten yards to my right! With wings whistling they flew across in front, heading to my left…straight into the pines and coming to perch among upper branches safely away from the human.

Happy I was, this loud sound was not made by a grizzly! Here grew an extensive patch of low crowberry shrubs loaded with ripe berries, countless little shiny black spheres…perfect sustenance for these black-and-white grouse. I stood still, enjoying their benign company: their flecked and spotted feathery beauty, their quiet but alert expression and their sparkling watchful eyes. And deep yellow blossoms of cinquefoil bushes randomly brightened the open boggy crowberry meadow here and there…bringing more of Nature's positiveness to this unique little space and time.

I picked a handful of the shiny black berries, throwing them into my mouth all at once. Quite tasty they were, a bit seedy but juicy enough to quench some thirst; no wonder these were a favoured food of grouse! Moving very slowly past the birds, not wanting them to fly away in a panic...thus possibly tipping-off their location to some nearby carnivore such as a fox or lynx...they remained silent and still as I moved on and into a tight, shady spruce forest. Here grew lichen of black, white, grey and cream colours thickly covering treetrunks, branches, standing snags and ancient logs...another beautiful silent living decoration...which was also staple food for woodland caribou.

Passing through this lovely caribou forest, I was soon back out and under sunshine on the grey gravel beach just south of camp. Along the shore I picked up a few driftwood sticks while heading northward. Back at camp the paltry pick of morels went into a rectangular wire-mesh tray for drying, placed in sunshine at the base of one large spruce tree just above the beach. Then I began building a campfire on pebbles near the gently plunking waterline.

Levelling gravel on the beach, I placed the driftwood there then gathered some dry woods brush and a piece of pitchy spruce-wood as fire starters. Of course, I had some old newspapers along for this purpose, too. Within minutes I had a crackling smokey fire going. The fire served three purposes: for keeping warm and dry, keeping mosquitoes at some distance and telling the grizzly sow and other animals where I was. This latter purpose may have been more wishful than factually valid: hopefully, to them a superior animal that controlled fire would be something to avoid!

With the fire burning nicely I sat down beside it, sinking slowly into the rolling, shifting pebbles. Not many mosquitoes were yet buzzing around which was a consolation. A few tiny black-spotted sandpipers came by, silently feeding along the beach with tails bobbing up and down as slender yellow beaks picked among pebbles close to water's edge. Three ducks flew swiftly by very low to the water, quacking steadily; so far out, I could not recognize them. The spruce and pine forest around camp was well-populated with red squirrels that chattered and squealed now and then from up in the trees. Two came hopping and bouncing over lichen and moss into camp then dashed up into the trees that stood above my tent. All of these little neighbours were so pleasant and entertaining! As I warmed my hands over the fire, the two squirrels squealed happily above. They were already accustomed to the quiet new arrival... almost fearless.

I had a long wait with not much of consequence to do, so decided to just appreciate the natural beauty that I was now trapped in! As the fire's fuel was used up, I walked the beach southward gathering more pieces of old dry driftwood. Now and then a sharp clunk or clack would jar the silence of the forest...as a squirrel snipped the stem of a spruce or pine cone, letting it fall and bounce from branch to branch or onto a groundsnag.

One chipmunk appeared, running along a tiny well-worn trail just above highwater line. A network of these chipmunk pathways ran between old stumps and roots where little burrow entrances were and along the upper bank edge. Several chipmunks lived here in a small colony, their wee trails connecting in a long narrow web-pattern that ran through lichen and moss at forest edge and down into fine dry dirt on the cutbank, just below the overhanging moss and little interwoven rootlets. I was happy to have so many little animals for neighbours. They would be good company during the long inactive wait!

As evening approached, sunset seemed to last and last. Orange, pink, grey and mauve clouds and deep navy-blue mountains to the west were mirrored as beautiful mottled reflections shimmering from lakesurface wherever the breeze blew. A fish touched surface not far from shore, sending small circles rippling outward. A few semi-transparent caddisflies floating with wings up quietly sailed near the pebbly shore, drifting along in the breeze...while little loose clouds of them flew their funny up-and-down pattern just above watersurface, as if teasing any fish that may be just beneath! The western sky changed imperceptibly from pale blue to lime green…then eastward and directly above to deepening shades of grey…as a few stars began to faintly appear.

Gradually the light of more and more stars became visible, shining stronger until their numbers were countless. As their lightrays brightened, larger stars flickered brilliant then dim and again brilliant. Many stars were coloured…and changed as they twinkled from pale red to orange to yellow and back again or from white to pale blue and back to white. Far distant stars, nebulae and galaxies were a faint fuzzy white or pale blue. Now the deep grey night sky shimmered and sparkled with colour, seemingly itself alive!

But now the squirrels and chipmunks were silent, resting in their burrows under large treeroots or stumps. The air had much cooled, so most mosquitoes were perched for the night in moss, dwarf birch and willow brush. Hundreds of shoreline pebbles clicked in a harmonious rhythm as they rolled together…pushed and pulled by little bubbling waves. And at times the gentle splash of a fish would accentuate this easy melody of Nature. One human sat quietly by the fire…experiencing, enjoying it all!

With a long driftwood stick I poked the burning wood, raising a few red, orange and white sparks skyward but to quickly fade away in the blackness above. Bright orange-red coals of the campfire squealed, popped and crackled. Among these squealing hot coals now and then appeared tiny pure medium-blue flames shooting out sideways or downward. The fire was dying out…and I was now fading towards sleep. Built low on the wide gravelly beach this fire would go nowhere, so I left it to sizzle out by itself, retiring to my puptent and hidden inside the plastic tarp fence.

Five to six feet high, this fence was closed on the ground all around except for a narrow overlapped entrance. With this I felt a bit safer. I could sleep better knowing that during the night blackness a bear or moose could not walk right to the tent, step on it or get tangled in its ropes. Also, if some large animal arrived in camp the fence would give me more time to identify it and respond appropriately. But even so, I was not looking forward to this first night…knowing that a mother grizzly with at least one cub was probably not far away!

I slept very lightly. But the night passed without incident and I had a good sleep-in next morning. Squirrels were up early chitchatting back and forth. Warm and cozy inside the tent, I lay half-asleep listening to them…a most pleasant way to start the day. Still in my semi-dream state as one squirrel rustled from branch to branch in trees above, there came a sudden loud thud on the plastic tentfly! Now abruptly wide awake, I lay still, tense and listening! Then I realized the cause.

The squirrel directly above had nibbled off a branchtip loaded with cones, then dropped it. Well, it was time to get up anyway! Pulling on my pants, I crawled out pepperspray-first from under the tentfly, tiptoed quietly on soft moss and lichen and looked over the tarp fence. Vertical greybrown treetrunks, black, white and pale grey lichen and ochre-green moss were all around…still and silent. The only animal visible in camp was the little squirrel just above, placidly crouched on a branch eating seeds from a pinecone.

As I walked towards the beach to rekindle the campfire, first thing I noticed was the nearly empty morel tray which I had left out overnight under the big spruce tree. Of thirty mushrooms only half-a-dozen remained! Very early this morning I heard something shuffling near the tree, sounding like a small animal…maybe a squirrel. I had not considered any chance of some animal taking them since such never happened in previous years. Now I had to assume that one of my squirrel neighbours carried them away to its winter food cache!

There were a few cone caches close to camp so after starting the fire, I checked them and around the woods awhile but could not discover where the morels were hidden. Maybe something other than a squirrel ate them? I wondered if a fox would eat half-dry morels. Oh well, it made no significant difference anyway since their value was merely five dollars or so — while the entertainment value of these little neighbours was far beyond that!

This day, I passed the time by keeping the campfire going and exploring north and south short distances along the beach and into the woods. Once an eagle flew over quite low going south in no hurry and ducks also a few times, almost skimming the lakesurface while winging quickly northward. But no large animals appeared. By evening clouds moved in and a steady light drizzle began. This easy rainfall was not a discomfort but actually more of a help by dampening the mosquitoes...now buzzing around nowhere. My little gravelly space was most comfortable beside the campfire, which kept me warm and fairly dry. Quite unusual, little wind came with this slow-moving storm. Lakesurface only rippled. At times, splashing of fish flipping out reminded me that I was not alone...that life teemed here in this remote place!

With the sky completely clouded over in a dark grey sheet, there was no sunset to cheer about and darkness came sooner. But even so, I remained on the beach feeding the flames with chunks of driftwood and was soon surrounded by night-time's blackness. I thought the fire's flame and smoke would be a small help in telling bears or wolves to avoid my camp. This night was actually so pleasant I spent much of it sitting cozily by the crackling, popping campfire. Eventually though, I crawled back into my little tent for another light sleep.

Overnight more drizzly rain came between intervals of calm silence...and by morning a bright white sky hinted that maybe sunshine would return. Up and rekindling the fire, I decided to cook some wild and brown rice for breakfast along with two cans of grub. Always tidy, both as respect to Nature and for safety from large carnivores, I thoroughly cleaned and flattened the tincans and put them with others into a plastic grocery bag which was then weighted down underwater with large rocks...garbage to be taken back out when I left.

As I sat on an upsidedown bucket enjoying a tasty breakfast and looking westward across the big bright grey lake, a sense of something nearby came upon me. Twisting sideways to look around, there...two yards away, a slender rusty-orange and black fox was standing still on the beach pebbles, quietly gazing at me. Behind its shining yellowish catlike eyes there seemed to be the thought: "I am hungry, too. May I have some food?" With benign pleading eyes the fox remained still but tense — ready to run!

Of course I had to share a bit, so very slowly moving left arm sideways, flipped a big spoon of Irish stew to the side, away from the fox...which it trotted to and lapped up. I fed this sociable little animal bits and pieces for about five minutes until it sauntered happily away with a mouthful unswallowed. No doubt a den with pups was not far away!

A light drizzle continued on and off most of the day while again I kept busy and warm by feeding the campfire. Two times, floatplanes flew towards then over the lake, raising a hope that my pilot had come back early. But no...they flew on...one eastward, the other southward. Even so, entertainment was very near in the lively presence of squirrels, chipmunks, sandpipers, ducks, one grouse, fish and caddisflies...all moving about in their own ways as I collected firewood along the beach and in the woods. And all this time, the surreptitious peacefulness of an all-powerful silence forced upon me a very relaxed state of body and mind. Soft peeps, little chirps, clucks and squawks that interspersed randomly during the day were so much in harmony they seemed to be themselves a part of the vast silence.

After this long but peaceful day...darkness finally arrived. Rain continued once again for much of the night. But by next morning it had stopped and in early afternoon the sky opened into patches of blue as the quiet grey sheet drifted eastward, soon replaced by high puffy white summer clouds. Now the weather was just right for an afternoon of exploration! South of camp along the beach I collected a handful of little oddly-shaped rocks that were naturally sculptured by wave action. Walking long distances along lakeshore observing rock types, geological formations and looking for hints of nonferrous metal, was most interesting...so time sped up somewhat. This area was mostly limestone and related rock with a touch of quartz but carried no obvious metallic ore.

By late afternoon I went back to the tent for a rest and getaway from lively mosquitoes which were out and about after the rain quit. Lying on my back in comfort and warmth I listened to the chatter of distant squirrels, the gentle splashing of waves and the clicking of little round rolling stones. Soon these easy sounds lulled me into a semi-slumber. After some unknown time, the sharp urgent chirping of a squirrel began from some distance into the forest...entering the background of my sleepy mind. Shortly, another squirrel, closer, joined...then another, closer yet.

As each squirrel joined the excited chorus, I woke up a bit more until finally almost awake. Three in all were now emphatically chirping out their loud danger call! Then I realized that there was either a large raptorial bird in the trees or maybe some large mammal approaching on the ground. Lying still on my back...I listened intently. For certain, a wild visitor was slowly approaching from northeast — but what? Could it be a furred predator, caribou or moose? Whatever...the squirrels were very upset by its presence!

Closer yet, another squirrel joined in with its harsh piping calls...then another even closer! More squirrels lived in this forest than I had realized. Now by the direction, distance and time intervals between each squirrel's persistent loud calls, I knew the animal was coming steadily and directly towards camp. And the speed and steadiness of its approach indicated an animal on the ground — not in the trees! In a hurry I sat up, buttoned on my jeanjacket, grabbed the rifle and one pepper spraygun. Just then a squirrel directly above the tent took its turn chirping hard and loud! The dangerous visitor was now very close! Without putting on boots, I quietly crawled out of the tent.

Standing up, I twisted sideways to peer over the tarp fence in that direction. The trees at the tent's eastern side were quite thick but any large or tall animal would still be visible through them. Nothing could be seen...it could not be a moose or caribou. Then turning and looking around three hundred sixty degrees, yet nothing animate appeared. I had expected a large animal, so now the tenseness eased slightly. Looking up into the trees...no large bird was there, either. I crouched low, tiptoeing across thick soft moss and lichen to stand right by the blue and orange plastic fence. These were tense moments even though I had pepperspray in my left hand and rifle in my right!

The squirrels continued on with their sharp emphatic calls and the one above my tent was now especially loud! This enigmatic animal was very close! I peeked over the fence...looking at the ground just outside it. Nothing was there, either! Again, tension eased...but much more, having seen no bear. "Must be something smaller but...where is it?" I thought. Whatever, the animal had moved at a very quick pace close to or right into camp, yet remained out of sight!

Silently looking all around...there was green and ochre moss, black, white and grey lichen on the ground. Thick-growing lichen on snags, treetrunks and branches was patterned in complex grey, black and white crisscrossing lines and curves. Looking towards the shimmering bluegrey lake, in shade beside the big scaley spruce treetrunk were my little lady's shovel, boxes of canned grub, Trapper Nelson packboard and bag. To left of these, in sunshine and shade was a brightly mottled maze of curves and lines: geometrically twisted, grey lichen-coated spruce branches and twigs.

Keeping completely still, I looked carefully…persisting. Focussing hard, my eyes moved very slowly…peering, scanning, looking for something animate. Then finally, from amid this busy geometric abstract, a vaguely different pattern began taking shape…faintly at first, as if materializing from some invisible realm or inner space. So…there it was! Erect and motionless, sitting beside my packboard only five yards away and calmly gazing out towards the lake: a lynx! "What a beauty!" I thought, as a jolt of cheerful excitement shot through.

It had not noticed me. With a breeze coming onshore from the lake and little waves splashing, it had neither smelled nor heard the human. The big relaxed-looking cat moved its head slowly, slightly, from side to side looking at the packboard and other camp supplies then gazed out towards the lake. Now I wished I had taken the camera instead of rifle from the tent! The big slim lynx' pale shades of mottled grey, white and ochre fur blend in perfectly with lichen, bark and branches rendering it almost invisible. This lynx appeared to be made of twilight…not matter!

I remained visually and mentally fixed on the animal, knowing that this visit would be short. Memory would have to replace the camera. The lynx sat about two-and-a-half feet tall and had very large forepaws. A bit humorous it looked, with long slender boney-kneed hindlegs and very large hindfeet that were shaped much like those of a snowshoe hare: oddly, the very animal that its staple diet consists of! A spontaneous smile came to my face…happiness charged mind and body, seeing for the first time a lynx in the wild! This was a most impressive big cat…and I was silently very excited!

After thus enjoying its presence for about one minute, the lynx' head slowly swivelled to the right and its fuzzy flat face turned back my way. With long black eartufts erect, calmly gazing around at the camp…finally, it noticed. Big pale yellow eyes stared at mine, fixed on my face looking steadily as the animal attempted to identify what it was seeing. Now not quite so relaxed and self-assured…for maybe ten seconds it scrutinized my face, all that was visible above the tarp fence. Smiling back at it, I kept perfectly still. Big yellow eyes suddenly opened wide as the lynx recognized something animate!

Keeping motionless, I was immensely enjoying this extremely rare experience! What a beautiful animal…even with its right ear partly chewed and mis-shapen, probably from a long-past bout of aggression with another lynx. I tried to not move at all but a slight motion on my face, probably my smile, had brought the cat to alert. Staring wide-eyed for a few seconds…then in a grey blur it turned quickly away — jumping in three lightning-fast zigzags — then suddenly stopped ten yards distant to stand broadside, staring back! It looked somewhat nervous while at the same time curious and uncertain about what I was…able to see only my head, face and neck. In this remote wild place the lynx would have probably never seen a human before.

A few seconds later the long-legged cat bound away to the south — hopping over lichen-covered groundsnags, zigzagging as it went in a natural escape response! Entering a thick treeclump, it slowed to a trot with short black-tipped tail up, then stopped about fifteen yards away. With tail-end my way, twisting head over left shoulder almost one hundred eighty degrees and looking back, the lynx was now barely visible amid mottled grey-and-white patterns of lichen and twisted branches. The lanky cat paused thus maybe half a minute…then turned and walked leisurely away. Dematerializing into colours and patterns of the forest maze, the lynx disappeared as if it be a ghost! Now in the near distance southward, more squirrels began their sharp danger calls! Then shortly, other squirrels too, called out in a sequence that curved to the east and then back northward, following the lynx' silent movement through the neighbourhood. Although it had been barely visible to me, not so the squirrels!

Charged with the excitement of this uncommon event, I belted on two peppersprays, put the rifle back into the tent then went down to the beach to stir up campfire coals…happy that this late afternoon visitor was only a benign lynx! With orange flames flickering, I fed them with dry wood chunks then sat down, sunk into the gravel…keeping warm. Breathing deeply, the air was a mildly pitch-scented pleasure. The ever-encroaching evening soon began to slowly colour clouds and sky with a quiet visual enjoyment. This peaceful calm and sensual beauty brought a natural unfabricated emotion of happiness and a sense of the deepness of life…an experience that would be impossible to describe at all in words.

But this beautiful wild place also stirred up thoughts, questions. Why is existence, life….be it human or animal…on our big-little planet, so harsh and so temporary? There must be more meaning to our existence than just eat-and-be-eaten, I thought. Kill-and-be-killed is a pervasive characteristic of both animal and human existence. We are all here for a short or long while: experiencing various pleasure and pain, caring, playing, fighting and dying. But humanity is supposedly superior; we can do and create more by far but likewise humanity also destroys far more. It seems that we human beings are not living up to our self-defined superiority, our self-defined civility, having not yet learned how to live peacefully with each other or with our beautiful animal companions! How are we superior?

Thoughts kept rambling on but not quite haphazardly, attempting to piece together the meaning of impermanence, interconnectedness, pain and pleasure…of phenomena and life on this planet. The natural realm of wild animals is a place of immense beauty yet deception and death are also integral with it. As material entities, all life forms…be they microbes, lichen, plant or animal…feed on each other while all of these are supported by the nutritious elements of Earth and also by energy that originates mostly with the Sun. The interconnection of these in Nature are well known due to humanity's evergrowing, albeit slowly, ability to think logically — with reason.

The logic of Science has discovered much about how natural phenomena, life and death function but has not answered…the why of it all! And this is where Religion in general has failed: the why of existence and death has not been properly explained…or if it has, is little understood. Humanity seems to have not yet found the right combination of reason, religion or spirituality, and social responsibility: that guarantees individuals, family groups and social groups will be civilized in the true sense…living harmoniously, not so selfishly, with each other and with Nature.

Now looking up at the sky…just one star was visible. The fire crackled and hissed softly as I warmed my hands near it. With almost no breeze, the lake was flat calm and hundreds of delicate caddisflies danced in the air above water along the shore. But being human, wanting to comprehend as well as experience, my mind continued flowing on with concepts, associated mental images and attendant emotions.

Science I thought must be very, very close to the why of our phenomenal existence…even though various disciplines of logic usually avoid this aspect, skirting by it. Matter and energy are interconnected as manifestations of existence and of life. With them exists another phenomenon called force. And all matter when viewed at its atomic and subatomic level is actually composed more of space, energy and force — none of which are matter. So…how close to the why could scientists, reasoners, be…while yet not seeing it?

162

Conscious, intelligent human minds have been observing and experiencing phenomena for millennia, yet lately have assumed that matter produces their very mind, their very consciousness. But the essential truth must be that a pre-existing deeper mind, consciousness or awareness, functions cooperatively with matter and energy...to produce conscious physical life forms — not vice versa! So...a type of mind must already be in the Universe, preceding material life. Life on Earth is all too complexly interconnected in a lively way to be merely chance, physical energy and matter only. Adding to this intricacy, everything is in motion at various speeds throughout an infinite Universe that extends physically both outward and inward...and it appears also mentally, consciously outward and inward.

My little neighbours here in the woods and lake and probably a few unseen large neighbours too, are conscious beings with mind, although different in some ways from humanity's mind. Animal minds are unique in their own ways yet have some commonality with that of human beings. Animal minds are also more direct, less complex, therefore easier to understand behaviourally than that of humanity; and animal minds being more direct are also more honest...less deceptive. Thus I pondered, asked and made effort to explain and comprehend the profoundness of existence, life and mind. Being alone in this remote deeply quiet place, encompassed by everything natural, allowed for and made this inner contemplation possible.

I felt as if I were partly absorbed into, somehow connected with the vastness of the beautiful sky just beginning to sparkle with starlight...light sent this way long before Earth was even born. Now my eyes burned and watered as the smoke of pine and sprucewood drifted my way bringing this sequence of thought to a halt. Forced to shift position, I stoked the brilliant orange coals, pushed a few small unburned logs farther in and over the hot hissing coals. So comfortable, so peaceful, so relaxing...this little secluded wild beach. The forest around was now very dark but the sky a vast expanse of minute bright lights.

The stars were now sparkling brilliant pale blue and white, pale pink and faint orange... suspended in the deep grey of Space. One large star to the southwest rapidly flickered in almost every pure colour of the prism: red, blue, green, yellow and orange. With my little neighbours all sleeping I sat alone but happy and certainly not lonely. This was my last night here, since tomorrow morning the floatplane pilot would arrive as preplanned, weather permitting...at nine a.m. manmade time. For a long while I remained still and silent, encompassed by night's darkness...savouring the presence and feeling the powerful peace of this quiet, very wild place. The fire's orange-pink and pure blue light slowly faded...its sizzles and pops became less frequent and quietened to almost mute. Then...leaving the animals of the night and retreating to the tent I joined the local squirrels, chipmunks and birds in silent slumber.

Togetherness

One blue-skied September day I was sitting on a big mossy rock munching down lunch beside roaring whitewater rapids. The deep swift water of the upper Skeena River was cold and clear green, reflecting little random streaks of golden yellow from the leaves of large ancient cottonwood trees at the far side and tall young poplars on this side. Icy water kicked up a fresh cool breeze…inviting some slow deep breaths as I gazed at this lovely, lively creation of Nature. Then, in the water just upstream there appeared the black heads of three bears coming around the bend…drifting and bobbing in the strong undulating white-capped current!

The sow held her snout high as two little cubs climbed up and held onto her back, then up onto her shoulders…as she tried swimming across to the other side. But a strong current pulled them very quickly downstream bobbing through big transparent green whitewater waves, closer and closer. Now in front of me only ten yards out — she was in trouble, with her head just slightly above water! Slowly, she sank down under the green and white frothing waves. Sinking under deep enough and long enough…she managed to escape the weighty cubs' grasp. They let go and — had to swim! Apparently, this risky drift was their first swimming lesson!

She surfaced again five yards downstream from the cubs. At first I was apprehensive for the cubs since this was very fast-moving water and wide, about forty yards to the far shore! In a few moments though, it became obvious that they were naturally good swimmers…even at merely six months out of their mother's winter den. Of course she knew what her cubs were capable of. One cub tagged along closely behind her as she now paddled leisurely across at a forty-five degree angle…while drifting a long way downstream. The other cub though, showed its independent nature by heading directly across from where I sat, swimming at a ninety degree angle and drifting only slightly with the current!

This second black cub won the race across. When its feet touched gravel bottom, it ran up onto the bar! There, it stopped, stood and shook soaking-wet fur with a rapid side to side motion…all around the cub a thin misty cloud of water droplets sprayed and sparkled in the sunlight. The little bear was drying off the same way that a dog does after a swim! The sparkling white mist quickly dissipated and the cub's thick black coat fluffed up back to normal. Standing motionless, it turned head, looking downstream at mother and sibling…still paddling across.

They continued drifting while slowly approaching the shore forty yards or so downstream. Surprising it was — to see what powerful swimmers these bears were! The first cub across took not much more than half a minute! The others were across in less than one minute, as they too, waded out and stopped on the wide grey gravelbar to shake themselves off. After that, the two bears slowly padded up onto a wide flat bench of tall dry yellowing grass and low pale green shrubs, stopping there momentarily. Then the first cub bound quickly along the pebbly gravel towards them…but before it could catch up, the sow bolted at high speed across the open sandy flat towards the forest edge! A split-second later, both cubs were leaping at high speed after her, stretching out almost flat in mid-air with each bound!

Safety under the thick treegrowth was of utmost importance to her. About fifty yards from riverside stood the tall, bright yellow and golden-orange forest. All three raced across…with ears straight back and glistening silver-black fur blowing flat back! In a few seconds they were out of sight, safely hidden within shadows under cottonwood trees and wild hazelbrush. The blackbear family would certainly be safe in there away from roads and hunters!

This uncommon meeting filled me with excited energy and a pleasantness beyond words. I knew the bears would not show themselves again. Even so, I remained on the rocky shore for quite some time…enjoying the bubbly translucent green and snowy-white waves, the roaring rapids and golden autumn forest where three blackbears were now safely out of human view. Amazed by the speed at which they — especially the young cubs — swam across this rapid current, a very fresh memory-movie kept running through my mind. No human would ever outswim them! As so often…my only regret was not having the camera handy.

About two weeks later but downstream somewhat I was walking along a deactivated logging road, looking at rocks…prospecting. Now and then I would stop to break a rock or two with my shorthandled two-pound sledgehammer then closely inspect the fresh breaks with a twenty-power pocket magnifier. Looking at the tiny crystal forms, colours and structure of rock was one more way that one could enjoy and appreciate Nature. This wee realm very often showed great beauty! It also indicated by geometry and light, the mathematical perfection of natural phenomena — some of the basics of modern Science. These many colours and often perfect geometric forms of microscopic rock constituents were another aspect of reality that few people ever see, unfortunately.

I quietly wished that more people would take time to look into this minute level where natural precision and beauty express in a way that is beyond the mundane! Although merely matter, crystals of rock…they have a mathematically precise, nonmaterial nature within and behind their formation. Here is another manifestation of the knowledge, or knowingness, that exists of itself on the Planet and in the Universe! Such perfection makes it obvious that existence and life must therefore have a very special meaning. Thus went my observations and thoughts…even though the only crystals now were perfect iron pyrite cubes shining silvery white.

Again moving onward and up, passing by several rockcuts that generated little interest, I was halted at one bluff by its different colour and texture. Kneeling down, I hammered an unusual-looking piece of rock. So hard and tough, it would break only after several heavy blows. Each time loud cracking sounds rang out, no doubt travelling a long distance through the cold still air. Finally, one piece snapped off. Now I went visually…and mentally…into its diminutive realm via the magnifier.

But within a few minutes I was brought back to the macro-realm by the distant rumble of a pickup truck slowly approaching from above. Placing the hammer behind a large rock and magnifier into pocket, I sat on the rock to wait. In a minute or two the brandnew fourwheel-drive arrived and came to a stop. It was a dark green crewcab Forestry vehicle seating six young people. The driver rolled down his window to inform me that a sow blackbear with two cubs were on the road only about one hundred yards up. They offered me a ride back down but I declined.

Showing him two pepper sprayguns holstered to my hip, I said that it was okay. I could defend myself. I would not go farther up and would soon be walking back down. They drove away. Then I resumed eyeing the piece of rock while periodically looking up the road for the bears. Continuing to bang rocks…I looked closely for particular colour, sparkle and shape that would indicate something of dollar value. But as usual nothing of any great interest showed.

Then again looking up the road — there she was! Peeking from behind a seven foot tall mountain hemlock sapling at roadside, the black sow stood facing me with pigeon-toed front paws solidly placed on the gravel. With steady eyes watching, fuzzy rounded ears on alert and tan-brown muzzle pointing my way, her shining black nose twitched slightly…testing for signs of danger, food or whatever. She arrived quicker than I had expected — only about three minutes after the foresters left! One cub soon appeared at the bend and quickly padded to its mother to stand beside her, where it also eyed me but in a somewhat shy way. The bears were just fifteen yards away. They were very healthy-looking with beautifully thick glowing fur and hair.

I was not certain what she had in mind — but walking the road was obviously on her agenda. And I thought she had come to assess what all of the cracking noises were about; this must have been the reason she arrived so soon! Standing motionless, she just stared in the typical bear fashion. Picking up the hammer, I slowly stood up with right hand on one holster while steadily looking back at them. Now a swishing sound of brush just below roadside indicated the second cub to be there just below its mother and sibling. Long moments passed in this nonverbal mutual regard; the sow seemed unwilling to move down the bank, off the road. The thought now came to me that I was in their way. Or maybe she was assessing me as a possible prey animal.

She continued steadily and without an eye-blink, staring…with ears straight up and showing no fear. I was becoming a bit apprehensive, not knowing her intention. Was she on the hunt, in carnivorous mode? After about one more minute of continuous looking at each other, she very slowly turned right, stepping down into the huckleberry brush below. The fuzzy round cub followed right at her heels. Brush rustled and branches crackled as they descended the steep slope…but only a short distance. Rustling brush ceased as the threesome stopped.

She would most likely be approaching along the slope just below the road, either to bypass or scrutinize me some more as a possible food source. Either way, if I decided to venture farther up the road I would have to be very alert when returning…not knowing where the bears would be by then. I thought not to risk it. Now it was my turn to move! I turned left, walking quickly away down the road towards the truck which was a good mile distant. This was disappointing, being cut short of my plan but I did not want to risk being so close to a fearless sow bear with two cubs!

Since over the years bears had been so accepting of my presence in their domain, I learned to respond similarly by showing them acceptance and respect. So here, I thought it was both prudent and appropriate to let these three bears have their space. They needed some peace, quiet and steady food-foraging: all crucial elements to their winter survival. My quick absence would benefit them for sure and maybe myself, too. Walking back down, now being cautious, I glanced back their way several times. I sensed that this mother blackbear may have began stalking me if I lingered too long. Luckily the bears never reappeared on the road, at least until I was gone from visual contact.

Walking at a leisurely pace, I remembered two previous times in other parts of northern British Columbia when bears came to inspect after hearing the sharp cracking sounds of my rock hammer. Both times the bear never showed itself but a low rustling of brush, at a bear's height, could be heard as the animal approached from the distance…then very slowly circled past about twenty or so yards away. One of those times the bear walked in a three-quarter-circle before leaving; the other did a half-circle. Both times I did some loud deepvoiced talking to ensure the bear that I was a risk to it, if it came much closer…that I was big enough to not be a potential food item!

I thought those bears were probably attracted to me because the sound of a heavy hammer hitting rock is similar to a rifle shot; many bears have been conditioned by hunters' rifle shots and gutted-out kills, so they know an easy meal often awaits after those sharp cracking sounds. Once again, I suspected that this mother bear came close for the same reason. None of these bears were afraid of such manmade noise but were instead…attracted to it!

Continuing downward along the road, I walked near the downslope edge for better visibility below; the upper forest had good visibility under the large old mountain hemlock and subalpine fir trees. From steep rusty brown mountain peaks far above, a cold thin mist began drifting down. Big drops of rain soon followed…at first only a few but within minutes became a steady and heavy downpour! Coming around one bend, just ahead, a lone porcupine was waddling downward along the pothole road. As I tried catching up, it sped up…then crossed over the road to the upper slope where it began climbing slowly upward under huckleberry brush. This sweet-faced little animal made me happy! It was quiet and gentle, looking quite huggable…if not for the sharp quills!

I watched the porcupine appear then disappear under shaking, rustling brush, slowly moving higher and higher. It would be safer from the bears up there than on the road! By now I was quite soaked, not being dressed properly, having not expected rain. I gave the little lone animal a "Goodbye," in thought and quickened my pace back to the truck. Along the way I thought of how many times seeing a single porcupine and only once were two together. They seemed to enjoy this silent aloneness and quiet lifestyle among the trees; but they were probably in communication with each other more than was apparent, via scent and maybe sound inaudible to a human. They would then be together even though at a distance!

Not until another year passed was I back banging rocks, but a bit farther north and east of this ancient forested mountainside. This time though, I carried a camera on my back. The morning was pleasant, cool and with bright grey sky spotted with a few blue openings that expanded, receded and constantly reshaped. I passed one black and white lichen-coated rock outcropping, then proceeded downslope through a patch of pale yellow-leaved birch and rusty-barked lodgepine trees. At its lower end the forest opened into a wide, green and pale yellow grassy field where as I approached…a most pleasing surprise stood about thirty yards away in the field's centre: three bears!

Two cubs were standing up on hind legs wrestling and batting at each other! They looked to be having a very good time and were quite oblivious of my arrival…so engrossed with play they were! These small yearling cubs were the same size but unusual…being of two different colours: one a creamy white and the other regular black. Their black mother though, down on four feet near her cubs, was immediately aware of my arrival. She stood there on alert, ears up and looking my way. But in a few moments, she dashed at full speed to the bordering forest! There she stopped just inside, still visible within shadows under dark bluegreen spruce and bright yellow poplar trees. Quickly reaching for the camera, I hoped for a photo of the cubs.

She whoofed four times…calling to her cubs! But they ignored her…so enjoying themselves and continuing to stand up on hind legs with forelegs around each other as if in a waltz, yet each trying to outmanoeuvre the other! Now with a barely audible sound, the sow kept calling her cubs with a drawn-out medium-high-pitched, gentle rolling sound, a sort-of cooing that lasted maybe two seconds with a very short pause between each call. Finally, just as my camera's three hundred millimeter lens was almost focussed, the salt-and-pepper cubs suddenly heeded her message. Both instantly lowered down onto fours — then darted at full speed across the field to her! As quick as that — they were gone to safety in the forest. Only slightly visible now through brush and lower branches...they just stood still looking back my way. I never got one photo...missing this great chance by a split-second!

Within moments this little wild family turned away and stepped farther into the forest, out of sight completely. Well, that was frustrating but I was also extremely excited in a most happy way. I had just seen my first Kermodei bear! This white cub was the first — and only — Kermodei that I have ever seen. It had a lovely, thick off-white coat of fur that was conspicuously visible...more so than that of its black sibling; the creamy white colour was the same as a polar bear's. Although now more than a year old these two cubs were still playfully childish and childlike. Even so, they had an exceptional mother and were in consequence healthy, happy and beautiful! Seeing this bear family proved to me what I had thought all along: that Kermodei bears are not a specie but actually a recessive genetic variation of the blackbear.

I sat down to wait...wishing the bears would eventually wander back into the open. Meanwhile, thoughts of the blackbear's variety came to the fore. The Kermodei is neither a separate specie, subspecie, nor a "spirit". Its paler colour of fur, nose and claws is just another recessive genetic characteristic. Besides white, there are cinnamon, blackish brown, light medium brown, chocolate brown, grey and yellow-orange fur colours: all recessive. These beautiful colours I have seen over the years at various places in western Canada: of more than two hundred blackbears about six percent were not black. I did notice that recessive colours show more in specific, limited local areas and of them, cinnamon is the most common. But in this area where Kermodeis are known, cinnamons have not been seen.

One could easily like these bears. It seems to me that all bears should be given some intelligent consideration in government-and-business planning. I think the best way, to start, would be to leave standing at all elevations some large oldgrowth forest. Bearproof garbage containers should be mandatory everywhere. High pagewire fencing around small remote towns, mining camps and logging camps would also help bears...besides cougars and people. Over and over I've heard and read about "problem bears" but the truth is...the problem human: who does not comprehend the needs, behaviour and value of bears nor the interconnectedness of Nature with humanity. That sort of human ignorance generates non-appreciation and no consideration for bears and other wild things. Such human negativity towards Nature is directing us all into social disaster: because economics, society and ecosystems are not separate entities.

With such thoughts...I waited for this rare family to show themselves maybe farther to the east in another long narrow meadow. But after some time they never appeared. Anyway, I had to continue westward on my own geological agenda. Even so, there was a good chance of seeing this white cub again next year or another since I would be back more than once to these beautiful remote wild mountains.

The following year I did return...both prospecting and scouting for pine mushroom habitat. On this day I was about sixty miles from the Kermodei-cub family's home range. I had walked long and hard through the woods of predominantly pine, mountain hemlock and subalpine fir...over and between the rounded lichen-and-moss-covered rock bluffs. All the while, the liveliness of small mountainside wildlife kept my mood up: squirrels chattered and chased each other; flights of kinglets, chickadees, tanagers and grosbeaks winged overhead at times, peeping and chirping their uniquely pleasing manners of speech. In shade beneath the trees, the cool air was clean and fresh with invigorating scents...released by live evergreen tree needles. Other than these enjoyments, the hours passed with little of consequence showing on the ground or in the rock.

As evening approached, a cloudless western sky changed in its slow timeless way…from light blue to pale limegreen. Making my way back to the truck, by the time I got there, twilight had arrived. In the semi-dark I wolfed down a hasty tincan supper then drove to a quiet secluded place where I could have some peace and sleep…away from human interruptions. By now the advancing night had turned the sky grey. Tiny pale white lights began blinking through the greyness of infinity.

Along one bumpy gravel road I found a good parking spot, stopped, then shuffled bags and blankets making a sort-of nest in the truck cab. Stretching out diagonally across the truck seat I lay on my back, raising tired legs up onto a soft backpack bag that was on the driver's side seat by the steering wheel. Relaxing, I looked up at the stars through a big sloping windshield: having this half-glass roof made my humble abode seem highclass!

Soon bright stars were shining and flickering in the millions…more distant ones as a pale grey haze glowing in the deepness of Space. Closer stars and planets constantly twinkled… their thin multipoints radiating outward. Alternating long then short then long again, these bright ephemeral spikes of light lit the sky in bright white, pale blue, red, pink, orange and yellow! What a beautiful way to end the day! Stars seemed to dance…as if living beings in the deep calm above, while black motionless conifer treetops and rugged hardrock mountain peaks stood silhouetted on the horizon below. As I lay watching this vast silent sky, feeling great wonder at such majestic phenomenon…an experience far beyond words…relaxation and peace, gently, surreptitiously came upon body and mind.

Looking out into the deepness of Space I waited and hoped for a meteor to streak across. Although countless aeons away, the brighter stars seemed to be very close…almost touchable! Time passed and the sky brightened with even more silent twinkling lights. Then finally, in the western sky a very quick thin white light streaked across — almost parallel to the horizon and moving southward. Within a quarter-second it flashed and vanished! With this short-lived excitement I made a wish, but not a selfish one. This was just for fun and would probably not come true…such things having no realistic connection. But even so, the reality of life was here before my eyes stretched in a complete circle around the black treelined and jagged mountain horizon; this starry sky expressed the essence of everything: light, space, motion and mind.

Two more meteors flashed across in quick succession from different directions and at different angles — one small and quick, another quite large and slow — to burn up and dissipate. The stars had now slowly curved a short way across the sky from east to west. Inside the truck cab, air was getting cold as heat radiated away. But I was cozily warm under a Hudson's Bay blanket and duckdown sleepingbag. Then another shootingstar with a long sparkling white afterglow tail, lit up in the western sky — this time a large, slowly moving meteor coming down at about forty-five degrees, streaking to the southeast. On seeing this one, I made a favourite wish for humanity: that they would become self-responsible, stop their selfish over-breeding and their selfish demands…thus begin living peacefully, realistically, with Nature and with each other! I knew that may never happen but this was a serious wish…far beyond the harmless traditional western peculiarity of wishing-on-a-falling-star.

One more lightning-quick thin streak appeared almost directly above, coming straight down. I wished another but more trivial wish. Now deeply relaxed, body and mind began to drift away from waking solidity…into sleep and dreams. Ever so slowly, waking mind's light-and-space was overcome. Oblivious now of the earthly space-time continuum, I was only vaguely conscious of dreaming…about or with someone and something…in that almost magical space where solidity and gravity seem to be subordinate to fluidity and lightness, where change could be instant and distance apparently nonexistent. After the passage of some unknown earthly time…a vaguely familiar sound, distant and unidentified, entered my dreaming consciousness. Thus pulled back into the waking state…although half-asleep…I recognized the howling of wolves!

With this recognition I was jolted back — now almost completely awake and very energized! These wolves were close…less than one hundred yards away! Slowly rolling down the passengerside window halfway for better hearing, I carefully, quietly sat up to listen. Their voices were a most cheering experience…unknown to them, they were bringing strong positive thoughts and feelings to this lone human. For a few moments, all was silent.

Then one very deep-voiced wolf began as a solo: this was an incredibly musical sound that changed continuously from very low through higher and higher pitches…with a few yodels simultaneously here and there…reaching a certain high pitch, then slowly lowering and ending with a very sad deep tone. This song was continuous nonstop musical vocalizing and perfectly harmonious! After a brief silence, the same adult wolf began the same song…but this time was quickly joined by two other adults that were not as deep-voiced as the first. Then three or four pups began following now and then, attempting to imitate the sound-pattern with their little high-pitched voices! There now seemed to be at least six or seven different tones of voice. As this beautifully melodious song continued, the wolves sang more and more in unison…as a chorus.

"Must be a pack of six at least," I thought.

They stood under pine trees at the same spot for about ten minutes, singing almost continuously! Their lovely voices sang out towards the endless starry sky…sounding out across the wide valley, then up mountain slopes…in such beautiful melody that no human voice could ever approach. These wolves were actually singing! They were definitely not howling. But their song, I soon noticed, seemed to be a song of much sorrow. Repeated over and over, each time it ended with a slowly lowering, deep, drawn-out, very sad sound that reached into the centre of my chest. This brought hot tears welling up into my eyes…tears trickled over, ran down my cheeks, over lips and dripped slowly from my chin.

The taste of salty tears was on my lips. As if frozen to my spot, I sat completely still… watching the silent stars twinkling brightly, lighting up the dark grey of Space: the stars seemed unresponsive to the wolves' beautiful but sad song. Such a beautiful song, I never heard before. It was as if a classical composition, carrying my emotions in happiness, pleasure and deep sorrow. I wondered. What were they singing about? What were they saying? Were they singing to the Universe, to the stars, or to other wolves on a distant mountain? Had a family member died?

A minute or two of silence passed. Again the wolfpack sang from another position in the forest to the southeast…but this time of shorter duration. More silent moments, then began another song of similar pattern with perfectly flowing pitch changes combined with lovely yodelling. The wolves were walking leisurely towards the south…bypassing my truck at a safe distance, stopping each time they sang. As they moved then stopped to sing, now each time the song shortened. I enjoyed another five minutes of these infinitely wonderous vocal sounds…as the wolves gradually moved farther and farther away. Then as suddenly, complete silence returned to the black forest.

The wolf family was moving quietly onward, padding between pine trees, under huckleberry brush and copperbush. Above them a myriad of multicoloured stars were silently sparkling. I lay back with two emotions running through mind and body: cheer and sorrow. Extremely happy I was, having this very rare experience of our living western wilds: a speechlessly enjoyable fifteen minutes of wolf song! But the sadness of each vocal ending brought me to sense that these wolves were in deep grief…which their emotion-filled melodious voices had pulled me into…also feeling such deep sorrow. Whatever their reason, this family of wolves had been vocalizing the most eloquent song this human would ever hear.

NOTES
Southern British Columbia

A DEEP RUMBLING

The 5000 Unit: the largest diesel engine of the 1960s, 70s and 80s, used by CNR and CPR, designated the SD 40-2. It is a V-16 with 3,000 horsepower, maximum 3200 horsepower.

Trainmen: a crew of usually — previously — five men.

Engineman: the trainman who runs, controls the engine.

Fireman: the trainman who monitors the engine's performance; in the past, he kept the fire going with wood, coal or oil as fuel, thus called "fireman."

Brakeman: the trainman who watches signals ahead, watches for danger, throws switches, goes flagging and performs various other manual duties. The headend brakeman also has the duty of pushing a special brake in case of emergency, which was called "plugging the brake." A second brakeman was in the caboose with the conductor…in the good-old days.

Cougar: the western Canadian word for our largest wild cat, scientifically designated: Felis concolor. This beautiful big cat is known as "cougar" in western Canada but in places where it either does not exist or is almost extinct, is called "panther" or "mountain lion," both misnomers. Large dominant males often weigh more than two hundred pounds. Mainland cougars are generally larger than those on Vancouver Island and are usually a pale tan colour while V.I. cats have either tan or auburn colours.

Miles, Yards, Feet and Inches: our traditional British, therefore Canadian system of measurement which I prefer to use, having grown up with it; this was and is an aspect of our identity. There is no good reason to let it be squeezed out by the foreign system, metrics. That is just one of the several "changes" emanating from eastern Canada that tramples on my identity.

We have a long tradition of using the British system which was also a part of our western and Canadian identity until "officially" and unnecessarily taken from us by a handful of Eastern politicians some years ago. I grew up with the system so always think with it. Metrics is alien, except in a science lab. A few conversion factors:

1 Imperial gallon = 1.2 U.S. gallon = 4.546 litres
3 feet = 1 yard = .9144 metre
1 mile = 1.609 kilometre
1 pound = .4536 kilogram
32° Fahrenheit = 0° Celsius.

SWISHING AND SNAPPING

Pepperspray: a concentrated essence of hot cayenne pepper, pressurized into a canister-type gun, designed for emergency self-defence against bears. This spray is usually effective and is more accurate than a gun-and-bullet. Pepperspray probably works just as well on any other wild animal such as moose, wolf, wolverine, cougar, etcetera.

Pepperspray Pointers: When going into the woods you should always carry at least one pepper spraygun for self-defence. But it is better having two, kept in holsters on a waistbelt. Know how to use pepperspray properly. It is to be sprayed only into the charging animal's face…especially eyes and nostrils. The average-sized spraygun lasts only about five seconds and is effective at ten yards or less. But be aware of wind direction!

The power of a spraygun's contents lasts about three years, so I'm told. If you are in a group, if possible each one should have their own pepperspray. Always keep it away from strong heat; it could explode if hot. When flying out, store pepperspray safely and separately from cockpit of plane or helicopter. Carrying pepperspray can and will save the lives of both human and animal: therefore having this sort of protection is most reasonable.

Squirrels' Cone Caches: These little animals work long and hard gathering cones for their winter food supply, a necessity for saving energy, thus for survival in very cold weather when cones yet high up are often difficult to access under snowy limbs or are ice-coated and frozen. Therefore commercial cone pickers who steal cone piles from squirrels should be delt with severely — that human selfishness should be penalized by law!

Spooked: frightened.

Grizzly: This omnivorous bear most often shies away from humanity but will be dangerous when in the carnivorous mode, when protecting its food source and territory, when surprised at close-range and when a female bear reacts to what she senses as danger to her cubs. The sow grizzly with cubs usually has a very broad personal boundary-line, much more than a blackbear equivalent has and more than a boar of either specie; so there is far greater probability of attack by a mother grizzly.

Wild Neighbours: Silent and Vociferous

Wolf: Wolves are sociable, social animals that live in family groups called packs. They are almost completely carnivorous, so will eat any animal large or small: mammal, bird, fish. Wolves are usually shy of humanity and mind their own wild business. Even so, they are carnivores capable of killing a moose or bison therefore would have no trouble with a lone human if they saw fit. I have heard of wolves threatening people in British Columbia but know not how valid the rumours are. Although I have been near wolves in the woods several times, they showed no aggression.

Pine Mushroom: an edible wild mushroom that, some seasons, is commercially viable generating several million dollars of activity in British Columbia. It is a tasty edible wild mushroom that is sold primarily to Japan where people buy it for either food or status. Classified into five grades, the button is number one…the status mushroom. As for taste, each grade differs, with the button the strongest; I like numbers two and three the best. We are losing this valuable renewable resource due to political neglect that is relative to archaic corporate economics. The clearcut is the foremost destructive force negating this mushroom's habitat.

In B.C., there are twenty or so known species of edible mushroom but most others are either poisonous or inedible due to taste or texture. Don't you take a chance…some edibles have close look-alikes that are poisonous. The destroying-angel mushroom grows all over western Canada and is probably the most toxic mushroom on the Planet.

Pets: We all love our pets as family members, don't we? But pet cats and dogs can and do kill or harass various wild animals. Cats are notorious bird-killers; they should be kept indoors at all times unless you build a small outdoor pen area; this way they will get fresh air and so will you by putting the litterpan there. Bells on collars do not work, since cats hide, wait and pounce or jump in an instant often from under or behind brush or branches: that is their genetically habitual style of hunting. Cats out at night will not kill birds but will kill nocturnal flying squirrels. Dogs chase, harass and kill deer, squirrels, ground squirrels, marmots, other small rodents and gartersnakes. Keep your dogs at home and under control. If you are walking in the woods don't let your dog run willy-nilly wild. If you ever see a hamstrung deer killed by someone's precious pet, you will understand!

SOMEPLACE REMOTE

Chanterelle: another edible and sometimes commercially viable mushroom that shows as two distinct species: one a pale orange, the other a creamy white.

Balsam tree: proper name is amabilis or subalpine fir, which are two separate species.

Humen: I use this word as plural of "human." In the English language, if the plural of "man" is "men," then the logic should be obvious. The word "humans" sounds crude. Most plurals end with "s" but there are several exceptions.

Wolf: The natural intelligence of the wolf...and other wild animals...is there. Intelligence is more functional than "instinct." There is an unfounded human prejudice that labels most animal behaviour as "instinct" but I think the wolf has no more instinct than does a human.

Conservation Officer: There has long been very little conserving of our wildlife by C.O.s. Most often they just shoot a "problem animal." There are better ways. If need be, why not livetrap or tranquillize the animal (bear, cougar or wolf) and sell it to a zoo, game farm or transfer it to eastern Canada where the specie was once-upon-a-time? This way would help keep up numbers and genetic variation...thus maybe keep our large carnivores extant. Along with this, hunters "bag limits" must be severely decreased, especially on the carnivores' staple food animals. And poachers must be severely dealt with.

Vancouver Island Elk: a subspecie of elk native to V.I., also known as Roosevelt elk.

PRESENT AND PAST

Copper Bloom: Copper carbonate is formed when copper, air and water interact. The bloom shows as shades of pale green, bluegreen or blue.

Mainline: a major logging road to which side-branch roads connect.

Wolfing down: eating in a hurry.

Marbled Murrelet: a tiny, fish-eating seabird that until recent years little was known about, since it tends to be nocturnal and nests in or near ancient forest, sometimes five miles or more from seashore. Unknown numbers die yearly when at night they fly into the guywires and lights of tugs, fishing boats and ships...since the murrelets' night-vision draws them to lights much as moths to lightbulbs. Maybe this bird's feeding areas should be designated as "lights out" zones. Ancient murrelets are also suffering for this same reason.

Gesture Communication: the nonvocal language used by almost all animals which involves position of body, head, ears, eyes, tail, etcetera. The gesture-language varies with species. When a person learns the meaning of such gestures, one will understand and appreciate the animal much more. With large animals such as bears, this understanding will make walking in the woods less dangerous...since on a close meeting one could read the message and know the appropriate way to behave. But beware...a stalking bear will attack lighting-fast from a motionless, apparently casual stance.

Logger: In B.C., men who cut down trees, buck them into logs, load and haul them out are called "loggers" not "lumberjacks," who are back East.

Fossils: on Vancouver Island, date at various times from 10,000 years ago to distant 263 million years ago.

Tap-Tap-Tap

Dewdrops and Raindrops: These act as beautiful prisms when sunshine passes through at a certain angle, emitting each colour of the spectrum one-at-a-time from different angles.

Pine: short for pine mushroom.

Flag: an open pine mushroom.

Button: a young mushroom with veil still closed over the gills.

Fairy Ring: a circular or oval growth-pattern of mushrooms.

Wormy: the presence of larvae in a mushroom, or the word used for such mushroom. Larvae are usually of a few fly species and beetles. They are grubs, not really worms. Several species take advantage of wormy mushrooms. Once, I saw a salamander standing still on thick moss directly under a pine mushroom flag waiting for flies. Ravens and varied thrush peck larvae out. One specie of brown spider, I have seen many times at the base of this mushroom also waiting for flies to jump onto…I call it the mushroom spider.

A Snap and a Track

Switchback: a hairpin-shaped curve on a road, usually built in steep terrain.

Clearcuts: both create and destroy — mushrooms, shade plants, moss and lichen die but sunloving plants begin to grow. Many open-ground plants are berry bushes that increase food supply for birds, deer, bears, chipmunks, etcetera. But certain birds such as woodpeckers, varied thrush and owls, also squirrels and pine marten suffer from their loss of food supply and nesting or denning space. Tree frogs and salamanders also lose their shade and semi-shade living environment. Clearcuts finish all-at-once large patches of shady ground habitat where shade-loving wildflowers grow, such as orchids, trilliums, white and pink fawn lilies and pink bleedinghearts.

The main trouble with clearcuts is: too many, too fast, too big. From the beginning logging has been poorly planned, with little reason put to looking at the whole picture so that besides immediate business there would be inclusion of other crucial factors, both ecological and economical. Many ecological facets have not been considered: changed water flows and percolation affect humanity, fish, especially salmon and all other life in that system; loss of nesting trees and snags for insectivorous birds affect those birds and other associated life such as flying squirrels, bats, tree frogs and even butterflies; absence of large hollow trees used as dens affect bears, wolves and cougars…large mammals that are very versatile but can take the bullying of human encroachment only so far.

Economics of human society has been and continues to be affected by this long-standing lack of ecological understanding, which leads to shallow-minded, limited reasoning in politics and business. Another example related to clearcuts is the human-growth mania and its attendant proliferation of lowland subdivisions, rezoning of forested and agricultural land: these are filled over with blacktop, buildings, foreign flowers, foreign shrubs and foreign trees…along with usually paranoid, fear-filled people who do not comprehend Nature and its non-human residents whose living-space they have just usurped and now live next to…if any remnant habitat remains. Woe be to a bear, cougar or wolf that comes too close in search of food! And what future is there with one of the economy's key health-indicators being "housing starts"? The cause and effect result will definitely be extinction of our large carnivores and along with that the end of a big piece of my western Canadian identity! Few bigcity people understand this, especially those in eastern Canada…and I'm sure they don't care.

Grey Copper: proper name is chalcocite, formula Cu_2S.

Gold: Over twenty-five years I've prospected and panned various parts of B.C. and Yukon. In British Columbia, little bits of gold colour can be panned from about seventy-five percent of our creeks and rivers…many outside of government's designated staking areas. Deep down in B.C. and Yukon's ground, more gold remains than what's been taken out so far; but in most cases the mining cost would be more than the gold's value. Besides gold, platinum and palladium are in a few creeks and rivers. The mountains and valleys of B.C. and Yukon are geologically rich and very interesting.

Carnivorous Cougars: Recorded killings of people by cougars in British Columbia are five in one hundred years. But three of these have been in the last thirty-or-so years. Besides this, numerous close-calls have also occurred when people were harassed, threatened, followed or cornered by hungry cougars…but somehow managed to escape. Even so, compare these figures with the human death-toll from bee stings in Canada, which are about three deaths per year or…ninety over the past thirty years! Of course, there are a lot more bees than cougars. The inconspicuous bees get little publicity but one cougar — big, beautiful and carnivorous — will make headlines! Government policy on the big cat far more resembles persecution than conservation. So does public attitude in general. And the C.O.'s ego is all-too-hungry to kill a cougar. Such be the consequence of irrationality, ignorance and fear. Why not live-catch a "problem" cougar and sell it to a game farm or zoo? Or plant some in eastern Canada where they are now most likely extinct.

Landing Site: an open flat area, usually bulldozed, where logs will be brought in, piled and loaded onto trucks. When logging begins, it is also called the yard.

Grapple Yarder: a large machine with boom, wire cable and giant iron tongs for grasping onto logs in the tree-felled area and pulling them to the landing site, or yard. The cable system looks like a huge clothesline.

Madill Steel Spar: a large machine with tall pipe-like iron mast that functions much like the traditional spar tree, for pulling logs into the yard area.

High Elevation Season: Summer is short and weather inconsistent causing sometimes shade-plant blossoms, open-area berries and mushrooms to coexist almost simultaneously; here were ripe huckleberries, orchids, wintergreen blossoms, pipsissewa flowers and pine buttons all on the same day.

Two Mistakes

Mushroom Spores: very minute seeds that blow on the wind.

Mycelium: the perennial living body of a mushroom specie that can be quite extensive although not visible, growing underground or in rotting or dying wood, etcetera.

Pine Mushroom Jargon: a "flag" or "hat" both refer to a large open-topped mushroom. "Hat" comes from the wavey upward curve of a very old pine, looking a bit like a cowboy hat's curl.

Breaking Camp: taking down tent, packing up supplies, etcetera, getting ready to move out. This day's pick: was $250 worth of mostly pine mushroom buttons.

Agility and Grace

Fisher: our second largest weasel with very sturdy-looking head and long slim body. Adults are more than three feet long, including tail. Scientifically named: Martes pennanti.

Wolverine: our largest weasel with bearlike head, face and paws. A fully grown adult can be almost four feet long, including its short bushy tail. Don't be deceived by its unusual body shape and odd motion on the ground; when up in a tree, the wolverine is the most agile and graceful animal I have ever seen. Back in the 1960s a pair of wolverines were kept at Stanley Park in Vancouver, giving me the opportunity to observe their behaviour. Then, I spent many hours watching them and at no time did they show aggression towards me, standing or crouching just one yard away. In the wild, I have seen only one at a distance. Tracks were in snow one time and twice in soft dirt. But trappers often see wolverine tracks in the snow leading to their trapsets for other furbearers where, almost invariably, the trap would be tripped intentionally...a most intelligent animal!

Full and Satisfied

Black Bear: Of more than fifty blackbears that I have met at close range in the woods, most were very polite and accepting of the human presence in their domain. Even so, circumstances vary and so does personality or temperament; potential danger is always there. Bears and other wild animals are dangerous at times so the best protection for a person walking in wild areas or on the fringes of wild areas...would probably be pepperspray. I always carry two in holsters, of medium-size. This size lasts for only about five seconds of steady spray, so you judge accordingly. Having these as self-defence will give you a sense of confidence...so you can better enjoy the beauties that abound in Nature.

If you are going out for a day or less, do not carry food or drink that's smell would bring a bear to you; best to have no food and just water to drink. If you meet a bear that seems nonaggressive but will not go away, one that tags along wherever you go, do not be lulled into thinking all is well because that bear would be assessing you as a potential food item...stalking you. In such case you should head back out. Don't give it time to overcome its initial caution towards the unknown human.

Other Advice: Another important item to have whenever you go into country that you do not know, is a compass...and learn how to use it properly. Get your bearing as you go into the woods and come back out by the same route, if possible. Observe...take mental pictures of natural objects and formations that are unique as you go in, which you can identify when returning. As you go in, look back frequently so you will recognize those natural markers when coming back out. Also carry a small knife, some matches, cigarette lighter, a bit of newspaper and a little piece of hard treepitch...all kept dry inside of tight plastic. A few large plastic garbage bags could be useful if one became lost, since these can be used as emergency sleepingbag or raincoat, with head-and-armholes cut into the bottom. Be careful with pepperspray when on the road, in the air or in camp — keep it away from heat! It might explode.

Seldom Seen or Heard

Cougars and Deer: Deer are usually the staple diet of cougars. If we want cougars to remain with us — and I certainly do! — we must keep deer numbers up, their crucial habitat intact and not fractured excessively. Deer hunting must also be kept at a minimum so that cougars need not seek food in form of dogs, cats and farm animals. It is only reasonable to include carnivores' food supply as a crucial part of government's formula when calculating the "bag limits" for hunters and fishermen, also. Years ago I wrote to British Columbia's Fish and Wildlife Branch about this issue but never received a reply...typical.

NOTES
Eastern British Columbia and Western Alberta

TRACKS IN THE SNOW

The Big Grizzly's Tracks: in snow were 14 inches long to clawtips.

Miles per hour: our traditional Canadian measurement of speed.

Fired it up: started the motor.

On-the-fly: nonstop.

Some Railway Terms:

Train Orders: messages to traincrews regarding movements of their train and other trains.

Train Dispatcher: the employee who creates orders that govern the movement of all trains within a rail subdivision and oversees such movement.

Train Order Board: also called a semaphore, a signal indicating to an approaching traincrew whether or not they need to get new orders at that station.

Hooped-up: train orders tied into a string-loop and ready for each trainman to catch with an outstretched arm, as the train passes by a station. Two devices called hoops were used to pass orders to the headend crew and caboose crew.

Cleared: For crucial safety, in maintaining precise orders from dispatcher to station operator then to train crews, the orders need to be "cleared" by the train dispatcher after his listening to a foolproof — almost — system where orders are repeated by each participating station operator, with all names and numbers being both stated and spelled out.

Tundra Swans: the new name of whistling swans, which look just like trumpeter swans except for two bright yellow spots on the whistler's black beak just before the eyes.

Railway Time: always on Standard time with hours numbered from one to twenty-four. Noon is twelve o'clock while midnight is twenty-four hours. This system was designed for consistency and safety; in it the zero is called "nought".

Conservation Officer: Once, I met in a wild area one C.O. who had travelled more than 200 miles from his Prince George office. He worked alone, he said, and had such huge area to cover…the impossibility of proper "management" — of hunters and poachers, not wildlife — was blatantly obvious. I had not seen poaching in this area but heard later that a few men on railway section crews did shoot moose or elk, using their friends' tags. Sometimes moose or elk were hit by trains, especially during winter: then railway employees would utilize some of the meat; one man in particular relished moose tongue.

One-Eight Hundred: Each western province and territory has a one-eight hundred or similar toll-free number to call for reporting poachers, polluters and various other wildlife infractions in wild areas. Trouble is, how many people have satellite cellphones? Too often, when the message gets through…the culprits are long-gone.

BROWN LAKE BLUE LAKE

Longtailed Weasel: scientifically named Mustela fremata, one of three small weasel species that when killed and skinned are called "ermine" by the deadly-selfish fur-as-decoration industry.

Beavers: One time near Chetwynd, B.C. I noticed a very large beaverlodge beside a pond, so walked quietly to it for a closer look. This lodge had two main entrances, one on each end like a duplex and in the pond were ten beavers lounging about, coming and going! This is the largest beaverlodge I have seen and the resident population showed that beavers are very much social animals.

Grand Trunk Pacific Railway: Around 1900 construction of this railway began from Prince Rupert to Prince George and along Fraser River towards Jasper, and vice versa. The two enigmatic railways were G.T.P and Canadian Northern. G.T.P. was completed in 1914.

Canadian Northern Railway: Construction began in Manitoba around 1899 to Jasper and onward along North Thompson River to Vancouver.

Canadian National Railway: Its construction began in 1919 and by 1923 had absorbed the other two financially malfunctioning railways.

Bangs and Thumps

Soopolallie: also called soapberry or buffalo berry, a bushy shrub having orange-red edible berries that are not very tasty.

Bear Behaviour: On three occasions I saw blackbears stamping front feet hard onto the ground. They stood facing directly at me and with ears up. Twice they were protecting an obvious food source; the other time may have been a territorial or personal-space warning since no food was apparent. When travelling both blacks and grizzlies often follow riversides, lakeshores, creeks and low brushy areas. Various animal trails are always in the woods, larger ones being used by bears, wolves, deer, elk, moose, woodland caribou, mountain goats and sheep.

In general, when one meets a bear at close range the bear will stare awhile and then walk away. But each circumstance is different and each bear is different, with its own personal characteristics and experience…therefore could respond otherwise. On three occasions over the years a blackbear saw me while I was unaware of its presence nearby…but it noisily ran to hide behind a large treetrunk! I saw the bear only as it ran. After a half-minute or so, the bear slowly re-appeared to show itself and observe the human. But if these, and several more at other times and places, were in carnivorous mode, I would not be here to write about them.

Garbage Bears: Such bears become "problem bears," as do ones that feed in orchards or grain fields; they are often shot, not necessarily by a conservation officer. Bears are also ran over on highways, usually at night. Why doesn't our government use their gall bladders as a dollar source to use in fish and wildlife habitat enhancement? Letting them rot makes no sense.

Beside a Whitewater Creek

Moose: During spring and summer in a part of eastern B.C., I got to know the summer habitation of eight adult moose along a ten-mile stretch of gravel road. They were a real pleasure to watch. But the road was soon paved, bringing an onslaught of hunters in the fall. That first season, five moose were shot and two years later none were to be seen. That happened in the 1970s. Moose calves always have a beautiful rusty auburn colour. Moose adults when angry show it by ears flat and pointing back, while hair stands erect from top of the head, all along the spine to stubby tail.

A CHANGE OF HEART AND MIND

Dolly Varden Trout: actually classified as a char.

Bonk: slang for a bumping sound.

Fishing: This human activity that has been done as personal entertainment for many years is erroneously called a "sport." People who do this enjoy the peaceful presence of Nature while simultaneously intent on killing a small living part of that same Nature. How absurd can humanity be?

Human Being: Many times when out in wild places I have thought about humanity's role and responsibility vis-a-vis animals, be they wild or domesticated. The idea of being kind and sharing with our nonhuman earthly companions seems an almost impossible one to actually live by in this confused world of humanity where various ideas, beliefs, cultures, races and commerce constantly push their particular ways — sometimes in agreement but more often competing and clashing. Well, with all of that, how is one to behave in a benign and constructive way? The best and most natural way to live on this Planet is with a kindness that allows wild beings enough living space to perpetuate alongside humanity. I think it is our duty to be good companions to them...to try as much as we can, even if not always possible.

Kelt: a spawned-out, dying salmon at end of the Pacific salmon's life-cycle. Presently our wild salmon are dangerously low in numbers due to years of political ignorance in Ottawa and Victoria, the consequence of pompous bigcity politicians who do not comprehend the word habitat nor how crucial are salmon to our whole westcoast ecosystem, both in the sea and on land.

Here is a message on how to solve that problem: the least expensive way, the ecologically clean way, the most economically and ecologically productive way to bring back our wild salmon — and the whole related system — is to dig spawning channels in already-existing gravelly lowland areas...but not too gravelly so the water sinks out of sight...and direct lakewater from nearby large lakes into these manmade creeks. Waterflow could be cheaply and effectively controlled by electronically activated gates at the top end; water can be aerated with little low manmade waterfalls that are jumpable by fish; bends in the channels, boulders and even logjams would create deeper pools for young steelhead and salmon species that by habit remain longer in fresh water. Such control channels could be quickly and easily cut by a few D-12 caterpillars.

The wild fish will come on their own but maybe initial introduction would speed up the process; once there, the salmon themselves will do the rest! No need for expensive gene-depleting hatcheries, not to mention taxpayers' dollar depletion...for what?

Areas where this concept would work are near Port Alberni, Courtenay and Campbell River on Vancouver Island. Each of these has one or more very large lake higher up and many miles of good glacial gravel in low-lying areas, ideal ground for digging such special spawning channels — manmade creeks. I know this system will succeed because when a boy in Alberni, salmon came up the town's open sewer ditches to spawn; they spawned right next to our house in the manmade ditch and next spring we could see little fry swimming there. The wild salmon did it on their own after ditches were dug in gravelly ground...no need for human input beyond that! Since the town was small and rainfall lots, the sewer ditches were relatively clean...good enough for the salmon.

I suggest this be done, since it is based on direct observation at the ground-level...where reality is! This same concept can be applied to already-existing small creeks where salmon once were, if there's a large lake above that can be utilized for maintaining steady water-flow levels.

FUR AND FEATHERS

Owls: Often owls will stand on gravel roads either gathering tiny pebbles or watching for a vole or mouse to cross. While at this sometimes they are ran over by people who, so into themselves, do not recognize the bird or else run it over on purpose. Several times I have seen dead owls ran over on gravel backroads; I have also stopped for live ones standing there and oblivious of my presence as they looked down the road away from my approaching vehicle.

More Thoughts About Nature, Life and Humanity: As I have come to know, Nature's reality is profound: far superior to any human convention be it philosophical, social, cultural, political or religious. For thousands of years little cultural groups have gradually developed into cities, civilizations…and in the process have also fabricated conceptual, emotional and physical boxes that separated their humanity from natural reality. So…in consequence there was a manmade unknowingness and a deadly serious phantasy-world that they lived and died by. Today, even with reason and science, humanity is not much different.

Although Nature is the great provider, it is not an infinite giver; one of man's incorrect assumptions has long been that wild animals — and everything else natural — exist primarily for meat, clothing, decoration and other human use. The exalted human being, the top predator, has either forgotten or not yet realized that such high position also necessitates giving, protecting, conserving — besides merely taking! Many recent extinctions of wildlife and destruction of vast habitat areas are the cause-effect consequence resulting from that irrational premise.

Planet Earth's living ecosystems consist of multifarious life-forms where the more evolved animal species are also conscious beings. It is not only we who are special; something special also looks at, observes, the world from behind those shining animal eyes. Natural ecosystems are places of evolution as well as both playground and battleground of conscious beings — physical beings with minds of their own.

The reality of Nature is this flow of conscious life, innate knowingness, energy, matter, space and time. We are all a part of it. Although manifesting separately on the physical level, we are connected subtly on a deeper level of mind. Whoever walks the wildlands as a benign visitor will have an opportunity to experience something nonconceptual, extremely valuable and maybe…even slightly profound.

LITTLE WHITE DOTS

Mountain Goat-antelope: This beautiful animal is biologically more antelope than goat but with beard and horns more like a goat, is usually called a goat. Most of their time is spent high, on or near steep precipices but during spring often lounge at lower slopes for awhile. During winter they are often again lower. One little-known fact experienced by only a few people, mostly prospectors, is that old abandoned mine tunnels at high elevations are often used by mountain goats for bedding down away from storms. Those old adits, at all elevations, are also frequently used as dens by bears and cougars; I know of two that cougars use and one by a blackbear. Since old mine adits are useful manmade bits of habitat for these wild animals, the British Columbia government's Mining authorities should cease their policy of permanently sealing them shut.

Two Voices In One

Pyrargyrite: a dark red to blackish silver ore.

Proustite: a bright red silver ore.

Corundum: a very hard aluminum oxide that is called ruby when clear red and sapphire when blue.

Ruby Crystal: hexagonal clear red corundum crystal.

Quartz Crystal: hexagonal crystal of silicon dioxide, usually white or clear and sometimes coloured.

Peace and Quiet: Wild places have a peace-inducing power that can be a good, quick-acting medicine for people whose nerves, bodies and minds have been overly stressed. And the more quiet the person is, the sooner will come a positive result. Just be still, silent and experience whatever is there. But of course, mosquitoes and biting flies will put a stop to it! Best times then to be out with Nature are early spring and autumn.

Sasquatch: Here in western Canada and the U.S. the myth of such ape-human has persisted for years and maybe centuries. Other areas of the Planet also have similar myths, so one can easily be influenced into accepting such as probable. But not a bit of real evidence has been found anywhere. Footprints in mud or snow can easily be fabricated as a joke or by someone wanting to make money from Sasquatch tales. The one film-footage of a supposed Sasquatch has been shown to be another falsity. If such creature were real, by now both its living-space and bones would have been found. But some people prefer exciting stories and phantasy over reason. Even so, the Sasquatch is only imaginary.

Regarding apelike footprints purportedly sometimes seen, the hind footpad of a black or grizzly bear is similar. Once I saw a grizzly walking in a completely silent manner, holding its large long claws tightly up in the air, so they did not rattle together as they normally do. By doing this, the bear's claws would also not show in sand, mud or shallow snow. Such tracks could be mistaken for something other than a bear.

Ogopogo: Okanagan Lake is the home of another manmade creature. But this one is based on more than hearsay since something large really lives in the lake, coming to the surface occasionally to flounder around. People have seen this but usually at a distance. Well, guess what…large sturgeon live in the lake and rise to surface sometimes for short moments. The sturgeon's whiskery snout and wavey-ridged back have something in common with the phantasy Ogopogo.

When a teenager, I lived in Vernon and once asked my Mum about Ogopogo. Was it real? She replied with the comment that it was just made-up by the Okanagan's tourist bureau. That was most plausible and still is.

Raven Calls: One time in early morning I was awakened by a raven perched straight above; I just lay motionless, listening and counting each variation in sound. It was croaking, squawking, yodelling, cawing like a crow, mewing like a gull and enouncing all sorts of distinctly different sounds. About ten minutes passed, then the big bird flew away…after bringing forth a surprising total of twenty-three completely different sounds!

Great Horned Owl: The strangest sound I have ever heard came from this bird early one evening. Coming from among evergreen trees, the sound filtered through at intervals, slowly getting louder and closer: a long, loud, raspy quack…a bit like a mallard drake! After several most curious minutes of this, an adult owl flew into view, perching nearby. Then its two silent fledglings also appeared in nearby trees. They continued on their way with the adult still quacking! This bird and the raven made unusual sounds that could easily be deceptive when heard from a distance on a forested mountain slope.

Social Animals

Elk: also called wapiti in Canada. We have two subspecies: Rocky Mountain Elk and Roosevelt or Vancouver Island Elk.

Royal Elk: a bull with six or more tines per antler.

The Elk Herd: Similar to other herding animals, groups of females and young live in a social way, co-operating and interacting with each other for mutual benefit. This co-operation is very close and strong during the spring calving time when cows aggressively guard the calves and birthing mothers. Bulls two years old and up, at this time and during summer, also live in loose herds usually higher on the slopes.

NOTES
Yukon
and
Northern British Columbia

RUSTLES, SHUFFLES AND WHIMPERS

Animal Tracks: I measure them with fingers, palm of right hand and arm length. The distance from longest fingertip to middle line of palm is five inches. With palm down and hand spread out wide, the distance from thumbtip to longest fingertip is nine inches. Distance from elbow to thumbjoint at wrist is twelve inches, and add four inches to front of palm.

Four Gallon Bucket: refers to four Imperial which is about five U.S. gallons.

The Sixth-sense: When one is out alone in wild places an unusual feeling can at rare times arise within, indicating that some large, possibly dangerous animal is nearby. The best way that I can describe it is: a mild inexplicable fear and feeling of being watched. Several times it has proven true. But this phenomenon is inconsistent, since several other times that I met bears or cougars this strange warning-feeling was absent.

Meeting Bears at Close Range: If a bear is not blatantly coming at you, it will usually just stand there, staring for awhile — often seeming like a very long while — as it tries to understand the circumstance: what you are and what your intention is. The way that you react to the bear will influence how it responds to you, in most cases. I almost always respond to a bear at close range by standing perfectly still, facing it and watching back. If I move at all, slow-motion will not excite the bear so that is how I get the pepperspray out. I do not step away but hold my ground. Silence is important, also.

The main point is to remain neutral so not to excite the bear into either self-defence attack or hunting attack. If you try moving away too soon, a third type of attack could ensue from the bear's sense of territory or a fourth from its sense of status. So I have found that remaining silent, still and fearless has been the best strategy. That way, a bear will not regard you as a prey animal and will not feel it has to fight: since you are neither running away in fright nor being aggressive towards it. Bears are usually cautious at first, not knowing your power, so if you remain still and quiet, the bear will probably not come at you from its sense of territory nor will it test your status. With me, every time the bear has just stared, assessed for awhile then slowly turned and walked away. Depending on circumstance I would not return to the area for three or more days or not at all.

Safety Wedge: a triangular piece that locks the pepperspray trigger shut until removed.

Yards: One yard is close to an average adult man's walking stride or pace; it is a traditional Canadian measurement that I grew up with, so naturally think that way, in spite of eastern politicians' meaningless but very expensive changes.

Moose and Caribou Mismanagement in Yukon: More than half of Yukon's 207,000 square miles is treed with ideal moose and caribou habitat yet one sees these animals infrequently. The human population is about 30,000 only. But they have preyed far too heavily on both moose and caribou. Woodland caribou in southern Yukon are almost nonexistent now. The problem is not the cold winters nor wolves but excessive human predation.

Wolves: When moose, caribou or sheep numbers become low, wolves are then more visible in the ecosystem, thus blamed for this…although mismanagement and overhunting are the real culprits! I was once told by a man living in Carmacks that in the mid-1990s one winter, two wolfpacks were fighting each other over tidbits in Carmacks' garbage dump. Guess why.

SIX ARE COMPANY SEVEN ARE NOT

Strychnine: a deadly poison, $C_{21}H_{22}N_2O_2$, that has been used to kill predators such as wolves and coyotes. But this poison persists in the dead animal and kills any other animal that scavenges on the carcass…so the whole ecosystem becomes devastated in consequence. The manmade ecological imbalance will last for many years!

Pro Pelle Cutem: The Hudson's Bay Company motto, meaning: "A skin for a skin's value."

Shrubby Cinquefoil: a bush with bright yellow five-petalled flowers, that grows unusually tall in Yukon and northern B.C. where I have seen it over six feet high.

Nodded off: fell asleep.

Blowdown: a tree or snag fallen to the ground, caused often by wind, heavy snow or soft ground.

Rounded up: gathered.

Snag: a dead tree either standing, leaning or on the ground.

Ground-snag: a snag lying on the ground.

Twenty-sixer: a standard large bottle of hard liquor of size containing about one-and-a-half pints.

Biting Flies: If one is out alone, a fly bite to an eyelid could swell it shut for two or three days: a definite danger. A tiny blackfly or no-seeum fly could do this and so could a deerfly or horsefly. In such case, a tablet or two of Benadryl would bring down the swelling much quicker.

Mosquitoes: Boreal forest is mosquito heaven but likewise hellish for most mammals and some birds. The year of this adventure was unusually heavy with mosquitoes but other years were not so bad. The irritation of mosquitoes buzzing and biting is a strong reminder that life on Earth is an imperfect combination of pain and pleasure, frustration and peace, ugliness and beauty. I think the best way to live in this earthly realm is to enjoy, appreciate the positiveness while simultaneously accepting, persevering with the negativeness. Both are important facets of our reality here. The positives and negatives in life and in Nature are very educational and can help you become stronger, more balanced inside. So, allow these qualities of appreciation and positive perseverence to grow within oneself.

Hunting Guides: They and poachers had driven woodland caribou and Dall sheep to the endangered level so there was a strong chance that wolves would have finished the decimation. A few years before this event, government enacted a massive wolf-kill in the area, shooting wolves from the air. But the use of strychnine by one hunting guide, in many ways degenerated the ecosystem even more. Trappers were irate, to say the least; they and guides had each other by the throat, metaphorically; too bad not literally. After that…Dall sheep and caribou numbers have remained low.

The Language of Wild Animals: Wildlife communicate with sounds, smells and gestures of body. They are very direct, simple and straightforward…honest. They do not argue, slander or deceive. When aggressive, they are direct and open about it…whether about territory, status, mating, food areas or the hunt. As such, it is easier to befriend a wild animal than a human being.

Camp Safety: After this event, I decided that next time I camp out alone in the wilds I would build a psychological barrier around my tent…in form of a tarp fence. That way, a small yard-space and visual barrier would prevent a large animal such as moose or bear from walking directly to the tent, especially at night. This would also give me a bit more time to react to any danger. And it would prevent a large animal such as a bear or moose from getting feet or legs caught and tangled in tent-ropes if walking past, especially at night…which would be dangerous.

On Steep Mountain Slopes

Cross-ditches: These deactivations are a ridiculous idea brought to B.C.'s Forestry from the U.S. They are one of the biggest wastes of taxpayers' money and that of any backroad driver. Having to drive usually in first-gear, my truck now burns far more gasoline. Twice the radiator has cracked from twist-stress going through the deep, angled ditches; besides, wheel alignment, balljoints and tierods are also stressed. These ditches are often dug where water rarely runs; or conversely, sometimes they just become deep mudpuddles. I suppose the theoretical purpose is to prevent road washouts but those happen infrequently; the cost to repair washouts would be much less than all of that ditch-digging cost. Crown Land belongs to all citizens, not only loggers and wood products companies so those mountain roads should be left driveable for "integrated resource" users, be they commercially motivated or not.

Stringers: thin veins of potential ore-carrying rock, usually quartz, that are often connected to a larger body or deposit deeper in.

Porcupines: Salted highways are killing far too many porcupines that find salty blacktop and gravel shoulders irresistible. This slow-moving forest animal does not understand technological danger since it evolved with quills and especially a quilly tail for self-defence. Now, on roads they merely turn tail towards oncoming cars or trucks then waddle away but often staying on the road. Up North, I have seen that ignorant people go out of their way to intentionally hit porcupines on or near roads: it is no coincidence that most road-killed porcupines were hit at the pavement-gravel edge.

Winter roads need sand and tiny pebbles, which brings death to many small mountain birds as they pick up sand, hit by cars or trucks, but salt is absolutely unnecessary for safety; in fact salt makes black ice where it would not otherwise be! So, for both safety and porcupines, salt should be banned on roads and highways.

One Wee Lake

Nontoxic Mosquito Repellent: Cooking oil is useful to some degree for keeping mosquitoes at bay. I have used canola oil on head, face, ears and hands and found that it works well but not perfectly. Mosquitoes do not like sucking oil into their probosces. But as oil rubs off or is sweat off, it thins enough for mosquitoes to bite through. So I carry a small bottle of oil for that purpose. A hat with mosquito net is not practical: it heats up too much, restricts vision and hearing which are crucial for safety in wild places. Oil keeps flies off somewhat, too.

Bug: a colloquial general word for any arthropod, etcetera.

Arthropod: scientific classification or phylum that includes most classes of "bug".

Insect: scientifically a class of "bug" but colloquially is a general term for any type.

Bedded down: lain down for a rest or sleep.

Nighthawk: a small hawk shaped similar to a swallow and that also feeds on-the-wing, on flying insects. This bird migrates thousands of miles every year, so deserves to have a peaceful nesting spot during our northern summer.

The Loon's Call: This bird has several different calls that I have always enjoyed hearing, especially when alone beside a lake or pond. Every Canadian should make an effort to hear and see a loon at least once…this bird is as Canadian as our beaver.

Wild Birds: Many bird species are crucial for keeping insect populations down and also for spreading seeds. Since excessive clearcuts, general land clearing, firewood cutting and even poorly-planned selective logging have destroyed — and continue to — all-too-many nest-trees: the birds need human help. Thus far, government people have done nothing of consequence in this area; civil servants are alienated from and little comprehend this reality…since they live and work predominantly within city confines, within big boxes called buildings.

But there is another kind of box that will help wild birds — the nestbox. You can help the natural forest and wild meadows by making nestboxes for more than thirty species that have evolved the habit of nesting in hollowed parts of trees and snags. It is best to use the thickest wood possible, especially if you put the box in a sunny spot since excessive heating inside can kill eggs or fledglings. Drilling a few small air-vent holes into walls will help with cooling. If possible put boxes up in places that are at least partly shaded.

For woodpeckers and chickadees put lots of wood shavings — not sawdust — inside of the box since these birds do not carry nest material from outside, having evolved with partly rotten trees. Such trees were naturally full of soft punky wood that was ideal for nesting. Do not put a perch at the entrance hole since it gives larger, carnivorous or more aggressive birds a place to land, harass and kill chicks. Likewise, for the same reason build the roof to overlap by at least two or three inches over the entranceway.

Some years ago an article in the Victoria Times Colonist mentioned that the work of one woodpecker is worth $1500 in pesticide cost per year. Well…reason, economics and ecology are telling how valuable and necessary bug-eating birds are. If our Forest Service were reasonable it would not allow snags and conk-inhabited trees to be cut down. It's for danger, they say… but more danger is in destroying our wild birds, so important they are in maintaining forest ecosystem balance.

Besides birds, small mammals, amphibians and insects also use tree-hollows for living space, shelter and nesting: squirrels, flying squirrels, bats, pine marten, fisher, treefrogs, salamanders, bees and even butterflies. Nestboxes would probably also be used at times by such animals. Anyone interested in making proper-sized nestboxes for various bird species can get dimensions, etcetera from the Federation of British Columbia Naturalists in Vancouver.

LIFE AND DEATH BESIDE A CLEAR CREEK

Northern Three-Toed Woodpecker: These sweet little birds have often been my only animate company when out walking the northern woods. Cheerful and friendly, they dissolve away aloneness.

Clouds: Especially during summer, clouds form, drift, disappear, reappear and change shape in ways that seem as if they be odd living beings…great for imagination and entertainment. Scientifically though, they are water, snow or ice particles freezing, condensing, blowing in the wind and evaporating in accord with changing air temperatures.

Lynx Paw: Information that I have on the lynx' maximum known paw size: it is just under five inches wide. The five-inch-plus paw in this event may have been a large lynx, not a cougar. Not enough prints were visible to assess the animal's stride and track pattern.

Dall Ram's Horn: Later, after drying out the horns and bit of skull which had been mostly chewed away probably by a porcupine or wolf, the weights were: three pounds twelve ounces for the single hollow horn, eight pounds three ounces for the horn with skull-part still attached.

Both horn-tips had been broomed off and also chewed somewhat, showing porcupine-sized toothmarks.

Broomed off: rubbed off by the ram probably due to restricted visibility as the horns grew to front of its face.

Yukon's Wild Sheep: Three different races of Thinhorn sheep live on Yukon's mountains: Dall, Stone and Fannon, the latter locally known as saddleback sheep. The saddleback is a genetic variation of Stone sheep and may also be a subspecie.

Wildlife Mismanagement: Dall sheep in Yukon and northern B.C. have been overhunted by big game guides and poached steadily by native indians: these are the main reasons for this sheep's decline, not wolves. When a large herbivore's numbers are down, wolves become more noticeable. But why do we still have some wildlife and unspoiled living wilderness in Western Canada? The primary reasons are: our relatively small human population, lots of rugged steep rocky terrain that hinders access and roadbuilding...and especially up North and Yukon, few roads. Not much realistic, intelligent planning has come forth that harmonizes economics with ecology. The four main aspects of our society that need to be combined in a balanced, viable way are: human population, ecology, economics and social doings. These must work together. Otherwise...we will lose our peace, our democracy and our Canadian identity.

CHIRPING SQUIRRELS

Boar's Nest: several fallen trees and-or snags on the ground, hungup together and crisscrossing, usually caused by stormy wind. Not mysteriously, they often occur along clearcut edges.

Bellered out: hollered; a very loud vocal sound.

Some Camping Tips:

Biffy: jargon for privy or toilet near camp but far away from lakeshore, creek or river, dug as a hole for human excrement. Best place is beside a log. Use wood ashes from your campfire to cover thoroughly each time, thus neutralizing and sterilizing it almost immediately. On your moving-out day fill in the biffy hole with fire ashes, dirt and gravel up to ground level.

Baking Soda: Sodium bicarbonate is all that is necessary for keeping teeth clean, plaque to almost nil and cavities to almost nil. It costs little and takes very little to neutralize acid in the mouth. It has a mildly salty taste. And swallowing a bit won't hurt but probably helps the stomach slightly. It is also good for minimizing body odours elsewhere. But it will stain clothes. Using baking soda on teeth can save even one person thousands of dollars over the years...healthier teeth and gums.

Food Containers: Always thoroughly, immediately, clean and flatten tincans. Store the cleaned cans inside of a bag, either secured and heavily weighted underwater or at some distance from camp so that residual food smells will not bring a hungry bear — or whatever — into camp. When you leave the area take everything back out. If you have dry or other food that can be detected by animals keep it high and out of reach, if possible up a tree on a rope and pulley. Up high, odours of food will be more dispersed by wind therefore its location less detectable by animals.

Nature Benefits Humanity: The peace and beauty of wild places can have psychological, emotional and physical benefit for people. If more people had such experience, they would better understand and in consequence do more to find ways for humanity to live harmoniously with Nature. We have the brain-power and the responsibility to do so. We can have logging, mining, farming, ranching, etcetera — without completely ruining ecosystems which are the crucial living-systems of both wildlife and humanity. But for this we need to have ecologically-sound limits on human population…sadly lacking at present! For Canada that especially means: no more immigration! Less foreign corporate domination would also be a big help.

Simple Beauty, Yet Profound: Enjoying and observing the beautiful deep yellow five-petalled blossoms and opening buds of a cinquefoil bush brings to mind the nonverbal, nonconceptual reality of existence: the reality of a pre-existing knowledge or knowingness in Nature and in the Universe. These flowers' colour, form and geometric pattern are expressions of mathematics: therefore manifestations of reason. Nature and the Universe must be functioning with some sort of consciousness or mind that is extremely diverse, yet co-ordinated. As the deep yellow buds slowly open, they are in motion…moving within and through space while simultaneously themselves, also being space, matter and energy.

TOGETHERNESS

Wild Families: This short-story actually consists of four separate occurrences that were in the same general area of about one hundred miles in radius. The Kermodei cub's family resides more than two hundred miles from the northern tip of Princess Royal Island and other Kermodeis have been seen another fifty miles north of their little grassy field. Princess Royal Island is known to be the area where this recessive white colour gene is most concentrated. But this white blackbear is also fairly frequently seen in the Skeena and Nass Valleys.

Bears: Over the years in various parts of western Canada I remember seeing two hundred four Blackbears. Of these, twelve had recessive fur colours: so just under six percent showed colours of cinnamon, blackish brown, chocolate, light brown, grey, white and yellow-orange. About two percent were cinnamon, the most common recessive. The yellow-orange bear was partly cinnamon and had auburn feet. Of the actual blacks, about two percent had a white vee or spot on the chest. One bear was two-toned with long black guardhair and pale rust underwool. Most of these rare colours seemed to be concentrated in certain limited areas. Blackbears on the Queen Charlotte Islands have two unique genetic expressions: about seventy-five percent have an all-black muzzle; the other less common recessive gene shows as four white feet and ankles that look somewhat like white boots!

During those same years, seventeen Grizzly bears presented themselves in daylight hours but usually for short moments. They were coloured mostly a medium brown but also blond, dark brown, blackish brown, grey and mixed. About forty percent were medium brown, thirty percent blond and twenty percent blackish brown. One bear was a greyish colour. The most unusual one though, had several colours that blend together all along the body length, gradually changing; this bear's head was dark chocolate, neck and shoulders lighter brown, grading along back and sides into auburn, cinnamon, then blond to white on its butt end and upper back legs; its feet were dark chocolate, then lighter brown going upward. The white butt was the same pale creamy white as a Polar bear or Kermodei.

These numbers show a ratio of Blacks to Grizzlies at about 12:1. The ratio of black Blacks to recessive Blacks is about 17:1.

Stars, Galaxies and Time: On a moonless night, soft colours of light emanate and twinkle from stars and galaxies. I the puny human, enjoy and observe in the present moment…light that began its multibillion-year journey from almost measureless distance away, at an almost measureless past time. I look at the distant past in the present moment. But now some of those stars would no longer exist…having burnt out or whatever. Such be the relativity and limitation of time, which is just the measurement of motion through space. What moves through space? Energy, light, forces, matter and no less…mind…all do!

On The Road Somewhere

This poem was experienced and written in October 1996.

Driving on a dark, rainy night…
Black shadows, poplar and pine
Along highway sixteen
Beside Skeena River;
Big water glowing.

Heading westward, pouring rain…
Can't see much…
Concentrating on the highway
Black, dark, glaring;
Rain streaks sparkling.

Something black and small ahead…
On the centreline;
It's moving…something alive…
I slow down to see
A porcupine!

Walking away slowly, as usual
Tail-end my way,
Its habitual way of protection;
I honk the horn a long time…
Hoping it will move off.

Should I stop
To chase it off…as I've done before?
Too dark, too narrow,
No place to safely park —
So just keep going.

Two days later coming back eastward,
At the highwayside, lay alone
Its body motionless, lifeless…and I stop;
Sudden sadness runs all through…
Hot tears fill my eyes.

Trickling down cheeks, dripping from chin
Onto greyblack pavement
Mixing with quills, broken, scattered…
And a little friend's dark red, drying blood…
Tears minutely reflect the infinite sky above.

Pale blue and brilliant white, the sky too,
Is silent and still…
As my little friend's body…
Both beyond reach, now for awhile;
Little porcupine-mind sparkles still, out there, in there…somewhere.

A Profile of The Author

As a boy in the little rainy town of Alberni, British Columbia, wildlife of all sorts were almost daily experiences for him and other boys of the neighbourhood. Their playground was most often in the woods and along creeks near town. He and several other boys raised young crows as pets. And almost all of them went barefoot every summer, all summer…when school was out. His early years being so saturated with Nature's living things, his identity developed much tied with them.

Teenage years were in the semi-desert north Okanagan town of Vernon, B.C. where hiking the cactus hills above town was a favourite pastime; his first experiences with bluebirds, meadowlarks, magpies and gopher snakes were there.

Then he went to the big city for a few years, to University of B.C. and Simon Fraser University with wildlife biologist as goal but did not succeed. Afterward he worked in various capacities for MacMillan Bloedel, Canadian National Railway, Canadian Pacific Railway and Ministry of Highways. During those years he would often wander the woods, hills and mountainsides as a part-time prospector. For about fifteen years he worked in the edible wild mushroom business while simultaneously prospecting. All of these occupations brought him to rural and remote places where contact with Nature's life would maintain and reinforce his appreciation of our little-understood non-human earthly companions.

During his early years he had a natural inclination for drawing animals, but which went into neutral through teenage years and later. Then in the 1980s and 90s he carved hardrock and burlwood and also began to paint his lifetime love: wildlife and Nature. Now, he's just began producing from his paintings: limited edition prints with image size about sixteen by twenty inches. These beauties, printed on canvas by the Giclee process with archival ink, are real limiteds at fifty-five only and can be viewed at his website: www. mountainwild.ca.

ISBN 141203447-7

9 781412 034470